SHAKESPEARE'S PRO

William Witherle Lawren
1876. He was educated in
Leipzig, taking his M.A. and Ph.D. degrees at
Harvard University. He was on the faculties of
Harvard and the University of Kansas and, for
almost thirty years, Columbia University, where
he was Professor Emeritus in 1936 and died in
1958.

Among his other books are *Medieval Story*
(1911), *Beowulf and Epic Tradition* (1928) and
Chaucer and the Canterbury Tales (1950). He edited
Goethe on Theatre (1919) and was a regular con-
tributor to philological periodicals.

SHAKESPEARE'S
PROBLEM COMEDIES

William Witherle Lawrence

PENGUIN BOOKS

Penguin Books Ltd, Harmondsworth, Middlesex, England
Viking Penguin Inc., 40 West 23rd Street, New York, New York 10010, U.S.A.
Penguin Books Australia Ltd, Ringwood, Victoria, Australia
Penguin Books Canada Ltd, 2801 John Street, Markham, Ontario, Canada L3R 1B4
Penguin Books (N.Z.) Ltd, 182–190 Wairau Road, Auckland 10, New Zealand

—

First published by Macmillan 1931
Revised edition first published in the U.S.A.
by Frederick Ungar Publishing Co. 1960
This edition first published in the Penguin Shakespeare Library 1969
Reissued in Pelican Books 1985

—

Copyright © Frederick Ungar Publishing Co., 1960
'Suggestions for Further Reading' copyright © Penguin Books, 1969

—

Printed and bound in Great Britain by
Cox & Wyman Ltd, Reading
Set in Monotype Fournier

TO

A. C. BRADLEY

Interpreter of English Poetry and
of Shakespearean Drama

CONTENTS

PREFACE TO THE SECOND EDITION   9

PREFACE   11

SUGGESTIONS FOR FURTHER READING   15

1. INTRODUCTION   19

2. 'ALL'S WELL THAT ENDS WELL'   43

3. 'MEASURE FOR MEASURE'   80

4. 'TROILUS AND CRESSIDA'   115

5. THE WAGER IN 'CYMBELINE'   156

6. LATER SHAKESPEAREAN COMEDY   181

   NOTES   204

   INDEX   217

NEARLY thirty years have elapsed since this book was first published. In the interval, much able and stimulating criticism of the plays of which it treats has appeared, and I am glad to think that this may have been due in some small measure to the first detailed analysis of these plays as a group. It would be quite impossible to reissue my book with due attention to all this without a complete rewriting, which would greatly increase its size, and perhaps distract attention from the main points which I endeavoured to present. I have therefore restricted the alterations to a few unimportant corrections and changes, so that the present volume stands substantially as when it was first issued.

As has often been remarked, the term 'problem plays' as applied to these dramas as a group is not wholly satisfactory, but it seems better than its alternatives, and I am encouraged by its wide adoption, and by its employment by E. M. W. Tillyard in his excellent book, *Shakespeare's Problem Plays* (London, 1950 [reprinted in Peregrine Books, 1965]). The main point to keep in mind, I think, is that criticism of this group requires a different approach from that to modern 'problem plays'. It is hard to get Hedda Gabler and Paula Tanqueray out of our heads, but, as I have emphasized, Ibsen and Pinero started with the problem, and made action and character illustrate this, while Shakespeare started with old stories, the main outlines of which he retained, and in each case explored character and action in terms of what I have called 'a perplexing and distressing complication in human life, presented in a spirit of high seriousness'. This involves some technical discussions of sources and analogues, and of changes in social and ethical convictions with the passage of time. What Shakespeare's audiences felt is important for his work, since he appears always to have been sensitive to the reactions of those gathered in the theatre.

I wrote this book in the hope that it might do something to dispel the perplexities which the problem comedies arouse in the minds of thoughtful readers and spectators today. But still more I cherish the hope that these plays, so flawed in some respects, so brilliant in others, may be an increasing source of pleasure when we see them on the stage, or read them, as they should be read, 'with the feet on the fender', not thinking of the critics and their utterances, but entering with surer feet into the enchanted realm which Shakespeare has opened for us.

June 1958　　　　　　　WILLIAM WITHERLE LAWRENCE

THIS book is, to a considerable extent, the result of preoccupation with the Middle Ages. For the past twenty-five years, I have been working in medieval language and literature with graduate students in Columbia University, and for nearly the same length of time I have given a course in Shakespeare for undergraduates. Discussions in this course have often shown that perplexing questions connected with Shakespeare's art may be solved by a consideration of his inheritance from earlier times. By this I do not mean the usual 'source study', but something much more comprehensive. His plays are, of course, not complete re-creations of older themes in the spirit of his own age, but a combination of Elizabethan conceptions and medieval survivals. No Chinese wall separated him from the Middle Ages; the Renaissance, that much-abused and yet shadowy term, means not a new birth after death, but a new spirit in a living and developing body. Most of the medieval elements in Shakespeare's work are not obscure or difficult to understand, though considerable study is required to make clear the subtler issues. Many problems which baffled the older critics, and which are still subjects of controversy, may by this general method of approach be much better understood, and often definitely settled.

My original intention was to write a book illustrating the general importance of a study of medieval literature and life for an understanding of Shakespeare's plays. During the past quarter-century, however, much highly significant research has been published, historical in method, rather than appreciative or impressionistic or philosophical. At the present day there is assuredly no need of elaborate argument to prove that the man who would understand Shakespeare must have some knowledge of the centuries preceding. The dangers of taking a purely modern point of view have often been stressed with striking results, as in the criticism of *Hamlet*.

It happens, however, that the so-called gloomy comedies, *All's*

Well That Ends Well, Measure for Measure, and *Troilus and Cressida,* which are singularly well adapted to this method of approach, have, with the exceptions of portions of *Troilus,* been very little so treated, and never, I think, as a group. They present very great difficulties, and critics are still far from agreement in regard to their proper interpretation. Their relation to Shakespeare's other plays, and to literary and social changes in his day, is still imperfectly understood. Both plot and characterization are greatly illuminated by study of medieval analogues and customs. Such study carries us on, with *Cymbeline* and *The Winter's Tale,* into the era of the Dramatic Romances. Perhaps the attempt to solve the definite problems presented by this group of plays will have a concreteness and an interest which a more extended treatment of Shakespeare's work as a whole might lack.

The Notes have been reduced as much as possible. I see no need of repeating easily accessible information. The bibliography of Shakespeare is now so large that it is impossible to give credit for every borrowed idea, or indeed to be sure that ideas which one thinks original may not lurk somewhere in print. I have, of course, relegated to the Notes discussions of matters too specialized for the main text, but such discussions, which might be almost indefinitely extended, have been sternly subordinated. Portions of Chapters 2 and 5 have appeared already, in somewhat different form, in the *Publications of the Modern Language Association of America;* and some passages in Chapter 4 have been taken from an essay of mine in *Shaksperian Studies by Members of the Department of English and Comparative Literature in Columbia University,* New York, 1916. Detailed references will be found under the appropriate chapters, in the Notes. The Modern Language Association and the Columbia University Press have courteously accorded permission to reprint. Quotations from the plays in the present volume follow Neilson's text in the Cambridge Edition, Boston and New York, 1906.

My colleagues Professor Ashley H. Thorndike and Professor George C. D. Odell have given me assistance which I gratefully acknowledge. Professor William T. Brewster has had the great kindness to read the entire book in manuscript, and I recall with

gratitude the friendly interest and counsel of the late Professor
Brander Matthews. The obligations of the worker in Shakespearean
drama to the published researches of others are too great to be stated
in detail.

May 1930   WILLIAM WITHERLE LAWRENCE

SUGGESTIONS FOR FURTHER READING

THE following represents a selection of the more important writings on Shakespeare's problem plays that have appeared since the second edition of this volume. There are many other relevant articles in scholarly and critical journals such as *Shakespeare Quarterly* and *Shakespeare Survey*. Select bibliographies are provided in, for instance, the booklets on Shakespeare in the British Council series, 'Writers and Their Work': *Shakespeare: The Problem Plays* by Peter Ure (1961), and *Shakespeare: The Final Plays* by Frank Kermode (1963).

I. EDITIONS AND SOURCES

G. K. Hunter's new Arden edition of *All's Well That Ends Well* (1959) is the fullest and most helpful. J. W. Lever edited the new Arden *Measure for Measure* (1965) and J. M. Nosworthy the New Penguin edition (1969). The most recent detailed edition of *Troilus and Cressida* is Alice Walker's for the New Cambridge Shakespeare (1957); the Signet edition (1963) is edited by Daniel Seltzer. Of *Cymbeline* the two most recent editions are the new Arden by J. M. Nosworthy, 1955, and the New Cambridge by J. C. Maxwell, 1960. Nosworthy's edition includes the full version of *Frederick of Jennen*, discovered since Lawrence wrote (see page 162).

Geoffrey Bullough reprints and discusses the sources in *Narrative and Dramatic Sources of Shakespeare*. *All's Well That Ends Well* and *Measure for Measure* are in Volume II (1958), and *Troilus and Cressida* in Volume VI (1966). In *Shakespeare's Sources*, 1 (1957), Kenneth Muir discusses sources of the three problem comedies and *Cymbeline*. Stories that provided the basis for *Measure for Measure* and *All's Well That Ends Well* are also given in *Elizabethan Love Stories*, edited by T. J. B. Spencer (Penguin Shakespeare Library, 1968).

2. GENERAL CRITICAL WORKS

Several studies have developed or modified the notion of 'problem comedies'. Ernest Schanzer, in *The Problem Plays of Shakespeare* (1963), discusses *Measure for Measure* at some length, and in an Appendix argues that *All's Well That Ends Well*, *Measure for Measure*, and *Troilus and Cressida* should not be grouped together. A. P. Rossiter's *Angel with Horns* (1961) has chapters on the individual plays as well as a general one on 'The Problem Plays'. Both writers provide a useful history of the term 'problem play'. William B. Toole's *Shakespeare's Problem Plays* (1966) considers *Hamlet* as well as the other three, and suggests that they have an implicit Christian framework which links their structure with that of medieval morality plays. John Russell Brown examines 'love's ordeal' in *All's Well That Ends Well*, *Measure for Measure*, and *Troilus and Cressida* in his *Shakespeare and His Comedies*. The second edition (1962) contains an added chapter on the last comedies, including *Cymbeline*. *Measure for Measure* and *Troilus and Cressida* are considered in O. J. Campbell's *Shakespeare's Satire* (Oxford, 1943). *Shakespeare: The Comedies* (New Jersey, 1965), an anthology edited by Kenneth Muir, contains valuable essays on *All's Well That Ends Well* and *Measure for Measure*, and Peter Ure's *Shakespeare: The Problem Plays* (1961) has brief accounts of the three problem comedies along with *Timon of Athens*.

3. THE INDIVIDUAL PLAYS
All's Well That Ends Well

Most of the comment on *All's Well That Ends Well* is confined to the books already referred to, and to articles in specialist journals. There is, however, an extended treatment of the play in G. Wilson Knight's 'The third eye: an essay on *All's Well That Ends Well*' in *The Sovereign Flower* (1958) which regards Helena as Shakespeare's supreme expression of a woman's love.

Measure for Measure

Possibly the most balanced study of this play is still Mary Lascelles's *Shakespeare's 'Measure for Measure'* (1953) which examines the play as a tragi-comedy that leaves many questions unanswered. A less tentative account is *The Achievement of 'Measure for Measure'* by David Lloyd Stevenson (Ithaca, New York, 1966) which, in arguing that the play is a fully realized artistic achievement, acknowledges a debt to F. R. Leavis's 'The Greatness of *Measure for Measure*', *Scrutiny*, X, January 1942, reprinted in *The Common Pursuit* (1952, Peregrine edition, 1962). In *'Measure for Measure' as Royal Entertainment* (New York, 1966) Josephine Waters Bennett argues that it was written specifically for the entertainment of King James, as a result of which the play, via the Duke, 'echoes at a polite distance the image which King James instructed his subjects to see in him'. Lawrence himself contributed some further thoughts on the play in his *'Measure for Measure* and Lucio', *Shakespeare Quarterly*, 9, Autumn, 1958, in which he draws attention to the coarsening in Shakespeare's treatment of Lucio during the play.

Troilus and Cressida

In *Some Shakespearean Themes* (1959) L. C. Knights considers the theme of appearance and reality in *Troilus and Cressida*. Two chapters are devoted to the play in Nevill Coghill's *Shakespeare's Professional Skills* (Cambridge, 1964), showing how our sympathies are directed in favour of Troy. 'Discord in the Spheres: the universe of *Troilus and Cressida*' by Una Ellis-Fermor in *The Frontiers of Drama* (1945) sees the play as an attempt, which finally fails, to find an image of absolute value in either Troilus's love, Agamemnon's chivalry, or Ulysses's vision of the hierarchy of the state. In *Shakespeare's 'Troilus and Cressida' and the Legends of Troy* (Madison, Wisconsin, 1953) Robert K. Presson explicitly tries to revise Lawrence's view that Shakespeare was fully under the influence of medieval rather than classical conceptions of the tale of Troy. Shakespeare's attitude towards the Greeks is discussed by T. J. B. Spencer in ' "Greeks" and Merrygreeks": A Background to *Timon of Athens* and *Troilus and Cressida*' (in *Essays on Shakespeare and Elizabethan Drama*, edited by Richard Hosley, 1963). In *Shakespeare's 'Troilus and Cressida' and its Setting* (Cambridge, Mass., 1967), Robert Kimbrough tries to explain some of the difficulties of the play by a theory that Shakespeare was trying to reconcile the different demands made by the public and the private theatres.

Cymbeline

There is a detailed account of *Cymbeline* in *The Recurring Miracle: A Study of 'Cymbeline' and the Last Plays*, by D. R. C. Marsh (Pietermaritzburg, 1962). There are also extended discussions of the play in *Prefaces to Shakespeare: Third Series* by H. Granville-Barker (1930); *Shakespeare's Last Plays* by E. M. W. Tillyard (1938); *The Crown of Life* by G. Wilson Knight (1947); *Shakespeare: The Last Phase* by D. A. Traversi (1954); and *Shakespeare and the Comedy of Forgiveness* by R. G. Hunter (1965). The history of *Cymbeline*'s critical reputation during this century is set out in 'Shakespeare's romances: 1900–1957' by P. Edwards, *Shakespeare Survey II* (1958), and the play is also dealt with briefly in Frank Kermode's stimulating *Shakespeare: The Final Plays* (1963).

1968

RAYMOND POWELL
The Shakespeare Institute (University of Birmingham)

ONE

Introduction

In the Chorus preceding the Fifth Act of *Henry V*, Shakespeare, departing from his usual though not invariable custom, introduced the familiar contemporary allusion to the expedition of the Earl of Essex to Ireland, which dates the passage, and inferentially the completion of the play, in the year 1599. Other evidence confirms the conclusion that this was the last of his chronicle plays dealing with English history and written in the closing years of the sixteenth century. He was at that time approaching the height of his creative power; he had gained a solid reputation as a dramatist and a man of letters, and he had become a shareholder in a theatrical company whose prosperity was in part dependent upon his pen. Some ten years of great productivity lay behind him. He had written two tragedies, *Titus Andronicus* and *Romeo and Juliet*, but his greatest achievement had been in comedy. The range and variety of his work in this field are remarkable; the dates of the comedies are uncertain, but we know from Meres that he must by 1598 have written *Love's Labour's Lost*, *The Comedy of Errors*, *The Two Gentlemen of Verona*, *A Midsummer Night's Dream*, and *The Merchant of Venice*. To these, by the turn of the century, must in all probability be added *The Merry Wives of Windsor*, *The Taming of the Shrew*, and *Much Ado About Nothing*. What piece may be concealed under Meres's allusion to *Love's Labour's Won* is still a matter for speculation.

The playwright, least of all craftsmen, can pursue his art along fixed and unvarying lines. He must be alert to perceive changes in the public taste, he must be conscious of the value of novelty, he must study the successes and the failures of his fellows. As he grows in maturity and insight, he must put the best of his ripened powers into his work. If he fails to do these things, he will soon find himself falling behind, and becoming, not the entertainer of the present, but the memory of a bygone generation. Shakespeare made no such mistake.

He was singularly quick to perceive changes in theatrical fashions, to provide his public with new varieties of amusement, and to pour out the best which he had to give for their deeper reflection. This was characteristic of him down to the very end of his active career in the theatre. In *The Tempest*, perhaps the last play wholly from his pen, he adapted effective elements from the Court masques and from current tales of adventure in the New World, which were then stirring the imagination of Englishmen, with no hint of the fatigue or the indifference of the magician about to break his staff and drown his book.

Especially noteworthy are the new paths into which he set his feet midway in his career. He did not neglect types of drama which had already proved successful, and in 1600 and 1601, to set conjectural dates, he produced *As You Like It* and *Twelfth Night*, the most delightful of joyous comedies. But more serious themes were engaging his attention. He turned, probably first as early as 1599, in *Julius Caesar*, to tragedy based upon classical themes, following this later with *Antony and Cleopatra*, *Coriolanus*, and the collaborated *Timon of Athens*. Beginning with *Hamlet*, he was occupied with the four great tragedies in the first five or six years of the century. So prodigal an outpouring of masterpieces of the first rank in so brief a space of time hardly finds a parallel in literary history. This appears still more remarkable when we add *All's Well That Ends Well*, *Measure for Measure*, and *Troilus and Cressida*.

These three comedies mark one of the most striking developments of Shakespeare's genius. They were probably written between 1599 and 1605, though the date of not one of them is certain, and all of them show evidences of revision. While they were composed, no doubt, in alternation with other work, they resemble each other closely in style and temper, and may be conveniently studied together. The settings and the plots are still those of romance, but the treatment is in the main serious and realistic. They are concerned, not with the pleasant and fantastic aspects of life, but with painful experiences and with the darker complexities of human nature. Instead of gay pictures of cheerful scenes, to be accepted with a smile and a jest, we are frequently offered unpleasant and sometimes even repulsive episodes, and characters whose conduct gives rise to sustained questioning of action and motive. These pieces, in short, reveal to us a new phase of Shakespeare's mind, and a new type of comedy. The term 'problem plays' has been proposed for them by F. S. Boas, who would also include *Hamlet* in the group. 'All these dramas,' he says, 'introduce us into highly artificial societies, whose civilization is ripe unto rottenness. Amidst such media abnormal conditions of brain and of emotion are generated, and intricate cases of conscience demand a solution by unprecedented methods. Thus throughout these plays we move along dim untrodden paths, and at the close our feeling is neither of simple joy nor pain; we are excited, fascinated, perplexed, for the issues raised preclude a completely satisfactory outcome, even when, as in *All's Well* and *Measure for Measure*, the complications are outwardly adjusted in the fifth act. In *Troilus and Cressida* and *Hamlet* no such partial settlement of difficulties takes place, and we are left to interpret their enigmas as best we may. Dramas so singular in theme and temper cannot be strictly called comedies or tragedies. We may therefore borrow a convenient phrase from the theatre of today and class them together as Shakspere's problem-plays.'[1]

Application to the Elizabethan age of a term usually confined to the present day has obvious dangers, but its use appears allowable if its meaning is made perfectly clear. We may note the modernity of the work of Shakespeare in the pieces now under consideration; Bernard Shaw has observed that 'in such unpopular plays as *All's Well*, *Measure for Measure*, and *Troilus and Cressida*, we find him ready and willing to start at the twentieth century if the seventeenth would only let him'.[2] But we cannot escape the necessity of making a working definition. The essential characteristic of a problem play, I take it, is that a perplexing and distressing complication in human life is presented in a spirit of high seriousness. This special treatment distinguishes such a play from other kinds of drama, in that the theme is handled so as to arouse not merely interest or excitement, or pity or amusement, but to probe the complicated interrelations of character and action, in a situation admitting of different ethical interpretations. The 'problem' is not like one in mathematics, to which there is a single true solution, but is one of conduct, as to which there are no fixed and immutable laws. Often it cannot be reduced to any formula, any one question, since human life is too complex to be so neatly simplified. Familiar illustrations may be found in the prose dramas of Ibsen. For instance, various problems are implied in *An Enemy of the People* – the duty of the citizen to the community, the right of a husband and father to sacrifice family comfort to his conception of such a duty, the value of compromise as against outspoken opposition to social abuses, and so forth. The outcome proposed by the dramatist is not the only possible way out of the difficulties; several playwrights, working with the same characters in the same situations, might well reach different conclusions. Sometimes the personages are left at the end in the midst of their troubles; in the play just named, nothing is really settled at the end. Usually, however, some resolution of the complications of the plot is suggested. In consequence of the painful nature of the events characteristic of this type of play, the issue will often be tragedy, as in *Hedda Gabler* or *Rosmersholm*. Or the problem may be resolved in a way that is not tragic, as in *A Doll's House*. Whether we shall, in this latter case, call the play a comedy or not is a matter of definition and agreement; most readers feel that this particular piece is too serious in mood and theme for comedy.

The term 'problem play', then, is particularly useful to apply to those productions which clearly do not fall into the category of tragedy, and yet are too serious and analytic to fit the commonly accepted conception of comedy. Indeed, when the problem play becomes tragedy, it is, I think, best considered under that rubric; at all events, there is no difficulty in so classifying it. Moreover, it is often very hard to determine whether a tragedy may also be called a problem play, or may be better so named. For these reasons, I prefer to exclude *Hamlet* from the group of Shakespearean problem plays proposed by Boas. On the other hand, there is little ambiguity in classifying the Shakespearean problem comedies, which stand sharply apart from the comedies of a lighter sort. I am therefore limiting the present study to *All's Well, Measure for Measure, Troilus and Cressida*, and the wager-plot in *Cymbeline*, which affords a conspicuous illustration of the method in the Dramatic Romances.

Some further cautions and explanations are desirable. In the first place, the 'problem' mood must not only be prominent in the action; it must dominate it. Painful and even tragic complications may occur in comedy, they may even be used for a deeper purpose than merely as contrast to more cheerful matters, but they will not make a problem play unless they constitute the controlling interest. Thus in *The Merchant of Venice*, the clash between Jew and Gentile is set forth in a spirit of high seriousness, and is most significant for the play as a whole. Shakespeare was obviously greatly interested in it; he balanced its conflicting issues in his own mind, and gave compelling eloquence to Shylock's recital of Jewish wrongs. Nevertheless, he made it only a part of a complicated action, with separate plots, which taken as a whole must clearly be classified as romantic comedy. Probably we give to the Jewish problem greater stress on the stage today, and regard Shylock's misfortunes more seriously than did the Elizabethans, who took their amusements naïvely, and who retained much of the medieval religious hatred of the Jews. The case is similar in *Twelfth Night*, with the sufferings of Malvolio, a good and honest, but dull person, with no sense of humour, who finds his darling ambition shattered amid the ridicule of those whom he knows to be at once happier and less virtuous than himself. Here Shakespeare, with his marvellous insight, gave to comedy a subtlety which we rarely find in his fellow dramatists. But there seems little doubt that the tragic element was greatly subordinated in Elizabethan performances of this merry piece, and it may be rightly so. Nowadays we stress it unduly. Stage versions of the play are arranged to give prominence to the part of Malvolio, and many actors, among whom Irving was conspicuous, have darkened the bright sunshine of Illyria with Malvolio's misfortunes.

Still less do the tragic elements in a tragicomedy make of it a problem play. Tragicomedy is hard to define exactly, but it clearly lacks the seriousness essential if this term is to be used. It is not analytical but theatrical. As Professor Ristine puts the matter, 'The essential lack of the integrating qualities that make for lasting drama is the besetting fault of tragicomedy. It presents no transcript from life; it neglects portrayal of character and psychological analysis for plot and theatricality; it substitutes dramatic falsity for dramatic truth; it emphasizes novelty, sensation, surprise, startling effect.'[3] The controlling spirit in a problem play must obviously be realism. No serious analysis of the difficult issues of life is possible unless the

23

dramatist comes to grips with things as they actually exist. The theme itself may have grown out of popular story, and may still retain the irrationalities of such story, but it must be taken as a real human problem, and discussed as such. For example, the conditions imposed upon Helena by Bertram, or upon Isabella by Angelo, seem fantastic, and the means taken to fulfil them almost equally so, but we are made to feel the reality of the sufferings of these unhappy ladies, the grim necessity which drives them to remedies so desperate. The 'problems' which confront them are taken by Shakespeare seriously and realistically, not with the easy geniality of romance. Contrast the romantic sufferings of Rosalind or Viola, which are as unconvincing as the serpent and lioness in the forest of Arden, or the shipwreck on the shores of Orsino's dominions.

It must be noted immediately, however, that realistic treatment is by no means maintained throughout Shakespeare's problem comedies. He was obviously far more interested in the complications of the action than in its resolution. He treats the development of the intrigue seriously and analytically, but he is impatient of reaching a solution by the same method. In *All's Well* and *Measure for Measure* he closes his play with the stock theatrical devices of romantic comedy. In *Troilus and Cressida* he stops the action abruptly; nothing is concluded. In *Cymbeline*, which begins in the full manner of the problem plays, he relaxes his grip on realities after the ending of the Second Act, throwing coherence to the winds, and pouring out his whole bag of stage tricks in a complicated and superficially effective close. We shall examine all this in detail later. It is characteristic of his general procedure in comedy. As Neilson says, 'the philosophical significance [of the comedies] stops short, as a rule, in the fifth act. The marrying off, at the close, of all eligible youths and maidens is more a concession to the convention of the happy ending demanded by the particular type of drama than the logical outcome of the characters or their deeds.'[4] Clearly, too, realism is much hampered by the demands of a pre-existing plot. This point hardly needs to be elaborated; we are all familiar with its importance in the consideration of *Lear* or *Hamlet* or *Antony and Cleopatra*. While Shakespeare exercised freedom in the alteration and manipulation of the plot-material which he had borrowed, he was also to a great extent controlled by it. His task was not so much the logical and realistic working out of a given situation as the psychological rationalization of a pre-existing story. In this regard his procedure was far removed from that of Ibsen or Sudermann or Pinero, and close to that of Chaucer in *Troilus and Criseyde*, or of Wolfram in *Parzival*, or of Wagner in *Tristan und Isolde*.

If the foregoing definitions and cautions are kept in mind, it appears legitimate to call these three Shakespearean comedies 'problem plays'. They represent a radical departure in his art: the serious and realistic treatment of a distressing complication in human life, but without a tragic outcome. Some phrase to designate them is highly convenient, and I know of none better than this, nor of any other as good, and I adopt it the more readily since it is not my own, but is borrowed from the distinguished English critic who was, I think, the first to give it this application.

There is a special reason for discussing these comedies afresh, which I have already suggested in the Preface – the distressing lack of critical agreement as to their interpretation. Oddly enough, they seem never to have been studied minutely and dispassionately as a group, and their complexities probed in the light of modern knowledge. The 'best authorities' are often directly contradictory, one praising a character for conduct which another regards as reprehensible; one perceiving a faithful transcript of life, and the beauty of heroism triumphing over great obstacles, where another can find only a gibe and a sneer. I have reviewed some of these disagreements in the chapters which follow. We shall see that Andrew Lang and Masefield have maintained as positively that Helena is despicable as Hazlitt and Coleridge did that she is admirable; that Dr Johnson thought that *All's Well* contains no moral, while Gervinus believed it is all moralizing; that Isabella, who is to most critics lovely and virtuous, seems to Quiller-Couch 'a bare procuress', and that the Duke, who is generally censured for being shifty and untruthful and for violating law and religious observance, emerges, from one of the most exhaustive and learned studies of the play ever made, as a portrait of James I, designed to tickle the vanity of that susceptible monarch. *Troilus and Cressida* still affords, in Tatlock's words, 'the chief problem in Shakespeare'. So with the reflection of the problem

SHAKESPEARE'S PROBLEM COMEDIES

mood in *Cymbeline*; Moulton perceives in the actions of Posthumus
Leonatus 'moral perversion', Hudson, 'noble sensitiveness'. In
short, the reader who looks to the Interpreter's House for guidance
finds affirmations and negations at once passionate and contradictory.
I venture to hope that it may be possible to arrive at a clearer understanding of the meaning of character and incident in these plays.

Moreover, the spirit underlying the composition of the problem
comedies seems to me to have been very generally misconceived. I
will not, at the present moment, attempt to discuss this in detail, but
will content myself with a single illustration. We often find it said
that these comedies reflect a mood of bitter cynicism, that Shakespeare
made use of disgraceful and dishonouring devices to gain endings
which can only be called happy in the ironical sense, and that he has
given us, as a result, mocking travesties of life and love. There is no
higher authority than Sir Edmund Chambers, who presumably expresses his final and measured judgement in the *Encyclopaedia
Britannica*,[5] in commenting upon 'the three bitter and cynical pseudo-
comedies, *All's Well That Ends Well*, in which the creator of Portia,
Beatrice, Rosalind and Viola drags the honour of womanhood in the
dust – *Troilus and Cressida*, in which the ideals of heroism and
romance are confounded in the portraits of a wanton and a poltroon–
and *Measure for Measure*, in which the searchlight of irony is thrown
upon the paths of Providence itself'. I shall take my courage in both
hands and say that I believe that this is (excepting in regard to
Cressida) absolutely wrong, and that careful objective study of the
plays and of the period will tend to show its falsity.

In any case, no matter where the truth may lie, a careful and detailed examination of this group of plays needs little defence. They
are of course greatly inferior to the better known dramas written by
Shakespeare in the opening years of the new century. We may agree
with Thorndike that 'all are confused in structure, uneven in style,
and constrained rather than spontaneous in manner'.[6] They betray
many signs of haste and indifference and reliance upon well-worn
theatrical tricks, and their themes and treatment are not pleasant to
modern readers and playgoers. Panegyrists of Shakespeare usually
treat them in apologetic fashion, and sometimes withdraw from
them in utter bewilderment. But they were, after all, written by

26

Shakespeare, and at the very time when he was doing his finest work. They contain many striking scenes, many vivid characters, much imaginative and brilliant verse, and again and again they reveal Shakespeare wrestling with the deeper mysteries of human life which find supreme expression in the great tragedies. Their plots may not seem agreeable to us, but these plots were popular in earlier days, in oral or written forms, or both. We cannot kick these secondary plays out of the way, while we lose ourselves in ecstasy over the great masterpieces. Moreover, an understanding of them is significant for Shakespeare's whole dramatic achievement at this time. If we know what he was aiming to do here, we shall better understand the great tragedies and the Roman plays, and comprehend more truly his technical methods in the supreme creative period of his life.

Two separate questions present themselves for our consideration. First, how did Shakespeare intend that these plays should be understood by his audiences? What do they mean? Second, how are their peculiar characteristics to be explained, in the general development of his mind and art? How did he come to write such pieces? The first of these questions is discussed in the chapters dealing with the individual plays; the second, an answer to which is dependent upon the first, in the concluding chapter.

I will not attempt to anticipate the results of those discussions here. Plainly, however, neither of the two problems can be solved by any one formula or method of approach. The plays are complicated structures, and while they show obvious resemblances and echoes, they are all different, each demands its own interpretation. Nor is their genesis in the poet's mind to be summed up in a phrase or two. If we are to attempt to penetrate the secrets of Shakespeare, who had the broadest human interests, read widely and penetratingly, and was in intimate contact with the varied and brilliant external life of his day, we cannot proceed in any simple and mechanical fashion. Critics have, I think, been too much inclined to emphasize one or more possible explanations of the peculiar characteristics of the problem comedies – personal misfortune or bereavement, disappointment in friendship or in love, the degeneration of the age, the demands of the theatre, the influence of prevailing literary and dramatic fashions, haste and carelessness, and so forth. There may be truth in many or all of these, and in other considerations as well. In particular the relation of these plays to contemporary and preceding dramatic work should be carefully observed. Much which came to fruition in the problem plays had been germinating through earlier years, and many of the distinctive characteristics of these plays are observable in later comedy and tragedy. The main point to keep in mind is the complexity of our task; no one 'open sesame' will unlock its mysteries.

The general method which I propose to follow in the detailed investigation of the several comedies must be made clear at this point. While we shall have many different matters to consider, which must be approached in different ways, we shall endeavour to base our primary conclusions upon definite and tangible evidence, discarding so far as possible the emotional and moral effect which the plays produce upon us today. It must be remembered that there is no evidence that the problem comedies were composed, any more than the more familiar plays, for the gratification of Shakespeare's aesthetic interests, or to give expression to his views on conduct and morality. They are, of course, permeated with thought and emotion, and are thus, like all true works of art, given validity and sincerity. But they were written in the first instance to entertain, which does not mean merely to provide diversion, but also to arouse and hold serious interest. I do not think that it will be questioned that they were primarily intended for representation on a stage, before an audience, and that they must in part be judged according to the immediate effect which they were designed to produce upon spectators. The most cursory examination shows how permeated they are with theatrical devices, and closer study reveals this still more strikingly. They are first of all stories, set forth with dramatic vividness.

The plots were neither new nor original; they had already proved their ready popular appeal, sometimes as narrative, sometimes as drama, sometimes in both forms. Shakespeare did not depart from his constant habit of taking well-tried, familiar tales, instead of inventing for himself. He was content to follow the plots of such tales, knowing that he could count on their acceptance, confident that his audience would go as readily with him into the land of make-believe as men of past generations had done. His achievement was to retell for his own day, in new and alluring form, what had already proved its power to capture the imaginations of men in the past. In this he was following the fashion of the dramatists who had served him as models during his theatrical apprenticeship, and of much of the prose and verse narrative of his times. His experience in the writing of chronicle history, which aimed to make vivid the pageant of earlier English reigns, while it could not substantially alter their events, had further accustomed him to this method, and made it doubly natural for him to take well-known imaginative stories, and follow closely their narrative outlines. Such a procedure was of course in no wise confined to his own day; we can trace it from the time of Euripides and Sophocles in their retelling of Greek mythology, to that of the unnamed authors of the English miracle plays, making vivid scenes from the Bible and Church legend. Nor is this procedure in any way restricted to drama; one of the most striking characteristics of medieval narrative, as we all know, is the reverence for existing plot-material, and the tendency to retain it, often in defiance of all logic and reason. The course of most of Shakespeare's plays was governed, in the beginning, by the adoption of an old tale, and of the conventions bound up with it – a very different procedure from that of the dramatist who builds his play about a character, and makes plot illustrative of character analysis and subordinate to it.

In our admiration for the subtler and profounder aspects of Shakespeare's work, which set it apart so strikingly from that of his contemporaries, we must not forget that it had a strong direct appeal for simple men (which it still retains today), that it was designed to provide entertainment for the ignorant as well as the educated, and that this appeal has first to be reckoned with in any attempt to fathom his deeper meanings. His work is not like a coin, with two separate and distinct faces, but rather like a bas-relief of intricate design, the main outlines of which are striking at a distance, but which, on closer examination, reveals new beauties of detail to the connoisseur. His plays did not have two meanings, one for the pit and the other for the gallery. He provided for the more intellectual spectators something which the groundlings, with their limited education and experience of life, could not perceive, but this was an extension of the simpler meaning of his play, and not at variance with it.

It is of particular importance, then, to examine carefully the medieval tales which form the basis of his story-telling, tales which are composed, in large part, of set themes –sometimes only single incidents, sometimes combinations of such incidents – which, in being told and retold in different countries and at different times, by word of mouth in ballad and tale, or pen in hand by the romancer or chronicler, assumed the most varied forms, and were set in the most varied combinations. The extraordinary thing is the persistence of what may be called the units of narrative, the consistency with which, in spite of all their transmutations, these units maintained a definite and recognizable form. Frequently they extended far beyond the limits of Europe and of the Middle Ages. They may have their analogues in India and in Africa, and nearer home among non-Aryan peoples like the Turks and the Finns. They often appear to have been old long before the barbarians overthrew classical civilization. It is as if the combined and universal story-telling experience of the world had evolved certain situations which had proved their right to immortality, and had provided succeeding generations with a basis for entertainment which could not fail of acceptance.

Such themes as these, with some of which we of today are most familiar through nursery tales, frequently seem, on any rationalistic basis, absurd. Yet the absurdities are usually necessary and fundamental; they cannot be removed without spoiling the story. Sometimes childish and irrational plot-elements, which everyone can recognize as characteristic of popular story, predominate; sometimes, as we observe them in the Elizabethan age, such absurdities are clearly the survivals of medieval habits of thought, archaic social arrangements, outworn moral convictions, and the like. But these absurdities were no bar to the acceptance of a story; the task of each succeeding teller was to clothe them in new guise, to interpret them afresh to each generation in such a way as would make a renewed appeal. With such narrative material the audience in an Elizabethan theatre was thoroughly familiar. The rude spectators in the pit would have become acquainted with it through oral tale and ballad, in the fields and at cottage fires, from the spinners and the knitters in the sun. The more educated playgoers might well have read it in more literary form, in print, though they, too, were not untouched by popular narrative traditions. We have to reckon with a time when many of the people at a play could neither read nor write, and yet were possessors of a richer heritage of narrative than the playgoers of today, who, although they are better educated in one sense, are far poorer in acquaintance with imaginative tradition which has gained authority through generations. Samuel Isham put the matter well, in commenting upon the mental attitude in the appreciation of pictures today, as compared with that of former times.

In our own time the importance of the subject [of a picture] is growing less and less. Reading and knowledge have become more miscellaneous and ephemeral, less simple and elementary. There was a time when in Protestant countries everyone knew the Bible and, in Catholic countries, the legends of the saints; when all educated people were familiar with classical mythology and even the uneducated could follow an allegory of Jupiter or Neptune. In those days artists could make elaborate figure compositions and have them understood. Now few facts are known in common by any great body of people, except the news contained in the papers of the morning; the news of yesterday is already forgotten. We have few visible subjects or symbols that appeal to any wide public.[7]

Investigation of medieval elements surviving in the work of Shakespeare is no rattling of dry bones, no shaking of dusty documents over bright pages; it is the demonstration of the continuing vital spirit of an earlier time in the splendidly creative age of Elizabeth. Perhaps I may quote some unpublished words of the late Sir Walter Raleigh, who perceived with his accustomed clearness of vision the point upon which I am here insisting. 'It is only the best scholars (and some simple human beings quite unscholarly) who do not fall into the trap presented by the words "Middle Ages" and "medieval". The Middle Ages were inhabited, not by a strange people across a dark frontier, but by ourselves. The frontier was built (and the name invented) by the arrogance of the newly intoxicated Renaissance. There are differences, of course, chiefly in the means and methods of civilization, and especially in the literary art. They accepted a story, and told it, as a story, without critical preoccupations.'[8]

A solid point of departure, then, for the interpretation of a Shakespearean play founded upon traditional story, is to inquire first of all what its theme would have meant to an Elizabethan audience. The direct source of the play may have been in literary form – Boccaccio or Bandello or an old play – but in spite of all modifications, and, in a sense, irrespective of the direct source, the vital theme emerges, with its old charm and authority, and asserts its power once more. Shakespeare knew that it could be trusted to make its appeal, and unhesitatingly used it for the very foundations of his play. Like story-tellers in all ages, he made changes, introducing new material of his own, altering details of plot and motivation and character, but – and this is the important point – seldom running counter to the fundamental conceptions which his theme involved, not making, for example, a hero out of a villain, or a heroine out of a wanton. He not only retained irrationalities, but he himself sometimes introduced, as in *Measure for Measure*, traditional but irrational elements into a rational situation, where no previous story-teller had done so.

Such a method of approach is particularly applicable to *All's Well*, *Measure for Measure*, *Troilus and Cressida*, and to parts of *The Winter's Tale* and *Cymbeline*, because the significant parts of their plots are drawn from the common stock of narrative tradition. Investigation of the meaning which these themes would have had for an Elizabethan audience is, however, as I have emphasized in the Preface, quite different from source study of the usual sort. Comparison of a given play with its direct source or nearest analogue reveals only a part of its significance. It is necessary also to examine as many different analogues as possible, to see what is fundamental and typical, and to distinguish it from special and individual features. The whole must be studied as a narrative theme, or, what is more usual, as a composite of such themes. Each play determines its own method. Sometimes the key to the meaning will lie in the retention of archaic plot-material, or of conceptions of life and manners characteristic of folk-tales. Sometimes guidance must be sought rather in aristocratic conventions, which, like those of the peasantry, developed a logic of their own, often equally at variance with common-sense. This is particularly true of the survival and revival, in the days of Elizabeth, of the observances of chivalry, which involved artificial ethical and social principles often contradicting the sturdy every-day morality of the British people. Careful study is often necessary to determine the alterations which chivalric principles have undergone, in passing into Elizabethan tradition. Curious and outworn customs and modes of thought, whether aristocratic or popular, are often quite inseparable from the plot, because they alone explain it properly, and make clear how its apparent irrationalities could still have been accepted as story-telling, although in actual practice in real life their validity had long since departed. So with characterization, which is often greatly influenced in a similar way.

An illustration or two from familiar plays will make these considerations still clearer. As we all know, *The Merchant of Venice* produces upon the spectator or the reader an impression of reality, largely through the remarkable naturalness of the characters. This impression vanishes if, instead of taking the plot for granted, we subject it to analysis. Nothing, surely, could be further from real life than the absurd arrangements by which a husband is to be selected for Portia. Why should the lover who chose a leaden casket rather than one of gold or silver be rewarded with her hand? One would think that the Prince of Morocco or the Prince of Arragon showed more gallantry than he. Study of the Caskets story, which is not in the tale from Ser Giovanni's *Il Pecorone*, the closest analogue to the play, explains the situation. An early form of this story is represented by the composite *Barlaam and Josaphat*, written to exalt the life and teachings of Buddha, and containing a series of parables which enforce moral truths. '[A king] caused four caskets to be made: two covered with gold and precious stones, but containing naught but dry bones. The other two, however, he covered only with clay, but filled them with jewels and costly pearls. He then summoned the courtiers to him and asked them to give judgement as to the value of the caskets. They replied that those covered with gold must contain the royal jewels, while the clay could be of no particular value. Thereupon the King ordered the caskets to be opened, and pointing to the golden ones he said, "These represent the men who go about clothed in fine raiment but within are full of evil deeds. But these," he added, turning to the caskets of clay, "represent those holy men who, though ill clad, are full of jewels of the faith." '[9] The selection of a casket or of caskets of mean appearance rather than of splendid exterior came to be regarded, in story-telling, as an evidence of virtue, and as such was combined with various other themes, and became extremely familiar in Western European literature. So it was made to indicate desirability in marriage, as in a tale in the *Gesta Romanorum*, in which an emperor subjects a princess to the test of choosing from three caskets, one of gold, one of silver, and one of lead, before allowing his son to marry her. The princess, like Bassanio, chose the leaden casket, and the wedding duly followed. Shakespeare might have read this story in Richard Robinson's edition (1577) of the Wynkyn de Worde *Gesta*; it is by no means certian where he got it. Further traces of the folk-tale origin of the theme are visible in the penalties, particularly that of celibacy, inflicted upon Portia's unsuccessful suitors (Act II, Scene 9). Whatever its source, the situation was used by Shakespeare in all its absurdity, because he knew that it was so commonly accepted and understood that his audiences would not question it.

How far Shylock was meant to be sympathetic and pathetic has been much debated. Stoll has demonstrated that a Jew and a miser could have enjoyed no such consideration in the Elizabethan theatre.[10] This is further corroborated by study of the Pound of Flesh theme. It does not seem to have been observed hitherto, or, if it has been observed, not sufficiently emphasized, that in early versions in which the lender of the money is neither a Jew nor a miser he nevertheless appears as a cruel or revengeful man, who could not, by the nature of the plot, be sympathetic. That blood is the price of the forfeiture of the bond shows his villainy; that the borrower has obtained the money for the sake of winning his lady or of enjoying her favours, and that he is saved by her intervention, further indicate that all the sympathy in the tale goes to the lovers. In a version in the *Gesta Romanorum*, the individual tales of which were probably gathered into this collection in the late thirteenth century, but are themselves much older, the lender is a merchant, whom the lover meets on the the street—'*perrexit ad quendam civitatem et obviavit uno mercatori*'. No reason is given for the merchant's strange bond, or for his hardness of heart when it comes to the payment. But he is harshly unyielding. '*Ait mercator: Quid verba multiplicias? Jam dixi tibi, crede michi, convencionem asscriptam inter nos habere volo*', etc.[11] In the *Dolopathos* of Johannes de Alta Silva, a collection of the twelfth century, the lender is a wealthy slave, whom the lover had once, in a fit of anger, mutilated by cutting off his foot. The slave now sees his chance to get even. '*Verum iuvenis se esse delusum dolens, a quodam servo divite, cui quondam ipse iratus pedem abciderat, centum argenti marcas sibi mutuari rogat. . . . Cui servus accepte quondam iniurie non immemor, pecuniam sub hoc pacto concedit, ut, si infra annum ipsam non restitueret, ipse de carne et ossibus iuvenis ad centum marcarum pondus auferret.*' The slave is obliged at the end not only to forgive the debt, but adds a thousand marks '*pro reconciliatione*'.[12] In other and later versions, the lender is made a Jew and a usurer, which blackens his villainy, but is not the deciding point in showing that he could not have been made sympathetic. With their background of popular narrative tradition, Shakespeare's audience knew that a man insisting on the blood forfeiture of a bond made with a lover who was staking all for a lady was up to no good, Jew or no Jew, and was to be regarded with aversion. They did not question that such a compact might be proposed and accepted, because they knew that such things happen in the world of story-telling. And Shakespeare knew it too.

The importance of examining social conventions may be illustrated by Shakespeare's treatment of chivalry. Many a teacher is asked why Romeo can, after his ardent devotion to Rosaline, forget her so quickly, or how Duke Orsino can love Olivia so strangely at long distance. Most mature readers of the plays have acquaintance enough with chivalric customs to understand such elementary matters, but with more subtle issues considerable explanation is often necessary. One such case I have discussed below, the wager in *Cymbeline*, which critic after critic has misunderstood. Everyone admits the influence of chivalry in the plays of Shakespeare, but it is extraordinary how little they have been studied against that background. When he put on the stage the adventures of the highly born, whether occurring on the walls of Troy or of Elsinore, in the park of the King of Navarre or of Leonato of Messina, he interpreted them in large measure according to contemporary courtly fashions. Chivalry, as a practical rule of life, was moribund in the fourteenth century, yet it was splendidly observed at the court of Edward III, it was ostentatiously practised during the Wars of the Roses, as for example by Malory's theatrical patron Richard Earl of Warwick, Henry VIII gave it magnificent expression at the Field of the Cloth of Gold, and it experienced a veritable rebirth under Elizabeth. A Virgin Queen enthroned gave new stimulus to elaborate and courtly compliment. From the time of her coronation, when Sir Edward Dimock rode on horseback into the hall, offering to fight any man who should deny Elizabeth to be the lawful sovereign of the realm, down to the days when, aged and wrinkled, she still demanded of her supporters the attentions bestowed by knights upon their lady-loves, chivalric observances ruled the outward manners of the court. Nor was the situation otherwise under James I. His accession was celebrated by a splendid tournament, and the glories of his state were sustained by lavish expenditure on knightly ceremonials. Prince Henry was especially fond of chivalric exercises, and excelled at tilting. All this, as a rule, bore small relation to the actual life of the time, just as tilting had no significance for actual warfare as then practised. Something of the true spirit of chivalry remained, however; the exaggerations of Raleigh, the bombast of Essex, were balanced by the true gentleness and courtesy of Sir Philip Sidney.

Medieval conceptions of the virtue of friendship explain much apparently exaggerated sentimentality in the relations between men in Shakespeare's plays. A true friend, so the Middle Ages believed, should stick at nothing to prove his devotion. Thus in the well-known tale of *Amis and Amile*, so charmingly retold by Pater,[13] Amile kills his own children in order to heal the leprosy of his friend. In the *Decameron*, in the eighth tale of the tenth day, Boccaccio tells how Gisippus, betrothed to Sophronia, and finding that his friend Titus is passionately in love with her, renounces all his rights as a husband, giving her to Titus. No account, apparently, is taken of the feelings of the lady. *The Two Gentlemen of Verona* has been very generally and wrongly taken to be mainly a love-story, whereas it is really a tale glorifying friendship. Even after the traitorous Proteus betrays him at the end, in a scene which generations of critics have misunderstood, Valentine is still the perfect friend, ready, when Proteus professes repentance, to sacrifice his lady, without consulting her, in order to prove the depth of his devotion to Proteus and the sincerity of his forgiveness.[14]

It appears, then, that Shakespeare was deeply influenced by

tradition, in the management of plot and characterization, and that no judgement of the subtler issues of his completed work is sound which refuses to take account of this. But its significance must not be misconceived or exaggerated. It ought to be superfluous to say that his imagination was confined within no rigid bounds, and that his artistic creativeness cannot be treated in any mechanical fashion. By the time he wrote the problem comedies he had long since emancipated himself from a slavish following of his sources; he took his own where he found it, but he treated it as he saw fit. He set his own personal and indelible seal upon it, altering it to suit his purposes, and lifting it into a sphere far removed from earlier play or poem or tale. The universality of his genius, which seems at times to transcend time and place, the modernity of his thought, carry us triumphantly, on a mighty surge, past many incongruities which appear disturbing upon more careful study. The rational way to account for those incongruities is not only to attempt to explain them logically, but to ask if they may not in part be due to Shakespeare's acceptance of traditions which are inconsistent with the logic of life as we understand it today – traditions the potency of which even he was powerless to escape. What I urge here, then, is a more careful evaluation of the elements by which his genius was to some extent controlled, as a corrective in that more difficult and subtle criticism which aims to follow him into the higher reaches of his imagination. Without such preliminary analysis, the most delicate and sympathetic appreciation, the most ardent devotion, the most rigid logic, will, I believe, go hopelessly astray.

This general approach to Shakespeare is of course in no wise novel. The necessity of following what is sometimes called 'the historical method', a large and vague term, has been often in the minds of commentators, though it has enjoyed less honour than impressionistic and aesthetic criticism. It is instructive to observe the fluctuations of learned opinion in the past. Despite the widespread admiration of Shakespeare in the eighteenth century, there persisted, in the conviction that classical standards should be the true guide to poetry and drama, an uneasy feeling that he wanted art; if he was not the '*grand fou*' of Voltaire, he was an untutored genius, whose defiance of dramatic conventions was to be deplored. The Romantic critics cried down such views with passionate emphasis, proclaiming him the model and copy from whom art and craftsmanship should be learned. Their adoration made them blind at once to defects and to processes of growth. Schlegel, Ulrici and Gervinus in Germany and Coleridge, Hazlitt and Lamb in England were little interested in how Shakespeare's plays came into being, but rather in their philosophical, literary and aesthetic import. This feeling continued well down to the twentieth century. The increasing knowledge of medieval and Renaissance literature too seldom led to the application of this knowledge to Shakespeare. Moreover, the plays were commonly viewed rather as poetry than as drama; one recalls Lamb's famous dictum that 'the plays of Shakespeare are less calculated for performance on a stage than those of almost any dramatist whatever'. The individualism of the Romantic school set men to interpreting the plays as they themselves felt them, seeking through their own imagination to point out new subtleties and excellences. Romantic criticism was, of course, anything that the critic chose to make it. It cannot be reduced to categories. But it is clear that it was little controlled by historical perspective; that it was mainly spun from within, from the critic's own mind. Much of it was of enduring value. The absorption of the most brilliant minds of Europe, from Goethe to Swinburne, in the plays of Shakespeare, produced a body of impressionistic criticism of the highest significance.

The necessity of more rigorous procedure, especially in the examination of sources and analogues, was perceived even before the time of Samuel Johnson, although little of practical value was accomplished. Johnson, himself, with his sturdy common-sense, saw that Shakespeare's achievement could not be correctly estimated without a knowledge of Elizabethan literature, and he read and took some account of this in pronouncing his critical judgements. He encouraged his friend Mrs Charlotte Lennox to publish her *Shakespear Illustrated*, which affords a general, if uncritical, view of the materials which Shakespeare utilized. Johnson's own work in historical criticism, and that of his predecessors and contemporaries, has been minutely and clearly set forth by Karl Young, who notes its submergence 'in the fine enthusiasms and transcendental insights of the critical schools that followed' – a submergence which lasted until the days of Rümelin and his *Shakespeare-studien* (1865), and indeed for long thereafter.[15] With increasing attention to technical investigations, in the closing years of the nineteenth century, a definite change became observable. Problems of text, of handwriting, of printing, of grammar, of semasiology; minute study of sources and analogues; investigation of folk-lore, contemporary science and medicine, research into the arrangements of the theatres and the theatrical companies – all this and much more proved its value as a check upon impressionistic criticism. The growing realization of its importance may be seen by following chronologically discussions of the enigmas of *Hamlet*. At the present day, no analysis, however subtle, can ignore the significance of technical investigations. It is obvious that nine-tenths of early aesthetic criticism went astray because of ignorance of the history of the Hamlet story, and of its effect upon the completed work of Shakespeare. The fundamental conceptions of the old Continental tale, and its later development at the hands of Kyd, as a Tragedy of Blood, combined with contemporary views of such subjects as revenge, madness, and melancholy, provide the surest avenues of approach to the elucidation of the vexed questions which generations of critics attempted to settle out of their own heads. The effect of this clear-eyed facing of the realities of dramatic history has been to show us another kind of Shakespeare from the idol of the Romantic school; not a god, but a man among men, working much as they did, and subject, in a large degree, to the same influences which moulded their lives; a man whose work is of varying artistic excellence, whose lapses are to be explained in human fashion, not as the nodding of a divinity, but a man, nevertheless, in whose heart and soul there burned a clear flame of genius such as the world has seldom seen.

Finally, in the last quarter-century, the gauntlet has been thrown squarely in the face of impressionistic criticism. The series of studies by Stoll, later collected into a volume, constitute the most important manifesto of the historical method, and of its significance for an understanding of the portrayal of character in the more important plays. Stoll was followed, in an aggressive and able book, by Schücking, who perhaps scarcely took sufficient account of earlier applications of this general method of approach.[16] It is clear that both

39

Stoll and Schücking formulate, in more vigorous fashion, a tendency of their time; it does not seem unfair to say that neither book could have been written fifty years earlier. When the twentieth century was well started, reaction was in the air. Romantic criticism could not continue along the old lines. The habit of looking at Shakespeare with an eye to historic fact as well as to imagination had been steadily increasing, and was bound to find its formal spokesmen. And the finest aesthetic criticism of our own times has been very different from that of the earlier romantics and philosophers. Dowden's aim, in his *Shakspere, His Mind and Art* (1875), 'to come into close and living relation with the individuality of a poet' started from the attempt to view him as of his time. 'It will be well first to stand away from Shakspere, and to view him as one element in a world larger than himself', the world of the age of Elizabeth.[17] And Bradley, in a classic of the application of logical analysis to Shakespearean tragedy (1904), spoke for those who 'read a play more or less as if they were actors who had to study all the parts. . . . This, carried through a drama, is the right way to read the dramatist Shakespeare' – the very antithesis of Lamb's position. Bradley continues, 'It is necessary, also, especially to a true conception of the whole, to compare, to analyse, to dissect. . . . In this process of comparison and analysis it is not requisite, it is on the contrary ruinous, to set imagination aside and to substitute some supposed "cold reason"; and it is only want of practice that makes the concurrent use of analysis difficult or irksome.'[18]

The application of the more rigorous modern method varies, of course, from critic to critic, according to his training and habit of mind. This is especially apparent in the final evaluation of Shakespeare's work. Any procedure which tries to hold in just equilibrium external influences upon the dramatist, and the mysterious ways of genius, is bound to err in details. Being human, the critic cannot always hold the balance true. So Legouis thinks that Stoll does not make sufficient allowance for Shakespeare's imaginative freedom. 'We may grant Mr Stoll,' he says, 'that the Romantic school [*le romantisme*] did not take sufficiently into account the theatrical conventions which limited the truthfulness of Shakespeare's delineations, but we can with justice reproach him for having himself represented Shakespeare too much as the slave or victim of these same conventions.'[19] On the other hand, it is clear that Schücking sometimes argues impressionistically and dogmatically. Feuillerat has noted that Stoll 'has applied the historical method far more rigorously than his successor', and that Schücking 'is not completely free from the tendencies which he attacks'.[20] One thing is obvious, at any rate; that when historical investigation has cleared the ground, aesthetic criticism must have the field in the final analysis. No matter how accurately we understand the influences which conditioned Shakespeare's work, these must always be secondary to that sympathetic appreciation which aims to follow the higher ranges of his genius, and to interpret them aright. But I think we can agree, at the present day, that aesthetic criticism cannot wing its flight without a careful survey of the ground beneath. There are, and probably always will be, critics who frankly regard the study of historical conditions and influences as a hindrance to full imaginative sympathy. The dramatist means, they say, what he means to you. Break the fetters of purblind peering into musty tomes, and enter into the warm rosy sunshine of his great spirit. There is no law against such procedure, but no consistent and solid interpretation of Shakespeare's artistic purposes can ever result from it. The ultimate result is likely to be illuminative of the critic's own mental processes rather than those of Shakespeare. We can read Goethe and Coleridge with profit, wrong as many of their conclusions undoubtedly were, because they were themselves men of great imaginative power and keenness of perception. Their utterances are notable as the reactions made by Shakespeare upon minds of the first rank. If the interpreter is himself a man of intellectual and imaginative power, his conclusions will be worth attention; if he is not, they will be negligible in just the measure in which he himself falls short in those qualities.

The chief emphasis in the following pages is on the historical and social groundwork. This emphasis is deliberate. Apart from other considerations, it seems to me still very necessary at the present day. I prefer, then, to have these studies regarded as a point of departure as much as an attempt at final interpretation of the problem comedies, although I have tried to indicate the general nature of ultimate solutions. I begin with *All's Well That Ends Well*, since that play presents, in singularly clear-cut form, a concrete example of the applicability of the principles here set forth. *Measure for Measure* is more difficult, partly because of greater complexity, and partly because of greater imaginative freedom. *Troilus and Cressida* represents a still further modification of material to a controlling artistic plan, determined, in general, absolutely by tradition, but developed with far less attention to purely theatrical effect. The persistence of the mood of these plays in the Dramatic Romances appears strikingly in *Cymbeline*, where, however, realistic treatment is quickly subordinated to the spirit of make-believe. Having thus attempted to gain a clearer idea of the meaning of the several plays, we shall be in a position to consider, in the final chapter, the group as a whole, and its significance in Shakespeare's artistic development.

TWO

All's Well That Ends Well

IN the analysis of any individual play, the first thing to observe is the special difficulties of interpretation which it presents. This does not mean the ultimate 'problems', stated abstractly in social or ethical terms, but definite questions of character and motivation in regard to which the intention of the dramatist is not wholly clear. In *All's Well* we are, for example, to ask ourselves in the beginning, not what Shakespeare thought of the relations between husband and wife in general, or of the conflict between love and caste, or of the limits to which a maid may go in wooing, but specifically whether he meant Helena to be regarded as noble and admirable, or as a schemer and a harpy, why he blackened the character of Bertram and yet rewarded him at the end, and whether he meant the final reconciliation of Bertram and Helena to be taken as a prelude to future bliss, or ironically, as a union which must ultimately result in disaster. These, and other difficulties, are so interrelated that it is hard to separate them completely, and to discuss each by itself.

Critical explanations have nowhere shown wider divergence than in regard to this play, nor have the points at issue ever been more sharply marked. Preliminary interpretation along the lines suggested in the opening chapter may be very strikingly made, since the main plot is a composite of themes of popular story, to which Shakespeare added no action of importance, though he altered many details, and provided the whole with the Parolles sub-plot. This sub-plot is singularly independent of the main action; much more so than is usual with Shakespeare's mature work, and it offers little difficulty. I shall return to it and to the minor comic relief later, after more important concerns have been disposed of; for the present it may be disregarded.

The familiar main plot may be concisely summed up as follows: Helena, the daughter of a poor physician, is passionately in love with

Bertram, Count of Rousillon. He does not suspect this, and has for her only the feelings of a friend. When he leaves for the French court, she employs a ruse to win him: following him, she offers to heal the king of France of a dangerous malady which has baffled all physicians, if the king will bestow upon her the husband whom she desires, putting her own life at stake if she fails. Making use of a sovereign remedy left her by her dead father, she heals the king, and as her reward claims Bertram as her husband. The king then forces him against his will to marry her.

Bertram leaves Helena immediately, and sends her word that she is never to call him husband until she can get a ring from his finger, and show him a child which he has begotten of her body. She follows him in disguise, and in Florence finds that he is attempting the honour of a maid named Diana. Helena bribes Diana to consent, and to demand Bertram's ring, and then herself takes Diana's place in the night rendez-vous without Bertram's dicovering the deception. Later she confronts him with the evidences that his conditions have been fulfilled, whereupon he accepts her gladly as his wife.

For the sake of convenience, I divide this, as a basis for later dis-cussion, into two parts: first, the Healing of the King, which carries the action through the marriage of Bertram and Helena; and second, the Fulfilment of the Tasks, which continues the action to the reconciliation at the end of the play. These, as we shall see, are ultimately based upon well-known themes of popular story. The second is the more important, since it occupies the major portion of the play, and constitutes its chief dramatic interest. It may therefore be examined first. Before proceeding with our analysis, however, let us look at some critical opinions.

The most important and interesting single character in the play is without doubt Helena. But what did Shakespeare mean that we should see in her? She has had distinguished and passionate ad-mirers; Coleridge's remark that she is Shakespeare's 'loveliest character' is famous, and Hazlitt maintained that in her conduct 'the most scrupulous nicety of female modesty is not once violated'. On the other hand, Dunlop said of Helena that 'considering the dis-parity of rank and fortune, it was, perhaps, indelicate to demand as her husband a man from whom she had received no declaration or proof of attachment, but she certainly overstepped all bounds of female decorum, in pertinaciously insisting on the celebration of a marriage to which he expressed such invincible repugnance ... she ingratiates herself into the family of a rival, and contrives a stratagem, the success of which could have bound Bertram neither in law nor in honour'.[1] Andrew Lang, whose taste and common-sense need not be emphasized, wrote much the same thing in a more vivacious way. 'Everyone would prefer to see the worm in the bud feed on the damask cheek rather than to see "*Vénus toute entière à sa proie attachée*", as Helena attaches herself to Bertram. A character in many ways so admirable is debased when Helena becomes a *crampon*. . . . Had Helena regained her lord in a more generous and seemly way, we would still have to pardon the original manner of the wooing.'[2] Lounsbury, in a criticism well worth reading, remarks, 'Nor can any excellence in Helen's character counterbalance the fundamental fact that she has been untrue to her sex. She persistently pursues a man who is not merely indifferent but averse.'[3] Helena has been adjudged guilty, then, on two counts; first, of forcing Bertram into an unwelcome marriage, and second, of compelling his acquiescence in it by an indelicate stratagem. Severest of all her critics, perhaps, is John Masefield, who believes that Shakespeare deliberately meant to make her despicable. 'Helena has been praised as one of the noblest of Shakespeare's women. Shakespeare saw her more clearly than any man who has ever lived. He saw her as a woman who practises a borrowed art, not for art's sake, nor for charity, but, woman fashion, for a selfish end. He saw her put a man into a position of ignominy quite unbearable, and then plot with other women to keep him in that position. Lastly, he saw her beloved all the time by the conventionally minded of both sexes.'[4]

Bertram is, by common consent, an unsympathetic hero. Few people can reconcile their hearts to him any more than could Dr Johnson, who found him 'a man noble without generosity, and young without truth; who marries Helen as a coward, and leaves her as a profligate: when she is dead by his unkindness, sneaks home to a second marriage, is accused by a woman whom he has wronged, defends himself by falsehood, and is dismissed to happiness'. We have the best of evidence that Bertram was not meant to be agreeable; a comparison with the source shows that Shakespeare deliberately blackened his character. But why should this have been done? Why

45

should the man upon whom the heroine centres all her affection, and for whom she braves the greatest dangers, be made a cad, a liar, and a coward?

It is not strange, then, that the ending of the play has caused the sharpest dissent, and the very title been held a misnomer. *Does* all end well? Can a marriage so arranged, an agreement between husband and wife so fulfilled, end happily? 'The very nobility of Helena's nature', says Lowes, 'renders the story which Shakespeare retained less plausible.' 'It needs all the dramatist's power to hold our sympathy and to force us to an unwilling assent to the title', remarks Neilson. Oliver Elton expresses a similar thought in a graceful sonnet.

> *All's Well!* – Nay, Spirit, was it well that she
>   Thy clear-eyed favourite, the wise, the rare,
>   The 'rose of youth', must her deep heart lay bare,
> And Helen wait on Bertram's contumely?
>
> Must Love's own humble, dauntless devotee
>   Make Night accomplice, and, a changeling, dare
>   The loveless love-encounter, and prepare
> To tread the brink of shame? May all this be
>
> And all end well? . . .

On the other hand, if those who condemn Helena are right, if, in Andrew Lang's phrase, she is 'the thief, not of love, but of lust', the chances for a really happy ending seem even smaller. And Bertram is quite as hard to explain psychologically as Helena. After treating his wife with the greatest harshness, setting what he believes impassable barriers to their union, engaging in an intrigue with another woman, and 'boggling shrewdly' to lie himself out of a tight place, he is apparently transformed in the twinkling of an eye into a model husband.

> If she, my liege, can make me know this clearly,
> I'll love her dearly, ever, ever dearly.

But are things going to end well for Bertram any more than for Helena?[5]

The comic relief, provided by Parolles and the Clown, brings no sunshine. The Clown is certainly, in the words of the Countess, 'a foul-mouth'd and calumnious knave', and Parolles, to quote Krapp,[6] who thinks better of him than most of us, 'is one of those obnoxious creatures who make themselves too conspicuous to be disregarded and yet must be scorned and despised'. Why had Shakespeare, who had hitherto treated clownish humour and braggadocio genially, no pleasanter use for them here?

How all these things, in sum, affect us, has been succinctly put by Barrett Wendell. 'There is no other work of Shakspere's which in conception and in temper seems quite so corrupt as this. . . . There are other works of Shakspere which are more painful; there are none less pleasing, none on which one cares less to dwell.' The nature of the plot has kept *All's Well* almost completely from representation on the modern stage; Kemble, in his acting version, omitted the central episode of the main action altogether. 'Everyone who reads this play,' says the editor of the *Arden Shakespeare* volume, 'is at first shocked and perplexed by the revolting idea which underlies the plot . . . it leaves so unpleasant a flavour with some people that it is not tasted again.'[7]

And so we come to the final questions. What does it all mean? Why did Shakespeare write this strange piece? Here the critics are again hopelessly at odds. The reader will find the much-venerated Gervinus treating the whole play as a moral allegory on the theme that 'merit goes before rank'. In allegory, of course, one expects some violence to reason and probability. He will find Dr Johnson, on the other hand, arguing that Shakespeare 'sacrificed virtue to convenience', and, in his desire to please, wrote with no moral purpose whatever. He will find Raleigh and Schücking attributing the apparent psychological shortcomings of the play to Shakespeare's carelessness or creative opulence, 'a part of his magnanimity, and a testimony to his boundless resource'. Elton believes that the solution lies in remembering that love is not governed by reason, and that nature works in a wonderful way. In the closing lines of the sonnet from which quotation has already been made, Shakespeare defends his work thus:

> That Spirit, from his seat
> Elysian, seems to murmur: 'Sometimes know
> In Love's unreason hidden, Nature's voice;

In Love's resolve, Her will; and though his feet
   Walk by wild ways precipitous, yet, so
     Love's self be true, Love may at last rejoice.'

Seccombe and Allen frankly give up the problem: 'The plot is a fanciful imbroglio, and the situations, even when they seem most threatening, have no more reality than arabesques; to regard the characters too seriously is merely to court delusion.'[8]

I will state briefly in advance the answers to these queries, suggested by the following analysis. I think it will be clear that Helena was meant by Shakespeare to be wholly noble and heroic, and fully justified in her conduct, both in the winning of Bertram and in the manner of fulfilling his conditions for their union after their marriage; that the Elizabethan audience would have accepted these 'tricks' as valid without question; that Bertram's sudden change of heart was a convention of medieval and Elizabethan story, which must be expected to follow Helena's triumph; that there is no implication that their after life would be anything but happy; and that the blackening of the character of Bertram and the disagreeable qualities of the Clown and Parolles are explainable for reasons of dramatic contrast and dramatic motivation. Shakespeare's own attitude to the materials in which he worked, and his ultimate artistic purpose in transforming them, can hardly be summed up in a phrase or two; this will require longer discussion last of all. I shall not seek to prove that the play is a pleasant one, or that it seemed so to the playgoers for whom Shakespeare wrote. But I do believe that it is far more unsavoury to us than it was to them, and that the effect which it was intended to create has been generally misunderstood.

I. THE FULFILMENT OF THE TASKS

The main plot of *All's Well* is based on the ninth novel of the third day of the *Decameron* of Boccaccio, which Shakespeare in all probability got from the faithful translation in Paynter's *Palace of Pleasure*. In brief, the story as told by Paynter is as follows:

Giletta, the daughter of Gerardo of Narbona, physician to the Count of Rossiglione, fell deeply in love with the Count's son Beltramo. Upon the death of the Count, Beltramo went to Paris. The king of France was at this time suffering from an illness which no one could cure. Giletta, who had longed to follow Beltramo, now saw 'not onelie a lawfull occasion to goe to Paris, but if the disease were suche (as she supposed) easely to bryng to passe that she might have the Counte Beltramo to her husbande'. She offered to restore the king to health, and if unsuccessful, to submit to being burnt. The king proposed, in case the cure were accomplished, to give her in marriage to some worthy gentleman, to which she assented, reserving, however, the right of choice for herself. The king was healed, whereupon Giletta demanded Beltramo as husband. The young Count, 'knowing her not to be of a stocke convenable to his nobilitie', objected, but the king insisted that the marriage be celebrated. After this was over, the Count obtained permission to return to his own country, but instead went to Tuscany, and entered the service of the Florentines against the people of Sienna (the Senois). Giletta returned to Rossiglione, where she set the Count's affairs in order, and then sent two knights to tell him that if it were on her account that he was absenting himself from home, she would herself leave. He replied that she might do as she pleased; that he did not purpose to live with her until she should get upon her finger a ring which he wore, and have a son begotten by him. When this reply was made known to Giletta, she told it to the chief men of Rossiglione, and said that she was unworthy to cause the exile of the Count, and that her purpose was to spend the rest of her life in pilgrimages and devotions. She then made her way to Florence, and lodged in the house of a poor widow. The widow told her that Beltramo was in love with the daughter of a gentlewoman of the city, a neighbour. Giletta went to this gentlewoman, and selling the whole story of her marriage, proposed that the daughter thould consent to the Count's advances, and demand his ring as a pledge, while she herself should take the daughter's place in bed, and so, by the grace of God, be got with child. So the affair was arranged. The gentlewoman and her daughter were rewarded with a large sum for the latter's dowry, and rich jewels, and thereupon retired into the country. Beltramo, being called home by his subjects, and hearing that Giletta had left, returned to Rossiglione. Giletta stayed on in Florence, where two sons were born to her. After causing them 'carefullie to be noursed and brought up', she repaired to Montpellier, where Beltramo, on All Saints' Day, was entertaining many knights and ladies at a great feast. In pilgrim's weeds, Giletta entered the hall, her two sons in her arms, and made herself known to her husband, showing him his ring, and claiming the fulfilment of his conditions. The Count asked her to tell how it had come to pass, and she related the whole story. 'For whiche

49

cause the counte knowyng the thynges she had spoken to be true (and perceivyng her constaunt minde and good witte, and the twoo faier yonge boies to kepe his promise made, and to please his subjects, and the ladies that made sute unto him, to accept her from that time forthe as his lawfull wife, and to honour her) abjected his obstinate rigour: causyng her to rise up, and imbraced and kissed her, acknowledgyng her againe for his lawfull wife . . . and from that tyme forthe, he loved and honoured her, as his dere spouse and wife.'

Shakespeare followed closely the main outlines of his source, but he altered many details. Moreover, he made it more elaborate by the introduction of Parolles and the sub-plot, of the Countess and the Clown and Lafeu, and of a second ring in the final episode. Compared with Boccaccio's ending, Shakespeare's Fifth Act is exceedingly complicated. It is generally agreed that the play has undergone a process of revision.[9]

The direct source of Boccaccio's *novella* is not known, but neither of its leading themes, which I have called the Healing of the King and the Fulfilment of the Tasks, can have been original with him. The popularity of these themes is shown by various early narratives in prose and verse, from which instructive conclusions may be drawn as to the general significance of the story as told by Boccaccio and by Shakespeare. To these narratives we may now give our attention. I prefer, as I have suggested, to consider first the second theme, since this occupies the main portion of the play. Reduced to its lowest terms, the Fulfilment of the Tasks may be stated as follows: a wife is deserted by her husband, to be taken back on the fulfilment of apparently impossible conditions, one of which is to get a child by him. She performs these tasks, and wins back her husband.

I do not ally myself with those who think it possible to trace in detail the origins and development of popular stories. The material is at once too vast and too fragmentary, too widespread, too elusive, to allow of any certainty in results. We are familiar with the weakness of the theory, followed by a multitude of scholars, and popularized for English readers by Max Müller, that such tales represent the faded remains of mythological narratives and concepts, and of the hypothesis, formerly widely accepted, that their origins are mainly to be found in the Orient. Such origins as can be traced are to be sought rather in primitive manners and customs, in the domains of anthropology and folklore. But this is no part of our present task. We shall rather observe evidences for the wide distribution of the themes of traditional story, such as the one just summarized, which underlie Shakespeare's plots; we shall reduce these themes to their lowest terms, so far as possible, and note characteristic changes which they have undergone in various countries and at various times, under the influence of special conditions.

Oriental analogues are frequently of considerable significance, even though we realize that all our chickens are not to be hatched out of eggs from India. The following Eastern tale[10] presents, in simple form, the theme with which we are at present concerned.

A clever woman was married to a husband who said to her one day, 'I cannot stay at home any more, for I must go on a year's journey to carry on my business.' And he added, laughing, 'When I return I expect to find you have built me a grand well; and also, as you are such a clever wife, to see a little son!' The wife got the money by a series of ruses, and had the well dug. She then travelled a long distance in man's attire, until she found her husband. Then she disguised herself again as a cowherd's daughter. The husband was attracted by her beauty, but did not recognize her, and proposed marriage. So they were married. At the end of three months he said that he must return. She asked him to give her his old cap and his picture. She then went back to her home, where a son was born to her. On the husband's arrival, he was not pleased to see the baby, but she showed him the cap and the picture, and told him the whole story, pointing out the new well also. So all ended happily.

More elaborate is the following Turkish story.[11]

A certain prince had a Vizier, who was the father of a twelve-year-old daughter. Hearing the maiden's cleverness praised, the prince called the Vizier to him, and propounded a riddle, which the Vizier was to answer within three days, or lose his head. After three days had passed, and the Vizier could find no answer, his daughter gave him the solution. When the prince was told, he asked who had given the Vizier the answer. At first the Vizier asserted that he himself had guessed the riddle; then he admitted that his daughter had aided him. The prince answered, 'If that is the case, the maiden will do for my wife.' The girl demanded that before they were married, the prince should bring her a white elephant, and a man without sorrow. The elephant was procured, but the prince, after searching vainly for three years for a man without sorrow, returned home. He then married the Vizier's daughter, but did not live with her. Instead, he went off hunting, announcing that he should be gone nine years. Upon leaving he gave his wife an empty chest, the mouth of which was sealed with his seal, commanding her to fill it with gold and silver without opening it, and a mare who must give birth to a foal like his black horse. He also told his wife that she must bear a child, instruct him well, and send the child to him, mounted upon the horse.

After he had been gone three days, the wife attired herself like a king's son, dressed up four hundred maidens like men, and rode out after her husband. She pitched her tent near the place where he was staying, thus attracting his attention. Hospitalities were exchanged, the prince not recognizing his wife in disguise. They played checkers in the prince's tent. The pretended youth proposed that they should play for a stake. So each wagered his horse, saddle, trappings, and seal. The wife won, and retiring to her tent with the seal, she brought the horse and mare together. Opening the chest, she filled it with gold and silver, and sealed it with her husband's seal. She then sent horse, trappings and seal back to the prince. The next evening, the wife proposed that they play for a girl. She purposely lost, and told the prince that she would send him a beautiful female slave. Retiring to her tent, she then assumed that disguise, and came back to her husband. He was inflamed with love for the supposed slave, and lay that night with her. They drank spirits (Branntwein), and the slave gave the prince a box on the ear. Angry and drunken, he chased the slave away from his tent. The wife then collected her retinue, and returned home.

After nine months, nine days and nine hours, she bore a son, whom she well instructed as he grew older. The mare also bore a foal. At the end of the nine years, the prince returned. His son was placed on the steed, and sent to meet his father. The prince was told that the boy was the son of the Vizier's daughter. At first he was angry, thinking that the child was not his own. Then the wife showed him the chest, told him that the steed on which the boy was riding was the issue of the mare and his own horse, and related the whole story.

'Then the prince was extremely joyful over what the maiden had done; because she was exceedingly clever and well-instructed, he exalted her above all his other wives. After he had lived with her a long time, he finally died.'

The motivation of the husband's desertion varies. The Indian tale, 'The Clever Wife', just cited is unusual in that the husband lays his commands upon his wife as a jest. In the Turkish story there seems to be no reason for the husband's departure for a nine-year stay, immediately after the marriage, but I am inclined to think that a fuller form of the tale would reveal it as pique for the tasks laid upon him by his wife[12] – the procuring of a white elephant and a man who had known no sorrow. Oral circulation frequently obscures the motivation of popular stories. The introductory episode of the Turkish tale, in which the girl wins a husband by her cleverness, should be especially noted.

A pretty example of the theme comes from a collection of Norwegian ballads.[13]

King Kristian goes off to war, and lays three tasks upon his wife. She must build a throne shining like the morning sun, construct a magnificent hall, and have a child by him. She gets advice from an old man. After the accomplishment of the first two tasks, she follows her husband to Scotland in disguise, and is gotten with child by him. The king gives her a ring with his name on it, which serves as a proof of the paternity of the child when he returns home.

The strange compilation known as the *Mágussaga* or the *Bragtha-Mágus saga* well illustrates the introduction of the episode into a longer narrative. The material in the saga was in large part carried to Iceland by men who had listened to the tales of French minstrels, and after being further altered by oral transmission, was worked up into written form. In its present shape it cannot be earlier than the middle of the thirteenth century. The portion which is of interest for us may be briefly summarized.

Hlothver is king of Saxland. One day he asks his counsellor Sigurd whether there is a king equal to him on earth. Sigurd tells him that as long as he lacks a wife and children his power is not complete, and draws his attention to Ermenga, daughter of Hugon of Miklagarth. The marriage is arranged, and Hlothver goes to get his bride. Ermenga paints her face white with chalk-water, and brings Hlothver a roasted cock, asking him to divide it between her and her father and two brothers. Hlothver is annoyed, but divides the cock. He returns to his own land, but remembers the insult. A Danish army is besieging Treviris. Hlothver, on going to war, sets his wife, in revenge for the insult of the division of the cock, three tasks, to be accomplished within three years:

she must build a hall, as splendid as that of her father; she must get a stallion, sword and hawk, as costly as those owned by Hlothver; she must show him a son of whom he is father and she the mother. She builds the hall. She then gives Sigurd the regency of Saxland, goes to Miklagarth, and brings back sixty warriors to Treviris, which is held by the Danes. She calls herself Jarl Iring of Alimannia, and enters the army of the Danish king. Her brother Hrolf, who is with Hlothver, tells him he has seen a fair maiden looking out of a window of the city. Ermenga, as the maiden, tells Hlothver that she is captive of Jarl Iring and that she is a princess of Frigia, and beseeches him to free her. The king sends for Iring, who consents to give up the captive for the king's stallion, sword and hawk. She then puts on women's clothes, and is conducted by Hrolf to the king, who keeps her three nights. She gets possession of the king's ring. With the help of Hrolf she returns to Saxland, where a son is born to her. The king returns also in due time, and finds that the tasks have been performed.

The anger of Hlothver at the division of the cock – a widespread folk-theme – is not a plausible reason for the imposition of the tasks. The whole saga, indeed, quite lacks the artistry which transforms varied materials into a unified whole.

The appearance of the theme in literature of an aristocratic variety may be illustrated by the charming prose romance *Le Livre du Très Chevalereux Comte d'Artois et de sa Femme*. This graceful story, which reflects the full tide of chivalry, deserves especial attention. The hero and heroine are historical, but their adventures are fictitious. Philip I of Burgundy, born in 1323, the son of Eudes IV and Jeanne de France, Countess of Artois, married in 1338 the Countess Jeanne of Boulogne, who bore him an heir in 1342. Philip died in 1346. The title 'Comte d'Artois' was never properly his; it would have passed to him on the death of his mother, who survived him. The romance appears to have been written in the later fifteenth century for Rodulf, marquis of Axberg, count of Neuchâtel, a friend of the Duke of Burgundy. Devices in the ornamentation make it probable that one manuscript was prepared for the wedding of Rodulf's son with Marie of Savoy in 1476. Rodulf himself died in 1487. The important point is that the romance affords a faithful picture of chivalric conventions of the later fifteenth century, and that its purpose is in effect a glorification and exaltation of an earlier Duke of Burgundy and his wife. The theme of *All's Well* is much expanded by descriptions of the 'grans vaillances' of the noble count, after leaving his wife. These, with the introductory matter preceding the marriage, form considerably more than half of the whole work. The development of the main theme is thus greatly retarded.

The Count of Artois was united in marriage to the daughter of the Count of Boulogne, with great pomp and rejoicing. Two or three years were happily spent by the couple in their city of Arras, but no child was born to them. This put the Count into a deep melancholy. One day, as he was leaning at a window thinking of this matter, the Countess approached, and asked the reason of his dejection. He replied, 'realizing her devotion and good-will towards him', that he had formed a firm resolution. 'This is, that I shall leave this country, and not return to be with you, until three impossible things are accomplished: first, that you be with child by me, and that I know it not; second, that I give you my steed that I love so much, and that I know it not; third and last, that I give you my diamond also, and that I know it not.' Shortly thereafter the Count rode away, leaving his wife behind so sorely afflicted that it was long believed that life had left her body. The adventures of the Count are then related at length. After the first despair of her grief was over, the Countess cast about for means to accomplish the tasks laid upon her. Clad in man's attire, she set out to find her husband, attended by a faithful vassal named Olivier. Feigning that she was going on a pilgrimage, she followed her husband to Valladolid, where she recognized his lodgings by the arms outside the door. Taking the name of Philipot, she entered his service as page. Sleeping in his chamber, as was the custom, she overhears her husband sighing for the love of the daughter of the king of Castille. She reveals the Count's love to the duenna of the princess, and also tells the duenna her whole story. They arrange that the Count shall be told that the princess grants him her love, but that in reality the Countess shall be substituted in her place in bed. This is done; the trick is repeated secretly many times, and the Countess is got with child. In her disguise as page, she receives from her husband the diamond, as a reward for her services in the love-affair, and the horse as well, to heal the malady from which the page appears to suffer. The Countess then makes her way back to Arras, where she calls an assembly of the nobles and clergy, and tells them of her accomplishment of the tasks laid upon her by her husband. The Count is sent for by an embassy headed by the Bishop of Arras, who tells him of the fulfilment of the tasks. The Count is deeply impressed by the devotion of his wife, and returns to Arras, where a child is born to them. 'There they lived in happy tranquillity for the rest of their lives.'

The motivation of the story is not faultless. 'The Countess of Artois is abandoned by her husband, who imposes the well-known conditions because, after three years of married life, she has given him no child. It is, therefore, absurd for her to run all the dangers to which she exposes herself, in order to pass one night with her husband, with so problematical a chance of success.'[14] This blemish is very effectually concealed by the charm with which the whole is narrated, however.

It is time to consider the bearing of these stories upon the interpretation of *All's Well That Ends Well.*

In the first place, they exalt the cleverness and devotion of the woman; the wits of the wife are more than a match for those of the husband, and her purpose is a happy reunion with him. There are analogous tales, of a similar significance, of a wife lying unrecognized with her husband without the imposition of tasks. A pretty Spanish poem[15] treats '*del engaño que usó la reina doña María de Aragón, para qué el rey don Pedro su marido durmiese con ella.*' The husband is pleased, and summons witnesses. The queen has a child in due course of time. An Egyptian folk-tale tells of the marriage of a girl of the Clever Wench type with a prince. After they are married he refuses to live with her. She disguises herself three times and has three children by him. When he learned the truth he 'was very happy and recognized the superiority of his wife . . . and they lived in happiness and prosperity all their lives.'[16] In many other analogues an unmarried woman, not a wife, must perform difficult tasks before a man will marry her. The tale of Diarmaid and Graidhne will serve as an illustration; I quote Professor Child's summary.

The Graidhne whom we have seen winning Fionn for husband by guessing his riddles . . . afterwards became enamored of Diarmaid, Fionn's nephew, in consequence of her accidentally seeing a beauty spot on Diarmaid's forehead. This had the power of infecting with love any woman whose eye should light upon it: wherefore Diarmaid used to wear his cap well down. Graidhne tried to make Diarmaid run away with her. But he said, 'I will not go with thee. I will not take thee in softness, and I will not take thee in hardness; I will not take thee without, and I will not take thee within; I will not take thee on horseback, and I will not take thee on foot.' Then he went and built himself a house where he thought he should be out of her way. But Graidhne found him out. She took up a position between the two sides of the door, on a buck goat, and called to him to go with her. For, said she, 'I am not without, I am not within; I am not on foot, and I am not on a horse; and thou must go with me.' After this Diarmaid had no choice.[17]

Very numerous are the tales in which the Clever Wench gives more than one proof of her wit; first, before marriage, and then after her union to the desirable husband, generally of high station, whom her adroitness has won for her.[18] Among these tales is, of course, the *novella* of Boccaccio which serves as a basis for Shakespeare's play.

In the second place, the husband, in the tales of married heroines with which we are chiefly concerned, accepts the situation as an evidence of his wife's courage and love. Nowhere is there a suggestion that he regards himself as having been despicably tricked. Many of the tales emphasize his pleasure at the outcome. And his rejoicing has a good foundation, for all these couples seem, in the good old way, 'to live happily ever after'. The merits of the wife bring their reward. In the *Romance of the Count of Artois*, the duenna, whom the count interviews before returning home, in order to learn from her the whole truth, puts the matter plainly. '*Par foy, sire, fait-elle, le celer ne vous vault riens; si vous jure en ma conscience qu'à la plus léale et meilleure dame de quoy l'en puist tenir parole estez-vous mariés; et bien l'a monstré quant pour vostre amour a enduré telle peine qui ne puet à dame estre pareille, durant sa queste ennuyeuse, laquelle jà n'eust achevée ne fust sa science et bonne conduicte; si me fist son fait si grant pitié avoir au cuer, qu'à luy aidier ay mis l'onneur de ma dame et mon bien en adventure, dont il n'est en riens mesvenu, pour quoy je loue Dieu et la benoite vierge Marie sa précieuse mère, à qui je prie qu'ilz veullent changier vostre vouloir en telle manière que ce soit à la joye de ma dame la contesse d'Artois, qui si léalment vous ayme que bien vous en doit souvenir à toutes heures.*'[19]

In the sources of *All's Well*, then, we recognize a Virtue Story, exalting the devotion of a woman to the man who so far forgets his duty as to treat her cruelly. Analogues of other kinds will occur to the reader immediately; the adventures of Griselda or Fair Annie, in which a husband comes to realize the fidelity of his wife after she has been subjected to the most trying of proofs; the ballad of *Child Waters*, in which the heroine, though pregnant, is forced to follow her lover's horse on foot before the man relents; the *Nut-Brown Maid*, which exhibits various tests of the woman's fidelity, ending with the moral,

> Here may ye see that wimen be
> In love, meke, kinde, and stable.

All this directly contradicts the arguments that the actions of Helena in regaining her husband would not have seemed deserving of admiration. There is at the end of Shakespeare's play, to be sure, no formal recognition of Helena's devotion and cleverness. Perhaps it has been crowded out in order to sustain the dramatic suspense by making things seem to go against the heroine up to the last moment. We shall later examine in detail the elaborate interweaving of surprises with which Shakespeare closes his play. This complicated series of mistakes is far more dramatic as material for the Fifth Act than the pretty scene in the French romance in which husband and wife are united, or the elaborate banquet-setting in Boccaccio's tale. After these mistakes are all resolved, the final reconciliation of Bertram and Helena is curiously brief and bald, even more so than in *Cymbeline*, when Posthumus and Imogen are at last united. The reasons for this brevity of treatment in *All's Well* will appear presently. Here the point to observe is that for dramatic reasons the Virtue Story quality, so evident in the analogues, is somewhat disguised in Shakespeare's dénouement.

We are now in a position to refute the assertion that Helena is guilty of indelicate persistence in pursuing the man who has rebuffed her. Just such persistence, such single-eyed devotion to a good object, irrespective of all other considerations, was regarded as meritorious. It is one of the most striking features of the Virtue Stories. As Hales says[20] of the tale of Griselda, 'the story does not contemplate the virtue it celebrates in reference to other virtues. It does not concern itself with these; in its devotion to its one object, it may even outrage some of them.' We shall later observe an admirable illustration of this, in the wager-plot in *Cymbeline*. That a virtue might be carried too far, or that it might transgress the most elementary demands of common-sense and decency in making for its goal, seems to have been little regarded in medieval story. Fantastic exaggerations were common, and due allowance must be made for these exaggerations when we find them woven into the fabric of Shakespeare's plays.

Equally untenable, in the light of early analogues, is the idea that the bed-trick is immodest, unworthy of a refined woman. There is never the least intimation in these analogues that the heroine, in thus proving her devotion, is doing an immodest thing. The answer would have been: she is lying with her husband, as any chaste wife has a right to do. The objection that delicacy would prevent her from doing so under false pretences would have been met by an Elizabethan, partly by the obvious point that she has to do so in order to fulfil her husband's conditions, and partly by the conviction, which we have just noted, that virtue should stick at nothing in pursuing its course. This appears not only in popular but also aristocratic literature. Would the elegant chronicler of the adventures of the Count of Artois, writing in the late fifteenth century, in order to compliment the houses of Burgundy and Artois, have attributed this ruse to the elegant and virtuous Countess if it had seemed indelicate? Would Shakespeare, in *Measure for Measure*, have made the ensky'd and sainted Isabella, the gentle forsaken Mariana, and the benevolent Duke use a similar stratagem if it had been felt repugnant to modesty?

What, now, as to the psychological adequacy of the ending of the play? Shall we conclude that 'the triumph of Helena's love will be merely external', that a union so brought about will never be happy?

To argue thus is to miss the whole point of the Faithful Wife theme, whether in medieval and Renaissance analogues, or in Shakespeare. No matter how harsh the treatment of the woman by the man, no matter how unsuited they may seem to each other, it is a convention of the Virtue Story that they 'live happily ever after'.

> Ful many a yeer in heigh prosperitee
> Liven these two in concord and in reste,

says Chaucer, after the trials of Griselda are over. After their reunion, the Count of Artois and his wife '*vesquirent en bonne transquillité le résidu du temps qu'ils avoient a vivre*'. So Beltramo lived with Giletta, '*come sua sposa e moglie onorando, l'amò e sommamente ebbe cara*'. In the cold light of reason, these endings may not seem destined to bring happiness. So one may argue that Cophetua and the Beggar Maid would have had little in common; she might have longed to exchange palace etiquette for the delightful freedom of begging in the street. Would the Prince have really been happy with Cinderella, obviously of a very different social station, just because she happened to have a small foot? The answer is, of course he would; the cold light of reason is no guide in stories. The fulfilment of the task is not a logical settlement of the dislike or indifference of the man for the woman, but it has perfect validity in a tale. Bertram, in setting the tasks for Helena, was really only stating in picturesque fashion that he would never live with her. 'When thou canst get the ring upon my finger which never shall come off, and show me a child begotten of thy body that I am father to, then call me husband; but in such a "then" I write a "never".' Dorigen in the *Franklin's Tale* sets an impossible condition, as she thinks, in order to get rid of an importunate wooer, like the ladies in the analogous tales in the *Filocolo* and the *Decameron*. But when the seemingly impossible is accomplished, the promise has to be kept. In the tales which we have just been examining, the accomplishment of the tasks, like the fitting of the slipper on Cinderella's foot, seems miraculously to melt away all reluctance on the part of the promiser. The inconsequence of fairy tales in this regard has been delightfully satirized by Barrie, in *A Kiss for Cinderella*. The Prince is very bored with the whole business, and as Cinderella advances for the trial he says, 'Oh, bother!'

(These words are the last spoken by him in his present state. When we see him again, which is the moment afterwards, he is translated. He looks the same, but so does a clock into which new works have been put. The change is effected quite simply by Cinderella delicately raising her skirt and showing him her foot. As the exquisite nature of the sight thus vouchsafed him penetrates his being, a tremor passes through his frame; his vices take flight from him and the virtues enter. It is a heady wakening, and he falls at her feet.)

'His vices take flight from him and the virtues enter.' Could anything more perfectly describe what happens to Bertram at the end of the play than this? Or what happens to the men whom Julia, Hero, Mariana, Celia, Imogen, and other pure and beautiful heroines marry? 'We are astonished,' says Creizenach, 'how easily in these closing scenes the wrong-doers are pardoned, even when through their criminal devices they have conjured up the greatest dangers. . . . Furthermore, it often happens that in the closing scenes attempts at poisoning and the like are no longer reprehended. The most unbelievable forgiveness in this regard is that of the innocent and suffering women, who in many such pieces are forsaken by their husbands for a mistress, or even pursued with attempt to kill. *Conclusions about the moral convictions and feelings of the dramatists cannot be drawn from these scenes:* they are obviously a part of the style of the romantic and unrealistic drama, as in comedy, where all ends with general happiness; we shall also notice examples of such ready forgiveness in Spanish comedies.'[21] The reason why occurrences of this sort in drama were confined to no one region is that the conventions of story-telling which produced them were the common traditions of the various countries of western Europe.

We may now gather up the threads of the preceding argument. It is clear that, from the point of view of narrative traditions still accepted in Shakespeare's day, the conduct of Helena in fulfilling the conditions set by Bertram for their union was admirable; that she showed cleverness, devotion and courage; that she was guilty neither of immodesty nor of unwomanly persistency; and that the 'happy ending' was accepted as a convention of drama because it was also a convention of story-telling.

But what of the opening scenes? Does a similar method of investigation exonerate Helena from the charge of unworthy conduct in forcing Bertram into a marriage which he does not desire? Again, from the point of view of Shakespeare's own day, I think Helena is guiltless. The whole matter deserves separate consideration, and must be treated by itself, though fortunately it may be disposed of more rapidly than the episode which has just been analysed.

2. THE HEALING OF THE KING

This, like the theme which has just been discussed, belongs to the general type known to students of popular story as 'The Clever Wench'. The two have been noted in combination, so far as my knowledge extends, only in Boccaccio and Shakespeare. Tales illustrating the cleverness of a heroine both before and after marriage are, however, very common.[22] In a large number of these the girl wins a high-born husband by her adroitness, and then gives other proofs of her shrewdness after her marriage. This is the case, for example, in the Turkish story of the Vizier's Clever Daughter, already cited. The Healing of the King was obviously attached to the Fulfilment of the Tasks in a similar way, to explain how the heroine came to be married, and to illustrate her cleverness. Boccaccio probably found the two in a source not now known to us; it is possible, of course, that he made the combination himself.

Landau thinks the Healing of the King of Eastern origin. This may be true, but the best of his analogues, an Indian tale from the story-collection of Somadeva, bears, to my mind, only a slight resemblance to the incident in Boccaccio. I give a somewhat more detailed summary than he does, in order that the reader may judge for himself.

Kirtisenâ, the wife of the rich young merchant Devasena, is ill-treated by her mother-in-law at home. Devasena goes away on a journey, after urging his mother to be kind to his wife. But the mother-in-law treats her with great cruelty, shutting her up in a dungeon, and giving her only a little rice each day. Finally Kirtisenâ escapes, and putting on man's attire, joins a caravan, which is passing through the woods. She fears robbers and conceals herself in a hollow tree. The caravan is attacked by a robber band, and all are slain. Kirtisenâ hears from her place of concealment in the tree a female demon (Râkshasî) telling her children about the illness of King Vasudatta. While he was asleep a centipede crawled into his ear, and multiplied in his brain. The demon goes on to narrate how the king may be healed. Kirtisenâ, having listened to all this, determines to undertake the cure. Still disguised as a man, she goes to the court and announces her mission. The king promises her half of his kingdom if she succeeds. A night passes; on the next day Kirtisenâ draws a hundred and fifty insects out of the king's head. She refuses half the kingdom, but accepts other rich rewards. She then hears that a caravan led by Devasena is passing through the city, and so finds her husband and tells the whole story to him and to the court. The king, deeply moved by this fidelity, gives her the honour of calling herself his sister (Dharmabhaginî) and makes Devasena a citizen. In this city husband and wife settle down to enjoy happiness for the rest of their days.[23]

I do not think that it has been observed that the Healing of the King, as found in Boccaccio and Shakespeare in the *All's Well* story, is merely a variation of one of the commonest of popular themes: a hero wins the hand of a king's daughter by performing a difficult task, in which failure will cost him his life. Instances of this theme need hardly be cited. Shakespeare, or more probably the unknown writer whose work he touched up, utilized it in *Pericles:* the hand of the daughter of King Antiochus is promised to the man who guesses the king's riddle, but death is his portion if he fails. Pericles guesses the riddle. The reader may follow this at his leisure through the many versions of the Apollonius of Tyre story. In the *Mabinogion*, in the tale of *Kilhwch and Olwen*, Kilhwch seeks the hand of the maiden Olwen, the daughter of Yspadadden Penkawr, a fearsome giant, who has slain many ambitious youths. Difficult tasks are set Kilhwch which he must perform before the maiden may be his, which are accomplished with the aid of Arthur and his heroes. Closer to the situation in *All's Well* is a parallel from Campbell's *Popular Tales of the West Highlands*,[24] which, in spite of its modern dress, is obviously old folk-material.

Farquhar, a drover in the Reay country, gets supernatural wisdom. The king is sick, and no doctors can heal him. Farquhar knows that the doctors are keeping a black beetle in the wound, and himself undertakes the cure, which is successful. The doctors are hanged, and Farquhar is offered lands or gold or whatever he desires as a reward. He asks for the hand of the king's daughter, and a grant of land, to which the king assents.

The variation of the theme in Boccaccio and Shakespeare consists in having it told of a woman instead of a man. The type tale would run something like this: a girl heals a sick king, her life being forfeit if she fails, and is rewarded with the hand of the king's son. Themes of this sort, which attained great popularity, could be applied either to a man or a woman. The Clever Wench tales, according to Benfey, go back to stories of a minister who assisted his sovereign in riddle-guessing. Afterwards these proofs of wisdom were attributed to a maiden helping her father, or to a wife aiding her husband. The Choosing of the Caskets theme in *The Merchant of Venice* appears in the *Gesta Romanorum* with a female Bassanio. The maiden selects the leaden casket. 'And then said the emperour, O my deere daughter, because thou hast wisely chosen, therefore shalt thou marry my sonne.'[25] In an interesting collection of Filipino popular tales, many of which may be traced to Occidental sources, there is a variant of the Clever Wench theme, in which the heroine gets the prince as a reward. 'Then the king . . . said, "Marcela, as you are so clever, witty and virtuous, I will give you my son for your husband."'[26] In Shakespeare's play we are close to this situation. Helena is given a man as husband of whom the king says, 'My son's no dearer.' It will be noted that she forfeits her life if she is un-successful in healing the king, proposing the extreme penalty her-self, 'With vilest torture let my life be ended.' So in Boccaccio. '"Sire," saied the maiden: "Let me be kept in what guarde and kepying you list: and if I doo not heale you within these eight daies, let me bee burnte."'

In the popular tales there was, we may be sure, no reluctance to reward the girl by bestowing upon her the king's son. No one would have inquired whether he liked it, any more than whether a princess liked being married off to a prince who had done her father a favour, or performed certain difficult tasks. Common folk are always pleased, as the ballads abundantly testify, when a woman of low station marries a man of high degree. So when the king gives a nobleman to the heroine who has cured him of a grave disease, the business of that nobleman, according to the ethics of popular story, is to take her cheerfully, for better or worse.

This was in agreement with the customs of royalty, especially in the earlier and ruder period, before the doctrines of chivalric love and *fine amor* had established themselves. The *chansons de geste* afford various illustrations of the power of a king to marry a lady off at will to one of his knights. Frequently the lady was allowed to make the choice herself. This custom arose from actual conditions in the political arrangements of the times, which made it necessary for an heiress to marry, and wise for the king to act as mediator in the arrangement. The action of the king in Boccaccio and Shakespeare, then, is not to be regarded as a strange anomaly of romantic story, but the exercise of a well-recognized royal prerogative. A noble lady might demand a husband without being thought too forthputting. Gautier, who gives a most interesting discussion of this whole matter, cites the case of Helissent, daughter of Yon of Gascony. 'She ... enters into the spacious hall, inclines herself before the king, and says, without hesitation or circumlocution, "My father has been dead two months. I want you to give me a husband."'[27] It is easy to see how this custom would affect a popular tale, in which a girl like Giletta or Helena, not noble, but one who had performed the greatest of favours for the king, might demand a husband as a reward. In the more primitive of the romances, as in the *chansons de geste*, the lady is not ashamed to do the wooing for herself. We all remember the princess Rymenhild, who certainly displays no shyness.

> 'Horn,' heo sede, 'withute strif
> thu shalt haue me to thi wif;
> Horn, haue of me rewthe
> and pliht me thi trewthe.'

In the highly artificial and aristocratic society portrayed in the *Decameron*, conceptions of rank and of the conduct proper for a lady had undergone a change. The ruder fashions of popular story and *chanson de geste* had been left behind. The young people who gathered amid the delights of country life to listen to one another's stories were well versed in the subtleties of courtly tradition, in a period of the sharpest class distinctions. In their eyes, a nobleman would naturally resent being expected to marry a girl beneath him in station. They would have looked for just the line of conduct which Beltramo adopted.

The Counte knewe her well, and had alreadie seen her, although she was faire, yet knowing her not to be of a stocke convenable to his nobilitie, disdainfullie said unto the Kyng, 'Will you then (sir) give me a physicion to wife? It is not the pleasure of God that ever I should in that wise bestowe myself.' To whom the Kyng said: 'Wilt thou then, that we should breake our faithe, which we to recover healthe have given to the damosell, who for a rewarde thereof asked thee to husband?' 'Sire (quoth Beltramo) you maie take from me al that I have, and give my persone to whom you please, bicause I am your subject: but I assure you I shall never be contented with that mariage.'

The repulse of the heroine is thus admirably motivated. Beltramo is sympathetically presented as a man unwilling to lower his social station by marriage with a physician or a physician's daughter, much as a modern aristocrat might object to an alliance with the daughter of a barber. He is rather a good fellow; there is little suggestion about him of the cruelty, deceit and viciousness of Bertram.[28] In Boccaccio's tale of the patient Griselda, the husband puts away his wife on the ground that his subjects resent his having married beneath him, and made a peasant's daughter his consort. Griselda illustrates the strength of meekness and patience; she regains her husband by lamb-like acceptance of every indignity. But this is not the virtue illustrated in the Giletta-Helena story. Here the heroine is not passive; she bestirs herself very actively to gain the man she loves, by putting her life at hazard in the curing of the king. This is apparently contradictory to the conventions of courtly love so prominent in the medieval romances, and so noticeable in the *Decameron*. The earlier and ruder love-making had been displaced by the code which decreed that the man should do all the wooing, and that the lady should allow herself to be won only after suitable delay. Giletta does not proceed according to these laws. But it is to be remembered that she is not a noble lady of Beltramo's own rank, and that her courtship is not of the approved aristocratic sort. She is a poor physician's daughter, who loves a man out of her sphere with a passion which drives her to desperate means, '*oltre al convenevole della tenera età*'. Boccaccio's formula, then, is something like this: a girl loves with consuming passion a man above her in rank, and twice overcomes his natural opposition to marrying beneath him by signal proofs of her cleverness and devotion.

By Shakespeare's day social conventions had changed once more. The same gulf did not exist between a noble and a girl of the middle class as in the fourteenth century. Furthermore, Shakespeare emphasizes a point only implied in Boccaccio's pages: that the virtue and love of the heroine more than equalize discrepancies of rank. Bertram's 'A poor physician's daughter my wife!' is countered by the king's long speech to the effect that virtue is the truest nobility. How little the accident of birth should really count for Bertram is shown by the fact that the Countess favours the match. She exclaims, on hearing of Bertram's rejection of Helena,

> she deserves a lord
> That twenty such rude boys might tend upon
> And call her hourly mistress.

Indeed, Shakespeare goes farther than Boccaccio: he makes the rejection of Helena depend, in the last analysis, not upon discrepancies of rank, but upon Bertram's own vanity, intolerance of control, and inability to see the finer qualities of Helena. He turns Bertram, in short, into a thoroughly disagreeable, peevish, and vicious person. Bertram's feeling for his old playmate becomes downright hatred.

> I'll send her to my house,
> Acquaint my mother with my hate to her.
> . . . .
> . . . .
> . . . . . War is no strife
> To the dark house and the detested wife.

Shakespeare's formula is, then: a noble girl loves a self-willed fellow incapable of realizing her worth, though above her in station; she puts her life in jeopardy to win him, and he repulses her through false pride and stubbornness. With all this before them, and with the Clever Wench tradition of the popular tales in their consciousness, the audience cannot but sympathize with Helena, and the main theme of the drama, the Fulfilment of the Tasks, may proceed.

The blackening of the character of Bertram is one of the most sweeping changes made by Shakespeare in the story as a whole. As we have noted, Boccaccio's hero is not of this sort, and the medieval analogues to the Fulfilment of the Tasks story never exhibit a man so disagreeable. It is significant that in the retouching of the play, in which Shakespeare's chief interest was in the revision of character,

Bertram was left with all his imperfections on his head. The Helena of the later draft is much more mature and sententious, but Bertram was not altered.[29] The dramatic justification for giving Bertram so bad a character is clear, however; it makes his rejection of Helena and his incapability of understanding her finer nature more plausible, it explains his willingness to commit adultery, which the plot absolutely requires, and it creates added sympathy for the heroine, who is repulsed with singular cruelty and rudeness. In Boccaccio's day, when adultery was sanctioned, and even demanded, by the code of courtly love, no such explanation of Bertram's act would have been necessary. But the people of Shakespeare's day, as we shall see in examining *Troilus and Cressida*, thought very differently. They would not have condoned the violation of the marriage vows of a man wedded to a girl like Helena, even though he had been united to her against his will. And Shakespeare still further utilizes the baseness of Bertram for dramatic effect in Act V. The interest at the end of the play is sustained by the young Count's frantic efforts to wriggle out of the complications of the Diana intrigue by lying and slandering the girl to whom he had sworn eternal fidelity. All this could not have happened had Bertram been a sympathetic character. The difficulty for the modern dramatist would lie in making plausible the final union of such a cad and villain with the heroine. But this was a thing which bothered Shakespeare and his contemporaries very little indeed.

3. PAROLLES AND THE CLOWN

To the deliberate degradation of Bertram, which naturally makes the main plot far less pleasant, is due a great deal of the apparent cynicism in the treatment of Parolles, who is, after Bertram, one of the least agreeable of all the people in the play. On first thought, a sub-plot presenting so despicable a rascal as Parolles might seem to reflect bitterness on the part of the dramatist. But if the whole matter is carefully considered, I think it becomes clear that Parolles could not be represented otherwise without weakening the main plot. He is the boon companion of Bertram, as Falstaff of Prince Hal, but comparisons between him and Falstaff must be made with reserve. There is no valid ground for concluding that Parolles was either an early sketch for Falstaff, or, in Brander Matthews's phrase, 'a diminished replica of Falstaff'; the chronological evidence is insufficient, either way. And the two characters are in many respects different. As Krapp has pointed out, 'to the Elizabethan audience witnessing a performance of *All's Well*, it seems probable that the comparison which the character of Parolles suggested was not with any Miles Gloriosus or with Falstaff, but with those villainist and modernist time-servers who walked the streets of London in gaudy splendour. If so, Parolles may not be regarded as merely an echo of the braggart soldier of Renascence comedy or a weak reproduction of Falstaff. He seems rather a transcript from Elizabethan life.'[30] There is never-theless an analogy between *Henry IV* and *All's Well* which is inescapable. Each presents a youth of pleasure-loving disposition, with tastes which are not too refined, under the influence of an older man of pretentious exterior and bad character. The emphasis lies in the one case on the charm of Falstaff and, in the other, on the base-ness of Parolles. The distinction is important for the character of the younger men. Prince Hal sees through the vices of his companion, and carefully tells the audience so. He is only sowing – cautiously – a few of the wild oats which endear a vigorous young hero to our hearts. With so genial and agreeable a misleader of youth as Falstaff, the Prince's wild nights in the London stews seem excusable. No one can wonder at his falling under the spell of a man who fascinates everyone about him. But Bertram is completely taken in by a shallow rogue who deceives no one else in the play. And there is nothing of Falstaff's personal charm or lovable quality about Parolles. He is a cad, through and through, whose associates heartily despise him. We instinctively feel that only a boy of weak character and vicious tendencies would select him as a bosom friend. Were Parolles an attractive person, we should insensibly be led to feel more tolerance for Bertram's shortcomings. But Shakespeare does not make this mistake. In order to keep the baseness of Bertram constantly before us, he makes his most intimate companion an offensive rascal.

The Clown, too, is a thoroughly unsavoury fellow; his frivolities, as Andrew Lang says, 'are coarse and stupid, even beyond the ordinary stupidity of Elizabethan horse-play'. But this very coarse-ness serves a dramatic purpose, especially the banter in the First Act.

What Lavache says later on may be dismissed as rather poor comic relief. The Steward is about to reveal to the Countess that Helena is in love with her son, when the Clown thrusts himself into the company. He begs her to favour his marriage with her woman Isbel, and the Countess, allowing herself to be diverted by this licensed jester, listens to some pretty unsavoury japes about marriage. The Steward then asks her to send the Clown to bid Helena come to her, and the Clown catches up the name 'Helen' with a reminiscence of Helen of Troy.

> Was this fair face the cause, quoth she,
> Why the Grecians sacked Troy?

ending with the reflection that there is one good woman in every ten, then reducing the number, on second thought.

One in ten, quoth a'! An we might have a good woman born but o'er every blazing star, or at an earthquake, 'twould mend the lottery well; a man may draw his heart out, ere a' pluck one.

COUNTESS You'll be gone, sir knave, and do as I command you.

CLOWN That man should be at woman's command, and yet no hurt done! Though honesty be no puritan, yet it will do no hurt; it will wear the surplice of humility over the black gown of a big heart. I am going, forsooth. The business is for Helen to come hither. *Exit.*

Dowden, in a passage which is sometimes quoted with approval, comments as follows: 'A motto for the play may be found in the words uttered with pious astonishment by the clown, when his mistress bids him to begone, "That man should be at woman's command, and yet no hurt done." Helena is the providence of the play; and there is "no hurt done", but rather healing – healing of the body of the French king, healing of the spirit of the man she loves.'[31] The Clown's remark about man being at woman's command clearly refers, however, not only to the fact that the Countess is sending him off, but to what he has just been saying about good women in the world. The next sentence carries out this cynical jesting: even if a chaste woman be no stickler for purity, she will do no harm; she will cloak her pride under humility.[32] The implication is: if Helen of Troy acted as we know she did, why not Helen of Rousillon? Through the lips of the Clown we are given the cynical view of woman; the cheap and facile reproach that 'chastity is no Puritan' is what might be expected of this 'foul-mouthed and calumnious knave'. The real beauty of devotion and sacrifice such as Helena exhibits, and the main theme of the piece illustrates, is set in sharp contrast to the view of the low-minded and vulgar. To make the Clown's words a motto for the play seems to me to miss their whole point; they are a motto, in the sense in which they are uttered, only in that the whole play contradicts them. The Clown is not so much moved by 'pious astonishment' as by impertinent cynicism.

Much of the disagreeable atmosphere of the play, then, is due to the desire of the dramatist to contrast with the bright virtue of Helena the evil in the corrupt society about her, the weakness and badness of Bertram, the cowardice and treachery of Parolles, the vulgar cynicism of the Clown. So in *Measure for Measure*, the purity and nobility of Isabella are thrown into higher relief by the background of corrupt Vienna, with its bawdy-houses, panders, and libertines so much in evidence. Parolles and the Clown have none of the geniality with which Shakespeare often endows his depraved characters, whether gentlemen gone wrong, like Falstaff and Lucio, or gutter-snipes like Pistol and Pompey. They are much more like types deliberately introduced for theatrical effect, with a technical expertness unrelieved by human sympathy. And so the humour of the play, which might have gone far towards making it more pleasant, remains forbidding, grim, and in the last analysis artificial.

4. INTERPRETATION OF THE PLAY AS A WHOLE

The most difficult of all the problems of *All's Well* now confronts us. What was Shakespeare's artistic intention in writing this strange play? How did he intend that his audiences should understand it?

The simplest and most obvious answer seems to me the true one. Shakespeare's aim was to tell, in theatrically effective fashion, a story, the story of a noble woman passing through great afflictions into happiness. He did not change the main significance of the tale as he found it, but followed absolutely in traditional lines, exalting the virtue of the heroine, just as his source, and other narratives of its type, had done. The play was thus written with its general treatment suggested in advance. Both oral and literary versions which had gained wide acceptance confirmed the nature of this treatment. Shakespeare was free to alter details and characterization, to make Helena's husband a cad, to complicate the final scene, to introduce subsidiary personages, but not to turn the heroine into a wanton, to question the efficacy of her stratagems, or to cast doubts upon her ultimate happiness.

It has been repeatedly said by critics, however, that the impelling force behind such plays as *All's Well* and *Measure for Measure* was irony, that Shakespeare chose to make of Helena and Isabella women whose show of virtue covers the gravest faults of character and conduct. This view seems to be holding its own bravely at the present time. An anonymous writer, in an interesting leading article in the *Times Literary Supplement*,[33] expresses himself as follows: 'The treatment of love in [*Measure for Measure*] . . . is as near to pure cynicism as Shakespeare could get. . . . Whatever may be the dramatic purpose of this singular "comedy", the condition of mind from which it sprang is manifest. Life is hateful and contemptible, and as for love, your bawd is your only honest man. In *All's Well That Ends Well* – supremely cynical title – Shakespeare seems deliberately to take revenge on his own idealism of love. He deliberately makes Bertram detestable and shows that the bragging coward Parolles is the better man. Then he makes Helena fall in love, passionately, tenderly, delicately, with the unpleasant young nobleman, builds her up as surely as Beatrice or Rosalind, puts into her mouth the divinely hesitating reply to Bertram's purely brutal "What would you have?"

> Something, and scarce so much: nothing, indeed.
> I would not tell you what I would, my lord.
> Faith, yes.
> Strangers and foes do sunder, and not kiss.

Yet after all this she plays the Mariana trick. One wonders what can be the conception of the poet in the minds of those who imagine that he had written a romantic comedy with a happy ending. The self-torturing mood of the play, the bitter mood of "I'll show you a happy ending", is only too apparent.'

Such a view as this assumes a direct break with all the earlier forms of the story which it has been possible to examine. It is very important to recognize that Shakespeare was not free, as is a dramatist or novelist of today, to make such sweeping changes in the meaning of traditional stories, in situations made familiar to people by centuries of oral narrative. In modern times, Anatole France is at liberty to turn the tale of Bluebeard inside out, and maintain, with the touches of delightful satire with which his readers are well acquainted, that Bluebeard '*fut bon et malheureux, et que sa mémoire succomba sous d'indignes calomnies*'. In *Die Jungfrau von Orleans*, Schiller could make the glorious maid die on the battlefield, rather than at the stake. But does anyone seriously suppose that Shakespeare could do this sort of thing? He was writing, not for a public which delighted in clever perversions of familiar tales, like the readers of Anatole France, or for a public which had forgotten medieval traditions, like the spectators of Schiller's plays a century or more ago. He could not have made a wanton out of Helena any more than he could have made Richard III kill Richmond on the battlefield. He had to make his appeal to the lower classes as well as to the more cultured, in order to ensure the success of his theatrical ventures. A very considerable part of his audience were people of no education or literary training, but with a good acquaintance with traditional story. They looked to the stage to tell them the tales which they knew, and resented, just as children do today, any radical alterations. A perversion of old folk-tale situations, like those in *All's Well*, would merely have perplexed and baffled them. The case was quite different with plays like *Bartholomew Fair* or *The Alchemist*, which did not involve situations of this sort. When Shakespeare chose to satirize love, he did it in quite another fashion than by the irony which critics find in *All's Well* – in incidentals which do not affect the main romantic plot, as in *Twelfth Night*, or in a court piece, like *Love's Labour's Lost*. But even in the latter play he did not take a familiar story and stand it on its head. The plot is perfectly straightforward, not ironical. What traces of irony there are lie in the dialogue and characterization. Only in *Troilus and Cressida*, which by its very nature is an exposure of the hollowness of love-making, did he undertake the perversion of a romantic tale. But, as we shall see later, that treatment was not of his own choice. From the point of view of his own time, it was not perversion. The tale had already been perverted.

Ironical intent in a play is exceedingly difficult to disprove—or to prove. Nothing is easier than to make it seem plausible to the modern reader, who forgets the source, and the social and dramatic conventions of Shakespeare's own day. A student of mine recently spoke of the 'fine irony' of the erection of golden statues to Romeo and Juliet by their afflicted kinsfolk at the end of the play. One needs only to observe that the Montagues and Capulets put up a costly tomb, in the source from which Shakespeare chiefly drew. Arthur Brooke will hardly be credited, I imagine, with introducing 'fine irony' at this point. In his view, the suffering families were doing what they could,

> ... lest that length of time might from our minds remove
> The memory of so perfect, sound, and so approvèd love.

Tennyson's lines at the end of *Enoch Arden*,

> And when they buried him the little port
> Had seldom seen a costlier funeral,

seem, with that delicious word 'costlier', somewhat out of key. There are reasons enough for thinking that the poet would not have allowed irony to intrude upon pathos at this point. But who can *prove* it, one way or the other? So one cannot prove that ironical intent does not exist in the plays which we have been discussing, but still less can one prove that it does. The burden of proof, with so direct and straightforward a writer as Shakespeare is in general, seems to me to lie upon those who would seek to establish the presence of irony in *All's Well*.

Didactic intention is equally difficult to establish or to refute. If anyone thinks, with Gervinus and Creizenach, that Shakespeare was slyly preaching a sermon to the Globe audience under the cover of Helena's woes, that he was trying to persuade them that 'merit goes before rank', or that 'personal excellence is of far greater value than high birth',[34] I do not know how to prove him wrong. But I think that the burden of proof lies upon his shoulders. Shakespeare's first aim must have been to provide pieces which were sufficiently interesting to fill the theatre and bring in money at the doors. He did this by presenting the pageant of human life as he saw it, by showing the issues of greed and hatred and malice, and of love and self-sacrifice and generosity. That he balanced these issues against each other for an ethical purpose is another matter. There has always been a tendency to make a preacher or a philosopher out of him, from the days of Tate and 'that cheap moral which every one of Shakespeare's tragedies contradicts, "that Truth and Virtue shall at last succeed",'[35] to the *Moral System of Shakespeare* of R. G. Moulton, who observed, 'the Shakespearean Drama constitutes a vast body of creative observations in human life, made through a peerless instrument; they invite arrangement and disposition into general truths'.[36] The wise words of Raleigh may be pondered by those who are inclined to believe such a pursuit profitable. 'It is ... vain to seek in the plays for a philosophy or doctrine which may be extracted and set out in brief. Shakespeare's philosophy was the philosophy of the shepherd Corin: he knew that the more one sickens, the worse at ease he is, that the property of rain is to wet, and of fire to burn.... There is no moral lesson to be read, except accidentally, in any of Shakespeare's tragedies.'[37]

This subject must be considered again in connexion with *Measure for Measure*, in the plot of which ethical problems are constantly suggested. But Shakespeare's attitude in that play, as we shall see, is not different from his attitude in *All's Well*. Whatever his philosophy and ethics were, they were certainly mainly those of his own day. He was very much a man of his own time, not a lonely soul out of harmony with his age. He was no Ibsen, showing his countrymen the diseases in their private and public life, no Strindberg, ruthlessly and cynically baring the unlovely sides of human nature. He had his individual convictions, of course, which we may think we can see now and again beneath the mask. But even if we are right in our guesses, I do not think that we shall find that such convictions will build a Moral System.

Another difficulty demands consideration at this point. It is to our modern feelings exceedingly disturbing that Shakespeare should in this play, as in many others, have portrayed characters who appear natural and as real as living human beings, and at the same time that he should have retained plots which make the actions of these characters seem psychologically impossible. This has been vigorously set forth by Schücking. How does it happen, he asks in effect, that a dramatist who knew men and women so intimately should make them behave as irrationally as do the people in the sub-plot of *Lear*, or in the main actions of *Much Ado*, *All's Well*, and *Measure for Measure*? He notes the dramatic effectiveness of some psychologically unconvincing scenes, and makes allowance for the necessity of accepting the devices of romance in romantic stories, but believes that the explanation of the whole matter lies in Shakespeare's neglect 'to employ his highest artistic faculties', and that he 'lacked the conscience of the artist who is determined to do everything as well as he can'. In *All's Well*, he objects to the degrading of Bertram and the contrast between the apparent weakness of will which Helena sometime exhibits and her resoluteness in action, and he further maintains that 'the whole problem of regaining the love of the husband is superficially conceived. . . . That love can give no bills of exchange no one in the piece seems to realize.'[38]

A fundamental defect in Schücking's argument, a mistake which the modern reader of the play is likely to make, is failure to allow for Elizabethan conventions. Dramatic narrative had its conventions as much as did dramatic presentation. We do not take exception to lengthy soliloquies and loud 'asides', we do not object that the characters, even the most realistic of them, speak in blank verse, because these theatrical artificialities have survived on the stage down to our own days. But the conventions of popular story which were accepted as current in the days of Elizabeth and James seem to us today only absurd and impossible. I have discussed this whole matter at length in the preceding chapter; there seems no need to embark upon it once more at this point. It was just because love *could* 'give bills of exchange', because the fulfilment of difficult conditions *could* bring forgiveness and love and happiness, in the world of story-telling, that all the characters in the play accept the situation, and that Shakespeare could put it without hesitation upon the stage. Again, by thinking of the piece as fundamentally a Virtue Story, we see a partial answer to Schücking's other objections; the gentle and apparently dependent Helena shows her courage and resolution in that she can nerve herself for the supreme tests of healing the king and fulfilling her husband's conditions, and her virtue shines the brighter in that her love prevails not only over his harshness and disdain, but forgives his immorality and the brutality of his conduct in the Diana episode.

When we ask, therefore, why Shakespeare could have accepted conventions completely at variance with psychological truth, why he could have set before us real men and women, and then made them act in strangely irrational fashion, the answer lies in remembering that he was a man of his own time, that he shared its inconsistencies and contradictions, and that he must have been far less disturbed than we are by habits of thought accepted by his age. We must be cautious about censuring him for not employing his highest faculties when he follows the dramatic customs of his own day rather than of ours. Lytton Strachey has well emphasized the importance of this point of view for an understanding of the days of Elizabeth. 'It is, above all, the contradictions of the age that baffle our imagination and perplex our intelligence. Human beings, no doubt, would cease to be human beings unless they were inconsistent; but the inconsistency of the Elizabethans exceeds the limits permitted to man. Their elements fly off from one another wildly; we seize them; we struggle hard to shake them together into a single compound, and the retort bursts.'³⁹ Shakespeare, with all the universality of his genius, was also a true Elizabethan.

There is no doubt, however, that he sometimes deliberately chose to sacrifice psychological consistency to purely theatrical effect. This is strikingly illustrated in *All's Well*, in the closing scene, in which Helena proves to Bertram that his conditions have been fulfilled, and that he must accept her as his wife. The natural way to manage this would be for Helena to claim justice of the king, tell her story, and call upon Diana to substantiate it. But Shakespeare introduces a complicated series of tricks and misunderstandings, postponing the full explanation as long as possible, in order to sustain the dramatic interest. This has been noted already; to realize the total lack of plausibility consider especially the part played by Diana. The obscure Florentine maiden becomes an expert stage-manager, keeping everyone in the dark as to her real purpose, boldly bandying words with the king, driving Bertram into a tight corner, and finally producing Helena, as a grand *coup de théâtre*. She has sent the king a petition, begging him to force Bertram to marry her, since, as she says, he is a widower, and has seduced her. But Diana knows that he is not a widower and that he has not seduced her, and she has no desire to marry him. When confronted with Bertram, she plays out the same comedy, showing his ring as proof, and forcing him to dishonourable calumnies and to a confession of guilt. She then asks for her ring again. This ring has a complicated history. It has been given by the king to Helena, and then to Bertram by Helena in the night rendezvous. Bertram has earlier in the same scene offered it as a marriage-token to Maudlin, the daughter of Lafeu; it was then taken by the king, and is now on his finger. Diana knows perfectly well that it is not her ring, and the king knows it is not, for he had himself earlier given it to Helena. Bertram confesses (what he supposes to be true) that the ring belonged to Diana. The king then asks her about it, and she answers him in intentionally riddling and misleading fashion. In anger, the king orders her off to prison. Then Diana, having extracted from the situation all the surprises it can yield, produces Helena, as her crowning stage effect, and the play quickly ends. All this may be good drama, but it is bad psychology.

It is furthermore true – thus far we may agree with Schücking – that in *All's Well* Shakespeare was far less successful in suffusing formal and traditional plot-elements with naturalness and in vivifying them with human sympathy than in other plays based on folk-tale themes. *All's Well* is artificial in effect; almost entertainment provided according to a formula. The technique of transforming narrative into drama is in good order, but the imagination of the dramatist has seldom been kindled, or his sensibilities aroused. A curious hardness and indifference are often evident. There are flashes of tenderness and fineness, as in the portraiture of Helena and of the Countess, but these are all too rare. Parolles and the Clown lack the genial human qualities which make us love such eccentric characters as Falstaff and Touchstone. One is driven to the conclusion that Shakespeare, needing a play for the company, took a well-tried theme, developed it according to principles which he had by this time fully mastered, but never put his whole heart and soul into it. He relied for effect, not on emotion or truth to life, but on the familiarity and popularity of the story, and upon the theatrical effectiveness of individual scenes. And this, I think, is why the modern reader, who has no feeling for the traditions of story, and who cannot judge from the stage effects, finds *All's Well* highly puzzling.

The reconciliation of Helena and Bertram at the end of the play is managed with singular abruptness, as is often the case with Shakespeare's final unravelling of the tangled fortunes of his characters. He seems to have been far more interested in their trials than in their deliverances. Perhaps he recognized that an audience is likely to lose interest when the end of the piece has obviously arrived – we all know the restlessness in the modern theatre in the last five minutes of the average play.[40] But the same hurried endings appear also in the work of great masters of prose narrative. Andrew Lang, in commenting upon the novels of Scott, speaks of 'the haste of fatigue which set him, as Lady Louisa Stuart often told him, on "huddling up a conclusion anyhow, and so kicking the book out of his way". In this matter of *dénouements* he certainly was no more careful than Shakespeare or Molière.'[41] Whatever be the cause of it, the hurried ending does not, to my mind, alter the impression that things have really come out right. Virtue triumphs in the end over the baser elements in human nature; the purity and devotion of Helena shame the cruelty and neglect of Bertram, and the vulgar cynicism of railers against women like the Clown. In the sub-plot the cowardice and treachery of Parolles are exposed in their full ugliness. Even if the Devil mutters behind the leaves 'supremely cynical title', the play *was* named *All's Well That Ends Well*, and the closing couplet echoes the thought.

> All yet seems well; and if it end so meet,
> The bitter past, more welcome is the sweet.

THREE

Measure for Measure

WHAT Shakespeare failed to do in *All's Well* he achieved in *Measure for Measure*, a play surcharged with emotion, and suffused with sympathy for the frailties of mankind. Here his imagination was kindled by his theme, and flashed forth in white flame, in a brilliance all the greater because of the deep shadows of the background. In commenting upon Shakespeare as an artist in character-drawing, Saintsbury, who is indeed sometimes given to hyperbole, exclaims, 'the great scene between Isabel and Claudio so far transcends anything that English, anything that European, drama had had to show for nearly two thousand years, that in this special point of view it remains perhaps the most wonderful in Shakespeare'. The hardness and indifference which we have noted in *All's Well* are gone; we are not again given a clever piece of stage technique, redeemed by the felicities of genius. Artificialities there are, but they are, in the main, secondary, not fundamental. Despite tragic occurrences, the tone of the whole is less depressing. Instead of the bitter Lavache and the despicable Parolles, a whole series of strikingly contrasted figures offers comic relief – the fantastic Lucio, Mistress Overdone, Elbow, Pompey, Froth, and their fellows. And even these, degraded as they are, have, as Raleigh has noted, a geniality of their own. 'The wretches who inhabit the purlieus of the city are live men, pleasant to Shakespeare. . . . This world of Vienna, as Shakespeare paints it, is not a black world; it is a weak world, full of little vanities and stupidities, regardful of custom, fond of pleasure, idle, and abundantly human.'[1]

This heightened sympathy and realism are undoubtedly due, in part, to the nature of the theme which Shakespeare was recasting. It is commonly said that this theme is of the same sort as that in *All's Well*, but the truth is that it is very different, both in nature and origin. *All's Well* is a composite of archaic and illogical folk-tale situations. The basic theme of *Measure for Measure*, on the other hand, may apparently be ultimately traced to an episode in real life. In any case, such a situation might actually have arisen at any time, and probably has arisen more than once. It is not only poignantly real, but intensely dramatic. It presents one of those dreadful alternatives between conflicting demands of honour and affection which have in them the very essence of tragic drama. A beautiful and innocent woman pleads with a tyrannical official for the life of her lover or brother or husband, and is given the choice between yielding her honour to save the man she loves, or refusing, and thereby knowing that his death is assured. She consents – from this point the versions vary. Novelists and dramatists have provided different solutions, but the fundamental tragic complication remains the same. It is a human problem; there is nothing about it which is illogical or unbelievable. It has furnished the modern stage with very effective and popular plays, such as Sardou's *La Tosca*, almost equally famous in the operatic setting with music by Puccini, *Paid in Full*, and *The Darling of the Gods*.

In Shakespeare's play this realistic basic action is combined with plot-material taken from traditional story, and exhibiting the archaisms and improbabilities characteristic of such narrative. The introduction of these artificial elements was chiefly due to Shakespeare, not to his sources. This point seems generally to have been overlooked. The extraordinary thing is that while the main situation apparently stirred Shakespeare very deeply, and while he gave to it a power such as no other writer had attained, he made it in some respects more conventional, less like real life. The result has been confusion among the commentators. They have been puzzled by the contradictions arising from the fusion of realism and artificiality, and they have failed to understand the significance of the changes made by Shakespeare. 'What is wrong with this play?' asks Quiller-Couch. 'Evidently *something* is wrong, since the critics so tangle themselves in apologies and interpretations.'[2]

The solution of these apparent contradictions must depend, it seems to me, upon a careful separation of the elements which Shakespeare added from those which he borrowed from his sources, and upon an examination of the significance of these elements, in the light of narrative tradition and custom, and of the way in which they were combined with the basic action into an organic whole. Before we proceed with such an analysis, however, we must be sure that we understand clearly the difficulties of interpretation which the play presents. This may conveniently be done by looking at the comments of representative critics. First of all, a brief outline of Shakespeare's plot will be helpful, familiar as the play is, for the sake of bringing out clearly the essential elements of the action.

The Duke of Vienna, withdrawing from his court, deputes his power to Angelo, who proceeds to enforce neglected statutes. Claudio, betrothed to Juliet, has been guilty of anticipating the privileges of marriage, and is imprisoned. Claudio's sister Isabella, a novice in a nunnery, pleads with Angelo for her brother's life. He basely offers to grant her plea if she will yield him her honour. The Duke, now disguised as a friar, advises her to consent to Angelo's demand, in darkness and secrecy, and promises to arrange that Mariana, once betrothed to Angelo, but forsaken by him, shall take her place at the nocturnal rendezvous. This is done, but Angelo breaks his promise, and orders the death of Claudio. Again through the intervention of the Duke, another prisoner is decapitated in Claudio's stead. The Duke reassumes his power, and the villainy of Angelo is revealed. Through the intercession of Isabella, Angelo is pardoned and given to Mariana in marriage. Claudio is re-united with Juliet, and the Duke and Isabella provide, apparently, a third bridal couple.

The central figure of the piece, the pivot about which all else turns, is, as in *All's Well*, the heroine. And here, as in that play, there is the widest diversity of opinion as to the heroine's true character. At one extreme stand the dithyrambics of Mrs Jameson about moral grandeur, saintly grace, vestal dignity and purity, which spring, perhaps, rather from emotion than from cold analysis. E. C. Morris finds critical encomiums common, however. 'Isabella and Angelo . . . are perfect dramatic creations. . . . The beauty of Isabella's character is only equalled by the adequacy of its presentation. Always simple, natural, forceful in her unsullied purity, she is one of Shakespeare's most ideal women.'[3] With this we may contrast Hazlitt's often quoted opinion. 'The only passion which influences the story is that of Angelo;[4] and yet he seems to have a much greater passion for hypocrisy than for his mistress [i.e. Isabella]. Neither are we greatly enamoured of Isabella's rigid chastity, though she could not have acted otherwise than she did. We do not feel the same confidence in the virtue that is "sublimely good" at another's expense, as if it had been put to some less disinterested trial.' This seems extremely mild, however, beside Quiller-Couch's ferocious attack on Isabella. 'She is something rancid in her chastity; and, on top of this, not by any means such a saint as she looks. To put it nakedly, she is all for saving her own soul, and she saves it by turning, of a sudden, into a bare procuress. . . . We are all acquainted with the sort of woman who will commit herself to any deed without question, if it be suggested by a priest. . . . One never knows where to take this paragon. She will plead Claudio's lapse as a venial sin: at the first suggestion of her own sinning it is "O, you beast!" – but by-and-by, to escape this, she is mating a pair without wedlock; while at the end we are left to suppose that for herself mating is mainly a question of marriage-lines; and that, for a Duke, she will throw her novitiate head-dress over the mill.'[5] Even Bradley, who is usually so cautious, says, 'We know well enough what Shakespeare is doing when at the end of *Measure for Measure* he marries Isabella to the Duke, and a scandalous proceeding it is', and Tatlock, who seldom gets things wrong, remarks, 'Isabella, herself "a thing enskied and sainted", lends her countenance to a dubious intrigue.'[6]

Nor has the gentle and unhappy Mariana been spared. Schücking, in a discussion which will be examined in detail later, condemns both Mariana and Isabella for their acceptance of the ruse by which Angelo is deceived. 'To this woman, then, whose name is Mariana, Isabella hurries and asks her secretly to change places with her and in her stead go to the meeting with Angelo, which is to take place in the dark. What an unheard-of, what a revolting thing to ask of a poor forsaken girl! But will she not refuse to make this sacrifice of her dignity? Is not the other girl obliged to use entreaties and tears and go down on her knees in order to move her? Nothing of the kind! Mariana is ready in a moment to entrap the faithless lover by this union in the dark. It is astonishing to see with how little self-esteem a woman is credited here.'[7] The 'bed-trick' is of course repellent to modern feelings. Brander Matthews remarked, 'The artifice itself is unlovely, and it cannot be made acceptable.'[8] But we have seen, in discussing the analogous situation in *All's Well*, that modern feeling is not a safe guide. The situations in the two plays are not the same, and the whole matter, as regards *Measure for Measure*, must be reviewed carefully once more.

Again, what is to be said about the actions of the Duke? His exalted rank has not preserved him from liberal censure. H. C. Hart has arraigned him methodically, in an indictment which includes most of the objections to his conduct raised by earlier critics. It may therefore be quoted at length. 'The Duke hardly seems to be a person to delight in. It is not merely his didactic platitudes and his somewhat overdone pompousness that get on one's nerves, but his inner character. We first meet him too timid or irresolute to enforce his own laws and deputing his duty to another, while he himself plunges into a vortex of scheming and intrigue; concluding by falling into love with a votary. At III.2.167 does he not transgress against the confessional? Again, he must have known of Angelo's treatment of Mariana, at least we are left to suppose he did (III.2.228), and was not his (the Duke's) a very shifty way of bringing him to justice, instead of a straight prosecution? Then the freedom with which he lies (IV.3.108–115) is not prepossessing. I imagine Shakespeare was not in love with his Duke. "A shy fellow was the Duke." ... He upsets all his crafty schemes for setting up his tottering justice and infirm authority by a general forgiveness and gaol-delivery all round. So much so that even where he justifies the title of the play, "An Angelo for Claudio, death for death!" he is in his own mind making a mockery of it.' In amusing contrast to all this is the view of Dr Louis Albrecht, who, in a very thorough study of the sources and interpretation of the play, holds that '*Measure for Measure* was written by the poet as a compliment to the new sovereign (King James I) on the occasion of his accession to the English throne', and sees in the portraiture of the Duke a series of honeyed encomiums.[9]

But enough of the critics – our main business is with the play itself. Those who like to know solutions in advance, before reviewing arguments, will find in the closing pages of the present chapter such conclusions as I feel may be drawn with safety from an analysis of *Measure for Measure*.

I. CINTHIO AND WHETSTONE

Giraldi Cinthio, a nobleman of Ferrara, published in 1565, at Monteregale in Sicily, a collection of a hundred tales, divided into decades, on a plan analogous to that of the *Decameron*, which he called the *Hecatommithi*. It was printed in more complete form, in Venice, in 1566. The fifth story of the eighth decade, which treats of ingratitude, forms the starting-point of the literary sources of *Measure for Measure*.[10] This story Cinthio apparently liked so well that he later put it into dramatic form, in a tragedy entitled *Epitia*, published in Venice in 1583. Cinthio's collection of tales was well known in Elizabethan England; it was one of the books in Florio's library, Robert Greene drew from it for his *James IV*, and Shakespeare took from it the crude and sensational tale which forms the basis of *Othello*.

The particular story with which we are concerned took the eye of George Whetstone, a dissipated man of good family, whose printed denunciations of immorality in London were founded upon bitter experience. He seems to have embraced literature not so much for its joys as for its revenues. He had tried other pursuits; as a soldier he had been in the Low Countries, and he was something of a traveller, gaining bitter experience through participation in Sir Humphrey Gilbert's unlucky expedition to Newfoundland in 1578–79. In the very year in which he set sail for the New World he published a play in rhymed verse based mainly on Cinthio's tale, *The Right excellent and famous History of Promos and Cassandra: divided into two Comical Discourses*. It was a two-part play of five Acts to each part. After a visit to Italy, he once more seized his pen, and produced *An Heptameron of Civill Discourses* (1582). In this volume of prose tales he more than once drew from Cinthio again, and retold, as a part of the 'Fourth Dayes Exercise', the narrative which he had already put into dramatic form. The *Heptameron* was again published in 1593, as *Aurelia, the Paragon of Pleasure and Princely Delights, by G. W., gent*.[11] Whetstone's prose version is a retelling of the main story in his own play, with the secondary action and secondary characters omitted. There are slight variations; he may have followed in places Cinthio's *novella*. In both play and story he made an important departure from Cinthio's tale: he kept the brother alive, through the intercession of a friendly jailer, an idea which he doubtless got from Cinthio's play.[12]

The tale, as told by Cinthio and Whetstone, reduced to its lowest terms, is as follows:

A man who has committed an offence is condemned to death. His sister appeals for mercy to the governor who has jurisdiction over his case. The governor, inflamed with love for her, offers to release her brother if she will yield to his passion. She consents, and is dishonoured, but the governor breaks his promise. The brother escapes in disguise, another being executed in his stead (or he is actually executed, as in Cinthio's tale). The heroine appeals to the governor's superior, who forces him to marry her, and condemns him to death, but finally pardons him on her intercession.

Whence Cinthio derived the story cannot be determined with certainty; it seems very likely, however, that he was utilizing an actual historical occurrence reported in the year 1547. This is set forth in an important contribution to *Notes and Queries* for 1893.[13]

'The May number of the *Századok*, the official publication of the Hungarian Historical Society, publishes a letter written in 1547 by a young Hungarian, then studying in Vienna, Joseph Macarius by name, to a relative and benefactor of his living at Sárvár in Hungary, which, as pointed out by a correspondent in the June number of the same publication, contains the earliest known version of the plot of Shakespeare's *Measure for Measure*.'

An English version of the extract 'in Hungarian translation, the original being probably in Latin', follows. The story is in brief this: In a town not far from Milan, one citizen was murdered by another. The guilty man was thrown into prison, but his young and beautiful wife went 'before the chief justice – who goes by the name of "the Spanish count"', who offered to pardon her husband at the price of her honour. After consulting her relatives, she acceded to his offer. Nevertheless her husband was beheaded. She reproached the justice bitterly, who only mocked her. She then went to Milan, and laid the matter before Don Ferdinando Gonzaga, 'the brother of the Duke of Mantua, and his Imperial Majesty's vicegerent for that province'. He told her to say nothing of the affair, invited the justice to a banquet, and then suddenly reproached him for his offence, forced him to marry her immediately, and pay her three thousand ducats as a dowry. On the following day the justice was executed.

'The original of the letter', says the writer in *Notes and Queries*, 'is in the Hungarian Public Record Office (the Országos Levéltár) at Budapest, among the papers of the Nádasdy family. It is dated from Vienna, Oct. 1, 1547.' The writer further calls attention to the fact that the character of Don Ferrante or Ferdinand Gonzaga 'agrees very well with that of the avenger of the woman's wrongs in our story', and adds that 'everything seems to point to the probability that the events as related by the Hungarian student and the French story-teller really took place at Como or some other town near Milano in or about 1547'. The 'French story-teller' is Goulart, who tells what appears to be the same incident in his *Histoires Admirables et Mémorables advenues de Nostre Temps* (1607).[14] 'The town where the event is said to have occurred is given in this version [i.e. Goulart] as Como, in Italy, which agrees well with the version of Macarius that it was not far from Milano. The date 1547 is exactly the same as given in the letter. The Spanish Count is in Goulart's "Histoire" a Spanish captain; but the wronged woman makes complaint to the Duke of Ferrara.'

Such an event as this, in 1547, might easily have attracted the attention of Cinthio, and been utilized by him eighteen years later in his *Hecatommithi*. This view of the matter is taken by Albrecht, who cites similar conclusions by C. H. Herford and Oliphant Smeaton.[15] Many other occurrences of this theme, with the variations which are normally to be expected, have been cited by Shakespearean scholars, from the time of Francis Douce.[16] These are set in various countries, and at various times, and are reported by various writers, from St Augustine down. There seems to be little use in reviewing them here. In some cases the story may have been transmitted from one setting to another; in other cases an independent version, based on an actual occurrence of the same simple train of events, may have arisen. 'In short,' as Morris says, in summary, 'it was a common story in the south of Europe in the fifteenth and sixteenth centuries, and may well have had some basis of fact in several places.'

The realistic character of this theme must once more be emphasized. In the letter of the Hungarian student and the tale told by Goulart it does not sound in the least like a stray fragment of romantic fiction. And the same is true of the literary versions by Cinthio and Whetstone, making due allowance for elaborations. Whetstone, indeed, in the dedication to his play, censured the impossibilities of the comedies written by the Englishman, as compared with the Italian, Frenchman, Spaniard, and German. 'In three howers ronnes he throwe the worlde: marryes, gets Children, makes Children men, men to conquer kingdomes, murder monsters, and bringeth Gods from Heaven, and fetcheth Divels from Hel.'[17] Whetstone's play itself, despite its stiffness and awkwardness of treatment, is based upon a realistic and moving crisis in human life.

2. SHAKESPEARE'S INDEBTEDNESS TO WHETSTONE

For our purposes, a minute study of the indebtedness of Shakespeare to Whetstone is of no great consequence. His chief source seems to have been Whetstone's drama *Promos and Cassandra*, both for the main plot and for suggestions in the characterization and in the secondary plot.[18] This drama is the most detailed of all the versions which we have been considering. It is wretched stuff, from every point of view, ineffective dramatically, halting metrically, weak in characterization and unconvincing in motivation. The splendid dramatic situation at the end is terribly bungled. No wonder that the piece never achieved presentation on the stage! Nevertheless, a reading of it is well worth while, if only to realize the transcendency of a genius which could transmute such dross into gold.

(Part I) Promos has been sent by Corvinus, king of Hungary, to join with the local officers in the city of Julio in enforcing justice. Promos proceeds to apply the statutes against sexual offences, in the course of which reform a young gentleman named Andrugio is condemned to death, for indiscretions with his sweetheart Polina. His sister Cassandra appeals to Promos, who reprieves Andrugio. In a second interview

Promos confesses his love, and promises Cassandra her brother's life, and whatever else she wishes, if she will yield to his desires, coming at night in the disguise of a page. At first she refuses, but after an interview with Andrugio, she goes to Promos in the disguise suggested, and gives herself to him. He promises to marry her, and free her brother, but instead gives orders for Andrugio's death. The jailer affords Andrugio means of escape, and shows Cassandra the head of a decapitated felon as that of her brother. Cassandra resolves to tell the king of the crime of Promos, and then take her own life.

(Part II) Andrugio, in exile in the woods, resolves to return, on hearing news from the city. Cassandra's appeal to the king (not shown on the stage) results in her immediate marriage to Promos, and an order for the latter's death. Andrugio reveals to the king the device by which his life was saved. The king pardons him, and orders that he marry Polina. Cassandra pleads for the life of Promos, whereupon the king pardons him as well.

A large number of minor characters provide a background in both parts of the play, generally of comic relief. This material is of little plot-value, save perhaps for the figure of Lamia, a courtesan, loved by Phallax, a subordinate of Promos, and protected by him. She is haled off to prison in the later part of the story.

Some details in Shakespeare's play were apparently derived from Whetstone's prose tale, particularly the name Isabella, who is in the *Heptameron* the teller of the tale ('Reported by Madam Isabella').[19] It would appear that Shakespeare got from Cinthio's play, in which the '*sorella di Juriste*' is named Angela, the suggestion for the name Angelo, and perhaps Lucio from a certain Lucillo, '*consiglier di Juriste*'. He may possibly have seen Cinthio's *novella* in the original also. Neither set of borrowings seems to me of much consequence. The important thing is to observe his indebtedness to *Promos and Cassandra*.

It is worth remarking that the vivid picture of sexual impurity in Vienna was beyond doubt suggested by Whetstone. The tale in the *Heptameron* records that Corvinus, king of Hungary, gave Promos the governorship of the city of Julio, who then 'purged the cittie of many ancient vices, and severely punished new offenders. In this cittie there was an olde custome (by the suffering of some majestrates, growne out of use) that what man so ever committed adulterie, should lose his head; and the woman offender should ever after be infamously noted, by the wearing of some disguised apparrell: for the man was held to be the greatest offender, and therefore had the severest punishment.' In the argument of Whetstone's play a similar statement is made; the statute in regard to impurity is made the reason for the condemnation of Andrugio, and the relations between Lamia and Phallax are significant.

And wantons sure, to keepe in awe, these statutes first were made,
  Or none but lustful leachers, should with rygrous law be payd.

Cinthio, on the other hand, lays particular stress upon ingratitude rather than sexual vice; in his tale the fatal law which condemns the youth[20] is not part of a campaign for the moral regeneration of the city.

The writer of the article in *Notes and Queries* above referred to pointed out the probability that 'the special law enacted by Matthias Corvinus, king of Hungary, for the improvement of the morals of the town of Gyula ("Julio") is merely the work of George Whetstone's fertile imagination.' This certainly seems very probable; certainly Whetstone had civic corruption and reform much in his mind, as is shown by his *Mirour for Magestrates of Cyties* (1584). 'In 1584 Whetstone abandoned imaginative literature and produced an elaborate prose treatise reprobating the vices that prevailed among the young men of London. The title ran: "A Mirour for Magestrates of Cyties. Representing the Ordinaunces, Policies, and Diligence of the Noble Emperour, Alexander (surnamed) Severus to suppresse and chastise the notorious Vices Noorished in Rome by the superfluous nomber of Dicing-houses, Tavarns, and common Stewes: suffred and cheerished by his beastlye Predecessour, Helyogabalus" (London, by R. Jones, 1584. 4to). A new title-page introduced "An addition or a Touchstone for the Time", which gave a very detailed account of the disreputable aspects of London life.'[21] I thought it possible that Shakespeare might have derived some suggestions for his picture of the manners and morals of Vienna from this source, but a careful examination of the rare pamphlet does not show that he was in any way indebted to it.

3. SHAKESPEARE'S ADDITIONS AND ALTERATIONS

The most important of Shakespeare's modifications of the story is the ruse suggested by the Duke, by which Isabella feigns consent to the proposal of Angelo, and arranges that her place in the nocturnal encounter shall be taken by Mariana, Angelo's forsaken betrothed. This was beyond question suggested by the analogous incident, based ultimately on popular tradition, which we have studied in the plot of *All's Well*. It assumes a new guise, however, in being adapted to the situation in *Measure for Measure*. The reasons for its insertion are clear. The virtue of Isabella is thus preserved, and the necessity of her forced marriage to the villain avoided.

Of very great significance, too, is the alteration of the plot by the prominence given to the Duke. In the sources, he is a mere lay-figure, brought in at the end to see that justice is done. Shakespeare makes him an important personage in the action, and in the characterization and the moral implications of the play. The Duke proposes and does much to arrange the Mariana ruse; he delays the execution of Claudio, and suggests to the jailer that Angelo shall be deceived by showing him the head of another man than Claudio; he tells Isabella, of course falsely, that her brother is dead, and suggests her appeal to the returned Duke. In Act V he delays the final ending of the action until all possible surprises are extracted from it, and even goes so far as once more to resume his old disguise. Certainly, the Duke is the dramatist's right hand man. His disguise serves to give point and reason for his sudden withdrawal from power; he desires, under cover, to observe his people and the governance of Angelo (I.3). It is natural that as Friar he should visit those people who are in prison, 'to know the nature of their crimes', and also that he should minister to the afflicted (II.3). Furthermore, he not only acts as a *deus ex machina*, but almost as explanatory Chorus, as in his speech at the close of the Third Act, and in moral and reflective passages elsewhere. His sanction gives authority, in the eyes of the audience, to stratagems which involve strange deceptions and perplexing moral issues. Finally, he plays his part also in the low comedy scenes, bandying words with the vulgar, and listening perforce to Lucio's frank remarks about himself and his policy – a source of much effective dramatic amusement.

The mingling of a sovereign in disguise amongst his people is of course a very old theme. Analogues will come readily to mind from *The Arabian Nights* down. It was common on the English stage at this period, as Creizenach has shown.[22] Albrecht believes that it was 'certainly' suggested here by an incident in Whetstone's tale, in which Andrugio, disguised as a hermit, mingles with the priests attending the projected execution of Promos, and, out of love for his sister, resolves to save him. Andrugio therefore appeals to the king, and, throwing off his disguise suddenly, shows that Promos has after all not succeeded in compassing his death. To me it seems much more probable that Shakespeare was here merely repeating a device which he had already used more than once, whereby an ecclesiastic straightens out the complications of a difficult situation, and by his spiritual authority gives confidence and sanction to the execution of a ruse— Friar Laurence in *Romeo and Juliet*, Friar Francis in *Much Ado*. I see little parallelism between the self-discovery of Andrugio, and the exposure of the Duke by Lucio. Disguise was the commonest of Elizabethan stage devices, and we must allow to Shakespeare the wit for making a few simple combinations for himself.

These two striking and fundamental changes in the plot, which, as themes of traditional story, archaic and improbable, go far to lessen the realism of the main action, must presently be examined in detail. Meanwhile we may note two alterations which do not involve the introduction of new themes, but which are nevertheless of considerable significance, one for the play as a whole, the other for the final scene.

Shakespeare radically modified the plot in making the heroine refuse to surrender her honour at the price of her brother's life, on the ground that her personal purity is of greater importance. 'More than our brother is our chastity.' Her rigid virtue is doubly striking, of course, in contrast with the whole background of sexual corruption in Vienna, and the emphasis on sexual laxness in Claudio, Juliet, Angelo, Lucio, and the low-comedy characters. When she first appears, she is 'wishing a more strict restraint' upon the votarists of the order which she is proposing to enter. Lucio, the loose-lived libertine, recognizes her purity, and holds her 'enskied and sainted'. Indeed, the firm insistence of Isabella upon chastity reminds one of the medieval heroines of Virtue Stories, who subdue all other considerations to the one perfect quality which they keep ever before them.

A further change in the story was made by Shakespeare through the deception of Angelo, who is shown the head of Ragozine the pirate, which he takes to be that of Claudio.[23] The reason for this is evident. Angelo continues to believe that his order for Claudio's death has been carried out, even to the very time when the living Claudio is brought into his presence at the end, and the Duke exclaims,

> By this Lord Angelo perceives he's safe;
> Methinks I see a quickening in his eye.

The dramatic suspense and effectiveness of the final scene are thus increased. Moreover, with delicacy of feeling, Shakespeare thus avoided painful scenes – the exhibition of a head or a corpse to the heroine, which she believes is that of her brother (as in Whetstone's play and story, and in Cinthio's play), or the actual presentation to her of the body of her dead brother (as in the tale by Cinthio).

We have now, I hope, a clear idea of the genesis of the different plot-elements in the play, and can proceed with the more important task of its interpretation.

4. ISABELLA AND MARIANA

Nothing in the play has aroused sharper dissent than the device by which the honour of Isabella is safeguarded, and nothing has been more completely misunderstood. The Duke has been blamed for suggesting it, Isabella for consenting to it, and Mariana for carrying it out. Most readers feel it to be in no wise consonant with the refinement of the sweet swan of Avon. It must, therefore, have very careful consideration here.

The examination of the 'bed-trick' in *All's Well*, in the chapter preceding, has shown that there is no ground for the assertion, frequently made, that Helena's ruse would have been regarded as unworthy of a modest woman. In *Measure for Measure* the problem is a little different. In the earlier play a wife lies unrecognized with her

93

husband, who believes that he is embracing his mistress, in order that she may fulfil the condition which he has made for accepting her as his wife; in *Measure for Measure* a jilted girl lies with her former betrothed, in order that the chastity of a woman whose honour he is seeking to corrupt may be preserved. But Mariana and her adviser are in no wise culpable, nor is Isabella herself. The point of importance to keep in mind is the relation between Angelo and Mariana. The fact that they had earlier been affianced is of the utmost significance in drawing conclusions as to the morality of the story. One can find, indeed, in medieval literature, narratives which tell of the request of a heroine, who is obviously to be regarded with sympathy, that another woman take her place in bed, in order to help her out of a difficult situation, stories in which no moral obloquy appears to attach itself to either woman.[24] Such narratives are not of great importance for the present discussion, however, since they do not present the essential feature in the plot of *Measure for Measure* – that Mariana was fully justified in yielding to the embraces of Angelo, on account of her earlier betrothal to him. This simple and obvious point in the Mariana story has been strangely overlooked by those who have censured harshly the gentle lady of the moated grange.

Such a betrothal as Mariana's was held in Elizabethan days to have much the binding force of the complete marriage ceremony, and to confer marital rights. The Duke, before suggesting the stratagem to Isabella, explains the situation (III.1).

DUKE ... Have you not heard speak of Mariana, the sister of Frederick, the great soldier who miscarried at sea?'

ISAB. I have heard of the lady, and good words went with her name.

DUKE She should this Angelo have married; was affianced to her by oath, and the nuptial appointed; between which time of the contract and limit of the solemnity, her brother Frederick was wreck'd at sea, having in that perished vessel the dowry of his sister. But mark how heavily this befell to the poor gentlewoman. There she lost a noble and renowned brother, in his love toward her ever most kind and natural; with him, the portion and sinew of her fortune, her marriage-dowry; with both, her combinate husband, this well-seeming Angelo.

ISAB. Can this be so? Did Angelo so leave her?

DUKE Left her in her tears, and dried not one of them with his comfort;

swallowed his vows whole, pretending in her discoveries of dishonour; in few, bestow'd her on her own lamentation, which she yet
wears for his sake; and he, a marble to her tears, is washed with them,
but relents not.

ISAB. What a merit were it in death to take this poor maid from the
world! What corruption in this life, that it will let this man live! But
how out of this can she avail?

DUKE It is a rupture that you may easily heal; and the cure of it not
only saves your brother, but keeps you from dishonour in doing it.

ISAB. Show me how, good father.

And the Duke shows her. The stratagem will have the effect, he
says, of compelling Angelo to give Mariana her due.

DUKE ... If the encounter [i.e. the love-rendezvous] acknowledged
itself hereafter, it may compel him to her recompense; and here, by
this is your brother saved, your honour untainted, the poor Mariana
advantaged, and the corrupt deputy scaled. The maid will I frame
and make fit for his attempt. If you think well to carry this as you
may, the doubleness of the benefit defends the deceit from reproof.

He also reassures Mariana, in highly significant terms.

> Nor, gentle daughter, fear you not at all.
> He is your husband on a pre-contract:
> To bring you thus together, 'tis no sin,
> Sith that the justice of your title to him
> Doth flourish the deceit.

Claudio's union with Juliet was of this sort, as Claudio's speech to
Lucio (I.2) makes clear. They were betrothed; 'upon a true contract
I got possession of Julietta's bed'. But they lacked the 'denunciation',
that is the formal declaration of the final marriage ceremony; they
were waiting for the 'propagation', the increase, of Juliet's dower.
Meanwhile a long-neglected statute forbidding physical union before
the final ceremony of marriage was revived by the virtuous Angelo,
and Claudio was arrested. We do not need to take this 'statute' too
seriously; law in Shakespeare's plays is queer business. The important thing to note is that the usage in England in Shakespeare's
day was that here represented as the common custom of Vienna,
before the reform instituted by Angelo.

An understanding of the binding force of the Elizabethan betrothal is important. Spousals, or betrothals, and the final celebration of marriage were separate and distinct ceremonies; the latter following after an interval of not less than three weeks. 'Private spousals could be accomplished by any of the lovers' formulas of today for becoming engaged, and in public spousals there was also a certain amount of latitude allowed. In the most orthodox form of the latter, a priest was present, and a regular ceremony consisting of vows similar to those of a present-day wedding was gone through with.'[25] Such a union was recognized by both ecclesiastical and state authorities as valid, the law declared the offspring of a troth-plight legitimate, and the church imposed penalties for violation of the contract.

Betrothals may be studied in *Twelfth Night*, *The Taming of the Shrew*, *The Winter's Tale* (twice), *Much Ado*, and *King John*. The union of Posthumus Leonatus and Imogen in *Cymbeline* appears to have been of this sort, a 'handfasting', and the lines of the play leave no doubt of the celebration of the essentials of marriage. The custom explains completely the apparent irregularity in the relations of Shakespeare and Anne Hathaway. Joseph Quincy Adams says, 'If he [Shakespeare] took advantage of the privileges such a contract [a troth-plight with Anne] was supposed to give, it could not have offended the moral sensibilities of the Stratford folk: as Halliwell Phillipps puts it: "No question of morals would in those days have arisen, or could have been entertained."'[26]

In the light of these considerations, Hazlitt's remark about the virtue that is 'sublimely good at another's expense', and Quiller-Couch's assertions that Isabella is 'a bare procuress', and that she 'is mating a pair without wedlock', collapse like pricked bubbles. We have seen how insistent Shakespeare is upon the purity of Isabella, how he altered the plot, making her refuse to sacrifice her honour even for her brother's life, and how she desires the strictest restraint in the sisterhood which she is about to enter. The moral justification of the Mariana ruse would be shown, if by nothing else, by the instant readiness with which she accepts the plan and puts it into execution.

Schücking, however, in a comment which has already been

quoted, thinks the proposal an 'unheard-of' and 'revolting' thing to ask of Mariana, who 'is ready in a moment to entrap the faithless lover by this union in the dark. It is astonishing to see with how little self-esteem a woman is credited here. This solution corresponds to the mentality of Boccaccio, the son of the fourteenth century. It is on a level with the morality of the middle and lower classes of medieval society, but certainly not with the ideas of the beginning of the seventeenth century, the views of which regarding women, as we meet with them in Overbury, Hall, etc., after all represent a considerably higher moral standard than is found in those earlier times. Are we to assume, then, that Shakespeare, who in other places gives evidence of such an exquisite feeling for human dignity, was not alive to the questionable character of this solution?'[27]

We may dismiss immediately, in view of what has just been said in regard to betrothals, any doubts which we may cherish as to the morality of the episode. Whether it be a sacrifice of dignity on the part of a woman to entrap her lover, as Helena entrapped her husband, is another matter. But the answer is equally plain; it involves restatement of a point which has already been urged in the preceding pages. Shakespeare was utilizing, as he so often did, a bit of archaic plotting which is hard to reconcile with the naturalness of his characters. His heroines seem so real that we find it hard to accept them in artificial situations. But such situations had been deemed suitable for heroines in the earlier traditions from which Shakespeare was drawing, they were current in the story-telling of his own day, and he therefore accepted them for his own dramatic purposes. How far he was disturbed by them we cannot tell; but it would seem, from the frequency with which he employed them, that he felt far less their lack of reality than we do, even when they seem to involve psychological contradictions. If they were not felt as disturbingly artificial by the people of his own day, they are less likely to have worried Shakespeare. Parallels to the Mariana–Angelo episode cannot be drawn from earlier history, since it was not traditional, but rather the result of his own deliberate introduction of the *All's Well* theme into *Measure for Measure*. We have seen, however, in examining the former play, that the ruse practised by Helena was common in story, and that there is no evidence that it was conceived as humiliating, as Schücking feels it must have been.

Moreover, a little reflection on the themes of literature in the Middle Ages will convince anyone that this ruse was equally characteristic of aristocratic as well as plebeian society. We have seen it attributed, in a medieval romance of the most courtly type, to a lady whom the writer particularly desired to compliment. Everyone knows that chivalric love sanctioned and even exalted much which would seem degrading to a woman today, and that many episodes in the most aristocratic of romances do not square with modern ideas of feminine purity. But this is not the main point. The important thing is that Shakespeare's plays are to be judged, not by the works of Hall or Overbury, who wrote for a small circle, and were in no wise representative of the general thought of their time, but by the literature with which the audiences of Shakespeare were familiar, literature which had proved its right to be remembered through generations of men, high and low, rich and poor. An admirable means of getting an idea of this literature is afforded by the list of books in Captain Cox's library, which may be conveniently found in Furnivall's delightful edition of *Robert Laneham's Letter*,[28] a list which affords, as the editor puts it, 'a view of the literature in which the reading members of the English middle class in Elizabeth's time were brought up'. The good captain, who had 'great ouersight in matters of storie', read chiefly romances and popular tales, like *Huon' of Bordeaux*, *Bevis of Hampton*, *The Squire of Low Degree*, *The Tale of the Widow Edyth*, *The Nutbrown Maid*, *Sir Eglamour*, a variety of traditional ballads and popular songs, a few 'auncient playz', and miscellaneous material, ranging from *The Hy Wey to the Spitlhouse* to *Doctor Boord's Breuiary of Health*. The plays of Shakespeare were in large measure written for the Captain Coxes of his day, and for the even less educated fellows who crowded the pit of his theatre and upon whose pleasure the success of any public play largely depended.

Schücking nevertheless believes that Shakespeare made use of the Mariana–Angelo stratagem as 'the most convenient solution', although he must have felt 'its questionable character'. He believes, too, if I understand him, that Shakespeare, who 'created such infinitely sensitive and profoundly emotional women as, for instance,

Desdemona', had a different attitude towards the relations of the sexes from that of his public. I should, of course, be the last to deny that Shakespeare's spirit was finer and more sensitive than that of the majority of his audience, but that his attitude as to sexual matters was fundamentally different from that of the average man of his time seems to me to require proof. We must consider not only the delicacy in the portraiture of Desdemona or any other heroine, but also the occasional coarseness in his art, before we conclude that the Mariana–Angelo episode was really repugnant to Shakespeare's spirit, and due to a desire to take the easiest way out of a dramatic complication. We do not think that a plot which turns upon the substitution of one heroine for another in bed, in order to deceive a man in sexual inter-course, is suitable matter for the stage today, any more than we feel that the conversation of Helena and Parolles about virginity, or the badinage of Julia and Lucetta about details of male attire, or the joking of Beatrice about the cuckold's horns are proper for modest girls. One is often struck, in Shakespeare's plays, at the tone of con-versation in the best of mixed company, as to marital relations, the getting of children, and the like. But Elizabethan notions were different. The men of his day were probably no worse than we, but their conventions were not the same. When we consider the stupend-ous genius and achievements of Shakespeare, it is sometimes hard to realize the profound effect upon him of those conventions, and to realize that he was after all no isolated ethereal spirit, but very much a man among men, sharing their point of view, and insensibly deeply affected by their convictions.

One more stone has been cast at Isabella – that it is 'a scandalous proceeding' for her to marry the Duke, as she seems about to do at the end of the play, since she is a novice in a nunnery. Before we consider this question, however, it may be well to look somewhat carefully at the Duke himself, and see what is to be said about his part in the story.

5. THE DUKE

The great prominence of the Duke is, as we have already seen, one of Shakespeare's most important additions to the plot. The sources give the ruler of the state a part only at the end of the story; Shakespeare makes him active throughout the play. Whatever shortcomings may be charged to the Duke are, then, due to Shakespeare alone.

The ruler of the degenerate city of Vienna is, I believe, to be regarded as a conventional and romantic figure, whose actions are mainly determined by theatrical exigencies and effectiveness; he is, as it were, a stage Duke, not a real person. In this respect he contrasts strikingly with Isabella and Angelo and Claudio and Lucio, and the low-comedy people. Most of the misunderstandings of his part in the play have been due to failure to perceive this. Nothing shows more vividly the conventional elements in Shakespeare's technique than an analysis of the Duke's varied activities.

In the dramas written before *Measure for Measure*, two agencies stand out prominently as representatives of right and justice in straightening out complications of plot: the State and the Church. The former is represented by the person in supreme lay authority – a Duke in *The Comedy of Errors*, *The Two Gentlemen of Verona*, *Twelfth Night*, *A Midsummer Night's Dream* (Theseus as Duke of Athens), *The Merchant of Venice*, *As You Like It* (the Banished Duke); the King of France in *All's Well*. The latter is represented by priest or friar – Friar Laurence in *Romeo and Juliet*, Friar Francis in *Much Ado*, who suggest, respectively, the stratagems by which the Veronese lovers are united, and the honour of Hero vindicated. The law and authority in these pieces is romantic law and authority; it cannot be judged by strict legal ecclesiastical standards. The quibbles which are the undoing of Shylock are as much a part of popular story as the sleeping potion which sends Juliet to the tomb. Shakespeare used dukes and friars when the peculiar powers and opportunities afforded by their station would help his narrative. He did not bother himself about the strict legality or rationality of their actions. What they suggest or decide has in his plays the binding force of constituted and final authority, and was so understood by his audiences.

The Duke in *Measure for Measure* combines the functions both of State and Church in his person. As Duke, he is supreme ruler of Vienna, who returns at the end to straighten out the tangles of the action, and dispense justice to all. In his disguise as Friar, he represents the wisdom and adroitness of the Church, in directing courses of action and advising stratagems so that good may come out of evil. But the plots which he sets in motion and the justice which he dispenses are the stuff of story; they cannot be judged as if they were historical occurrences. And the Duke's character cannot be estimated on a rationalistic basis. If he really wished to set matters right between Angelo, Isabella, Mariana, Claudio, and the rest, he had a short and easy way of doing it. He was in full possession of the facts; he could have revealed himself, brought all before the bar of his authority, freed the innocent and punished the guilty in short order, and this would have saved Isabella and Claudio much suffering. Such an arrangement would, however, have been much less effective dramatically than his continued disguise, his suggested ruses, the prolongation of the suspense of the accused and the false security of the villain. No, he knows what is expected of him as a stage Duke, and makes the most of his part. Similarly, in *All's Well*, the King, assisted by Diana, squeezes the last drop of theatrical effectiveness out of the complications at the end of the play. Of course, as Hart complains, the Duke's way of bringing Angelo to justice is 'shifty', and not a straight prosecution. But it is just these shifts which keep the audience alert and interested. Of course the Duke 'plunges into a vortex of scheming and intrigue'; it is this which makes the play. Of course, as Hazlitt says, 'he is more absorbed in his own plots and gravity than anxious for the welfare of the State'; of course he 'upsets all his crafty schemes for setting up his tottering and infirm authority by a general forgiveness and gaol-delivery all round'. The audience were interested in the Duke's reforms only in so far as these served the plot. They did not care a straw about the triumph of his theories as a reformer or the moral welfare of Vienna. What they did wish was that the play should end, as a comedy should, in a general atmosphere of happiness, even for the sinful Lucio who had amused them by his drollery. Of course the Duke lies when he tells Isabella that her brother is dead (IV. 3), in order to spur her on to vengeance, and in order, as he himself says, 'to make her heavenly comforts of despair, when it is least expected', that is, to restore her suddenly to happiness later on, with dramatic effectiveness. Of course he lies when he tells Claudio that as confessor to Angelo he knows that Angelo's purpose is only to try Isabella's virtue; the plot requires that Claudio should believe that he is going to lose his life. It really does seem a little

absurd to accuse the Duke of 'transgressing against the confessional'.
His statement that Angelo had confessed to him appears to be only a
ruse for the deception of Claudio. Nowhere in the play does the
Duke in disguise come face to face with Angelo until the final scene;
it would appear that he was steering clear of him. Granted, however,
that Shakespeare meant us to understand that he had actually, in his
disguise, received Angelo in the confessional, it seems highly unlikely that Angelo would have confessed thus falsely. In any case, the
Duke, who knew Angelo's purposes, would not have been deceived.
But I do not think that Shakespeare intended us to think that there
had really been any confession at all. The Duke, in his capacity as
Friar, was telling a falsehood to Claudio in order that the ends of
justice (and of effective drama) might be served. He lies for a good
purpose again and again; in saying that he has come from the Pope
(III.2), in saying that Angelo is holy and just (IV.2), and he even lies
to Isabella at the end in his habit as the Duke (V.1.394 ff.). The
counsels of a stage friar are, however, *ipso facto* holy and just, and to
be obeyed without question. Quiller-Couch, however, scornfully
remarks, 'We are all acquainted with the sort of woman who will
commit herself to any deed without question, if it be suggested by a
priest', but we can find that sort of woman – or man too, for that
matter – in Hero, Juliet, Romeo, Benedick, Beatrice, and Leonato.

The 'scandalous proceeding' of the approaching union of the
Duke and Isabella, a novice of the sisterhood of St Clare, must be
judged in similar fashion. An Elizabethan audience was not likely to
be scandalized by the heroine's leaving a convent and pleading with
the deputy for the life of her brother, and finally being rewarded for
her trials and virtue by marrying the most distinguished man in the
play, in the good old story-book fashion. Small niceties of ecclesiastical infringement were not shocking to Protestant England in
Shakespeare's day. But the play makes it perfectly clear that Isabella
had not as yet taken vows. Sister Francisca says:

> It is a man's voice. Gentle Isabella,
> Turn you the key, and know his business of him.
> You may, I may not; *you are yet unsworn.*   I.4

Of course a Roman Catholic novice who has not yet taken vows in the order may forsake the religious life, and marry. It looks as if Shakespeare had deliberately prepared for the marriage of Isabella to the Duke, by making this point at the very beginning. It has been noted that she does not formally assent to the Duke's proposal, in the closing lines of the play:

> Dear Isabel,
> I have a motion much imports your good;
> Whereto if you'll a willing ear incline,
> What's mine is yours and what is yours is mine.

But I do not think that there is any doubt that Isabella turns to him with a heavenly and yielding smile. And I cannot see in the least why she should not.

It has been suggested that the Duke has borrowed some of the characteristics of King James I. Scholars now usually believe it probable that the play was produced at court on 26 December 1604, by the King's men, although grave doubts have been cast by Tannenbaum upon Malone's alleged transcript of a lost document, upon which evidence of such production mainly rests.[29] If the play had been presented at court, it would not have been surprising to find Shakespeare introducing flattery of the new sovereign, as Tyrwhitt suggested. The well-known dislike of James for crowds and popular greetings might under such circumstances be reflected in the words of the departing Duke:

> I love the people,
> But do not like to stage me to their eyes.
> Though it do well, I do not relish well
> Their loud applause and Aves vehement;
> Nor do I think the man of safe discretion
> That does affect it.   I.1

Angelo expresses a somewhat similar thought:

> Why does my blood thus muster to my heart,
> Making it both unable for itself,
> And dispossessing all my other parts
> Of necessary fitness?
> So play the foolish throngs with one that swoons;

> Come all to help him, and so stop the air
> By which he should revive; and even so
> The general subject to a well-wish'd king
> Quit their own part, and in obsequious fondness
> Crowd to his presence, where their untaught love
> Must needs appear offence.　　　　　　　　　　II.4

Shakespeare had occasionally inserted allusions to Elizabeth in earlier plays. The passages just cited, while not as definite as the familiar lines about the 'fair vestal throned by the west', or 'Our radiant queen hates sluts and sluttery', are something in the vein of the words of Theseus,

> Thrice-blessed they that master so their blood
> To undergo such maiden pilgrimage,

which look like honey for the Virgin Queen.

Chalmers, in 1799, remarked that 'the character of the Duke is a very accurate delineation of that of King James, which Shakespeare appears to have caught, with great felicity, and to have sketched, with much truth'. Albrecht believes that Shakespeare had an intimate familiarity with James's *Basilikon Doron*, which he thinks appears in *Measure for Measure* both in fundamental ideas and in forms of expression, that the Duke is a 'character-portrait' of James, and that the play contains many allusions to him and his times. I am not convinced by Albrecht's parallels. The utterances of the Duke and of James on the duties of a sovereign occasionally show some resemblances, but not greater than would be expected of two works treating this subject, while the verbal parallels seem to me entirely negligible. 'There is a river in Macedon; and there is also moreover a river at Monmouth ... and there is salmons in both.' It was not Shakespeare's habit, so far as we can discover, to insert full-length portraits of his royal contemporaries in his plays. There seems little ground for thinking that James I lent to *Measure for Measure* more than a touch or two, at most, and none whatever that Shakespeare utilized the *Basilikon Doron* for his play. We have to make due allowance for a certain number of accidental resemblances.

The essentially artificial character of the Duke may, as has already been suggested, be well illustrated by comparing him with the 'comic relief'. If, as is possible, Mistress Overdone, Pompey and Elbow were suggested by Lamia, Rosko and Gresco of Whetstone's play, they have been so transformed and made natural as to be scarcely recognizable, while a new and elaborate portrait, unlike any of the wooden figures in *Promos and Cassandra*, has been introduced, the impudent, dissolute, and engaging Lucio. Here we have striking studies of the riff-raff of the Southwark bank, the unsavoury yet amusing types of the Elizabethan brothels. They are unhampered in the play by incidents or characterization drawn from conventional story; they show us, in naked realism, the unlovely side of London life, etched deep with the penetrating acid of keen observation. But in spite of all their vices, they are likeable as well as human. To quote Raleigh's penetrating words once more, they are 'live men, pleasant to Shakespeare'. Pompey is 'one of those humble, cheerful beings, willing to help in anything that is going forward, who are the mainstay of human affairs. . . . Froth is an amiable, feather-headed young gentleman – to dislike him would argue an ill nature, and a small one. Even Lucio has his uses; nor is it very plain that in his conversations with the Duke he forfeits Shakespeare's sympathy. He has a taste for scandal, but it is a mere luxury of idleness; though his tongue is loose, his heart is simply affectionate, and he is eager to help his friend. Lastly, to omit none of the figures who make up the background, Mistress Overdone pays a strict attention to business, and is carried to prison in due course of law.'[30]

Beside men and women like these, full of vigorous life, the Duke, with his shifts and tricks, which strain plausibility to the breaking-point, seems a puppet, manufactured to meet the exigencies of dramatic construction. He is more important but quite as artificial as Oliver or the Usurping Duke in *As You Like It*, who are wicked as long as Shakespeare needs them so, and are then, with a grotesque lack of probability, converted, because it helps the plot to have them virtuous at the end. We cannot analyse such characters psychologically. The Duke of Vienna, on account of his great prominence in the play, has just enough plausibility of characterization to make an audience accept him; he has none to spare. Perhaps we may sum the whole matter up by saying that Shakespeare drew the Duke as he did because he needed him, and that he drew the main protagonists and the low-comedy people as he did because they interested him. Pompey and Mistress Overdone and the rest, in particular, serve an important purpose, in their very detachment from the artificial details of plot; they serve to make us forget the improbabilities which Shakespeare imported into the play, improbabilities which revolve about the Duke and his schemings; and they throw over the whole an illusion of vivid and unforgettable reality.

I imagine that some readers will take issue with me for regarding the Duke as an essentially artificial figure, elaborated to meet the requirements of plot, and as a study in character, of minor importance in himself, or for the play. Critics have frequently regarded him as the mainspring of the action, and his peculiar disposition as having profoundly influenced the development of the plot. This I believe to be quite the reverse of the truth.

Let us try to reconstruct the way in which the play took shape. In the first place, Shakespeare took from his sources the complete intrigue which forms the backbone of the plot, but introduced into it important new elements of his own. In order to set in motion these new elements, he hit upon the expedient of using the Duke as a *deus ex machina*. Whetstone had brought forward the King, whose function is to set right the errors of the deputy, and who is a prototype of the Duke, only in the Second Part of his play. Shakespeare, with the utmost adroitness, introduced the Duke at the very beginning, and then made him direct the action throughout, in disguise as a friar. It thus became necessary to make his withdrawal from power plausible. This Shakespeare did by depicting him as a man temperamentally unsuited to his high office, who 'cannot face the odious necessities of his position'. So the Duke's character was, in the actual writing of the play, determined by the plot; the plot did not spring from his character. By beginning the very first scene of his play with the Duke's retirement from office, Shakespeare indeed made it seem that this retirement was the direct cause of the events following; but we know that these events were already in the plot, and independent of the Duke's withdrawal from power.

We have no right to object to the remodelling of a play, no matter how this has taken place, if it results in a logical and consistent whole.

But in *Measure for Measure* no such result has been attained. The art of the expert craftsman has only partially concealed the stages by which his structure has been erected. The picture of the Duke at the very beginning, his retirement, and the appointment of a deputy, are natural and plausible, but what follows is story-book business – Haroun al Raschid disguised, Substituted Bride, Severed Head, and the various mechanical tricks and turnings of a complicated *dénouement*. As soon as the Duke gets into action, the artificiality of his figure is evident. Moreover, his very activity ill accords with his retiring disposition, his desire to lay aside power, and delegate it to another. More than any fictitious character in Shakespeare except Iago, the Duke is the directing force in the intrigues of the plot. Yet, says Lucio, 'a shy fellow was the Duke', and recent criticism has taught us that such comments from minor characters report truth. In a word, then, Shakespeare has not succeeded in making the Duke both serviceable to the purposes of drama, and psychologically consistent. Not only in origin, but in the effect which he produces upon the spectators, he is entirely different from Angelo and Isabella and Claudio. Their experiences are transcripts of actual human life, and usually in accord with their characters. They are real people. The Duke's part in the plot, excepting for his abdication, is little in accord with his disposition as sketched in the beginning, and little in accord with probability. He is essentially a puppet, cleverly painted and adroitly manipulated, but revealing, in the thinness of his colouring and in the artificiality of his movements, the wood and pasteboard of his composition.

6. ANGELO AND DRAMATIC JUSTICE

Coleridge, in a familiar passage, wrote: 'The pardon and marriage of Angelo not merely baffles the strong, indignant claim of justice (for cruelty, with lust and damnable baseness, cannot be forgiven, because we cannot conceive them as being morally repented of), but it is likewise degrading to the character of woman.'[31] Here are matters which deserve consideration. The 'strong, indignant claim of justice' extends, however, far beyond the pardon and marriage of Angelo; it concerns the whole solution of the action at the end, and the appropriateness of the title *Measure for Measure*. Analysis of the character of Angelo, and of the reasons why he does not get his just punishment, will form an admirable introduction to a discussion of the Duke, of how far the ends of justice are in general served by the decisions once more enthroned in power at the end of the play.

Let us begin at the beginning. Did Shakespeare mean Angelo to be regarded as a good, though narrow, man, suddenly gone wrong through an overmastering sexual temptation? Dr Furnivall said of Isabella, 'Her unhappy words, "Hark! how I'll bribe you," seem to have first brought out the evil in Angelo.'[32] Or was Angelo a villain from the start, who deceived the Duke as to his real character? I do not imagine that there is any way of settling this point. It is even possible that Shakespeare had not made up his mind about the virtue of Angelo, any more than Thackeray had – in a different sense – about the virtue of Becky Sharp. But it seems more likely that Angelo is to be regarded as having been a smooth rascal, who had been successful in concealing his baseness. His cruel and unjust treatment of Mariana, which has sent that unhappy lady to languish in her moated grange, his readiness not only to put Isabella in her dreadful predicament in order to satisfy his lust, but also to break faith with her and to kill her brother, do not point to native virtue. True, the Duke puts confidence in him, raising him to power above the older and more temperate Escalus, but even if this be regarded as a trial of his character, as Blackstone suggested, it proves little. Some of the most conscience-less of Shakespeare's characters, Edmund, Goneril, Regan, Iago, seem so effectively to have concealed their wickedness that the virtuous people whom they destroy have no suspicion of their real baseness. True, Mariana pleads for Angelo's life, and even Isabella, greatly as she has suffered, joins in urging that he be spared. But the complete repentance and forgiveness of the villain is a common dramatic convention, which Shakespeare found in Whetstone in this particular instance, and used frequently in other plays. A further piece of evidence seems to point to Angelo's native baseness; his flat refusal to temper justice with mercy, and spare Claudio, long before the dishonourable proposal is made to Isabella (II.2). One is reminded of Shylock and the trial scene by Angelo's stand, in this first interview with Isabella, upon the strict letter of the law, and the deaf ear which he turns to her eloquent appeal for mercy for her brother. Rigorous enforcement of the law is indeed no crime, but an audience would hardly see virtue in a man who insisted on sending a youth to death for a venial offence, in the face of moving appeals for mercy uttered by a beautiful heroine.

There can be no doubt, however, that as soon as Angelo has resolved to use his power to satisfy his passion, and at the same time to compass the death of Claudio, he must be regarded as a 'strong and fast'ned villain'. Against his double wickedness the Duke prepares a double stratagem: the substitution of Mariana, and the decapitation of Ragozine. Both of these ruses were, as we have noted, introduced into the play by Shakespeare. The Duke says, at the end of the Third Act,

> Craft against vice I must apply.
> . . . .
> So disguise shall, by the disguised,
> Pay with falsehood false exacting.

This balancing of one trick against another gives point to the title of the play. But the phrase 'Measure for Measure' also means, as Shakespeare has emphasized, the balancing of the penalty which Angelo meted out to Claudio for violation of chastity by a similar penalty against Angelo himself for a fault which he is supposed to have committed – 'An Angelo for Claudio, death for death!'

The whole passage is so significant that it must be quoted. The Duke says to Isabella,

405 For this new-married man approaching here,
Whose salt imagination yet hath wrong'd
Your well-defended honour, you must pardon
For Mariana's sake; but as he adjudg'd your brother, –
Being criminal, in double violation
410 Of sacred chastity and of promise-breach
Thereon dependent, – for your brother's life
The very mercy of the law cries out
Most audible, even from his proper tongue,
'An Angelo for Claudio, death for death!'
415 Haste still pays haste, and leisure answers leisure;

> Like doth quit like, and *Measure* still *for Measure*.
> Then, Angelo, thy fault's thus manifested;
> Which, though thou wouldst deny, denies thee vantage.
> We do condemn thee to the very block
> 420 Where Claudio's stoop'd to death, and with like haste.
> Away with him!   V.1

This has often been misunderstood and mispunctuated. Notice that lines 409–411 refer to Angelo's own misdemeanours, not to those of Claudio, who has been guilty of no promise-breaking. The Neilson text indicates this, but I emend the punctuation by ending the parenthesis in the middle, not at the end, of line 411, with the words 'Thereon dependent'. The sense of the passage is: Angelo's plot against the honour of Isabella may be pardoned, but not the breaking of his promise to spare the life of Claudio. Measure for Measure; the punishment must fit the crime: as Angelo condemned Claudio to the block, he must in like manner suffer on it himself. 'Measure' is sometimes 'used as a judicial term for dealing out justice' (Schmidt), as in III.2.256: 'He professes to have received no sinister measure from his judge.' The curious phrase 'leisure answers leisure' was probably influenced by desire for a rhyme to 'measure'.

Angelo has made full confession, and asked for death. It turns out, however, that Claudio has not been put to death, after all, and that Angelo has not succeeded in his plot against the honour of Isabella. Both of the women whom Angelo has wronged now plead for his life. What is the Duke to do? What does the 'strong, indignant claim of justice' require?

The whole point of the closing scene is that justice should be tempered with mercy. The mercy which Angelo had refused to Isabella is extended by the Duke in far greater measure, and under far stronger provocation. There is no stickling upon the letter of the law. Claudio is forgiven his venial offence. Even the wretched Barnadine, 'unfit to live or die', is pardoned.

> But, for those earthly faults, I quit them all;
> And pray thee take this *mercy* to provide
> For better times to come.

And Angelo is pardoned too. No doubt Shakespeare was influenced by the ending of Whetstone's play, in which Promos is not only forgiven, but restored to his governorship, but he took advantage of the conventional solution of the plot to lift the whole into a higher moral conception of justice than 'an eye for an eye and a tooth for a tooth'. The ending of the play, then, really contradicts the title. Our modern feeling may be that Angelo gets off altogether too lightly, but the pardon of the repentant villain and his union to a heroine was a commonplace in Elizabethan drama, and would certainly have been readily accepted by a contemporary audience. So Proteus, Oliver, Posthumus and Bertram are 'dismissed to happiness', despite their earlier cruelties. The claims of strict justice are secondary to those of stage entertainment. *Measure for Measure* is not a tract on equity, any more than it is on government; it is not an expression of Shakespeare's convictions in regard to the administration of law, but a story of human passion, sin and forgiveness.

In judging this situation, we are likely to be led astray by failing to realize the difference between conceptions of justice in medieval and modern times. The medieval attitude still persisted in the days of Elizabeth, especially in the minds of the common folk, and in literature reflecting their views. The modern idea of a progressive amelioration of the social body by far-sighted legislation, and its application to particular cases, was anticipated by the best minds of the Renaissance, but had by no means gained acceptance in the days when Shakespeare wrote. A passage in a book by the Dutch scholar Huizinga has an especial bearing upon justice in *Measure for Measure*, though obviously written to point no such application. 'Instead of lenient penalties, inflicted with hesitation, the Middle Ages knew but the two extremes: the fullness of cruel punishment, and mercy. When the condemned criminal is pardoned, the question whether he deserves it for any special reason is hardly asked; for mercy has to be gratuitous, like the mercy of God.'[33] Altruistic and advanced social philosophy like that of Coleridge, then, is no touchstone for judging an Elizabethan play.

Shakespeare might, after the dark shadows of the preceding intrigue, have ended *Measure for Measure* as tragedy, had he so chosen, but he determined that it should close in the spirit of comedy. The transition from the heights of tragic experience to the cheerfulness of a happy ending is too abrupt for the taste of modern critics, who like a play to be psychologically consistent. Shakespeare, however, did not shrink from violating such consistency, and executing a deliberate *volte-face* at the end. This is bitter medicine for those who claim that Shakespeare's works will appear as perfect and well-rounded wholes, if we only have the wit to look at them in the right way. We may as well admit that Shakespeare's art oscillates between extreme psychological subtlety, and an equally extreme disregard of psychological truth, in the acceptance of stock narrative conventions. To attempt to explain away the Shakespearean happy ending seems to me a hopeless task.

The one thing upon which the Duke insists is the good old conventional English demand that the wronged maid be made a recognized wife by marriage. So Angelo weds Mariana, and Lucio, though pardoned other offences, has to marry his punk. Coleridge's objection that Angelo's marriage is 'degrading to the character of woman' is that of a nineteenth century philosopher, strong in moral judgements, and weak in knowledge of Elizabethan narrative and social conventions. The same miraculous processes which lead to the forgiveness of erring male characters, and their conversion to the paths of rectitude, also automatically make them perfect husbands. The audience in the Globe Theatre, we may be sure, did not worry their heads over the illogicalities of the situation. They knew that the raptures of reunion and the music of marriage bells were a prologue to the good old story-book ending, 'And so they lived happily ever after.'

7. CONCLUSION

We may now review the principal results of the foregoing discussion, omitting the analysis of the sources and their relations to Shakespeare's play.

The essentially realistic character of the main plot, which deals with the fortunes of Claudio, Angelo and Isabella, a plot apparently based upon an episode from real life, was emphasized by Shakespeare's vivid and sympathetic treatment, and its realism was further heightened by the portrayal of the low-comedy characters

Mistress Overdone, Elbow, Pompey and Abhorson, and of Froth and Lucio, who, though of better social station, are fitly to be grouped with them. The elements added to the main plot by Shakespeare, which most affect the Duke and Mariana, offer a striking contrast, since those elements were drawn from conventional story-telling, and are thoroughly artificial. By his art in making them plausible, Shakespeare preserved, to a large extent, the illusion of reality produced by the play as a whole. But when we study the way in which the different parts of the plot were interwoven, and look with care at their motivation and their relation to the depiction of character, it becomes clear that the Duke, who plays so important a part in the action, is really a secondary and not an efficient cause in that action, and that his character was outlined and developed by Shakespeare in order to accord with it.

The ruse suggested by the Duke, agreed to by Isabella, and accepted by Mariana, has been shown to have involved, in the eyes of an Elizabethan audience, no moral laxity in any of those characters, mainly for the reason that Mariana had earlier been betrothed to Angelo, and that such a betrothal was held to confer the exercise of marital rights. It has further been observed that this stratagem was imitated from that in *All's Well*, where Helena must equally be absolved from having shown a lack of modesty or morality. The frequency of this episode in popular story, and the clear evidence that it was there held not only to be entirely worthy of a heroine, but praiseworthy as well, must also be taken into consideration. The marriage of Isabella to the Duke, which appears to be impending at the close of the play, must be accepted as proper, since she had not yet taken vows, and since the retirement of a novice from an order and her subsequent marriage was, and still is, in complete accord with Roman Catholic custom.

The machinations of the Duke, his deceptions that good may result, must be judged in the light of romantic and dramatic tradition, which may be studied in other Shakespearean plays. The Duke, in his own person, and in his disguise as a friar, combines the two agencies regularly used for the settlement of dramatic complications in accord with justice: the State and the Church. Neither his character nor his actions can be judged on a realistic basis. His state policies and his moral reforms must be viewed as belonging in the realm of story-telling, not as serious discussion of moral issues, or a transcript of life. Since he represents supreme authority, whether as Duke or Friar, whether secular or religious, other personages of the plot are not to be censured for entrusting themselves entirely to his guidance. In drawing his portrait, Shakespeare may possibly have been influenced, in a detail or two, by James I, but there is no adequate evidence that he knew James's *Basilikon Doron*, or was affected by it.

Angelo appears to have been conceived as a villain by nature, not as a good man gone wrong through sudden temptation. The play gains its name from the thwarting of this villain by the ruses suggested or practised by the Duke, and the suiting of proper punishments to Angelo's crimes, especially the infliction of the death penalty, since Angelo had apparently caused the death of Claudio. The title 'Measure for Measure' is, however, contradicted by the final decisions of the Duke, who concludes that mercy should temper justice, and that the strict letter of the law should not be enforced. The nature of the *dénouement* is due in part also to the claims of the 'happy ending'. In any case, it can as little be judged in accordance with strict logic or on the basis of principles of sound government as the sudden repentance of Angelo – a familiar Elizabethan convention – can be estimated rationally. The conversion of the villain makes him, as elsewhere in Shakespeare's plays, a suitable husband for a virtuous heroine. The true interpretation of the whole play, indeed, depends upon constant realization that while it seems real through the brilliancy and veracity of the portraiture of most of its characters, and through the intensely human struggle of the basic plot, it nevertheless exhibits improbabilities and archaisms which must be judged in the light of early traditions and social usages.

FOUR

Troilus and Cressida

THIS play, never a general favourite with readers or playgoers, and
indeed seldom performed on the stage, nevertheless bears un-
mistakably the seal and imprint of Shakespeare's greatest creative
period. It compels instant attention by the beauty of its verse, by the
telling imagery of its great speeches, with their pregnant wisdom and
mature philosophy, and by the acid brilliancy of its character-drawing.
It reveals, too, despite its reflective quality, something of that ir-
resistible power, that magnificent opulence of creative energy, which
we feel in *Antony and Cleopatra* or *King Lear*. Goethe, in talking with
Eckermann, ranked the play in this regard above *Macbeth* in the
achievement of Shakespeare, saying, 'would you learn to know his
unfettered spirit; read *Troilus and Cressida*'. But this brilliant play
has ugly features. Character and action are portrayed in a curiously
disillusioned and unsympathetic fashion; the most careless reader is
struck by the pettiness and bickering of the Greek chieftains, the
futility of the great struggle about the walls of Troy, the sensuality of
Helen and Cressida. As interpreters stand the elderly lecher Pandarus
and the foul-mouthed Thersites. The very atmosphere is close and
unhealthy; cowardice, rancour, boasting, wantonness, and even obscenity are constantly in the air. Moreover, how strangely the whole
ends! All these plottings and schemings, all the rhetoric and philosophy, all these amorous intrigues, all these big words and blaring
of trumpets bring at the last no settled issue.

The commentators have been hard put to it to explain the mani-
fold difficulties of *Troilus and Cressida*, from Coleridge, who remarked that he scarcely knew what to say, and that 'there is no one of
Shakespeare's plays harder to characterize', to Barrett Wendell,
always clear-sighted and sensible, who gave up the task as insoluble.
'A puzzle we found *Troilus and Cressida*, ... and a puzzle we must
leave it; our best comment must be guess-work.' The curious reader

115

may follow at his leisure the many attempts at elucidation, often strongly coloured by personal impressions, critical preoccupations, or philosophical theories. They agree as little as do the explanations of the two plays which we have just reviewed. Although many stimulating suggestions have been made, a survey of earlier critical theories hardly seems profitable, since no really satisfactory solution, commanding general acceptance, has been provided. The past twenty years, however, have brought new contributions to the problems of the play. These contributions have been much concerned with the effect of literary and social traditions upon the work of Shakespeare. Never was there a better illustration of the importance of the general method of approach upon which the present volume is based. It was indeed recognized by Lee, Boas, Neilson, Deighton, and others, that allowance must be made for medieval traditions and social ideals surviving in Shakespeare's play, but intensive study of these matters was first completed about fifteen years ago. Much of the credit of insisting upon such study is due to Tatlock. Detailed researches were published by him and by two other American scholars, working independently at about the same time. The general problem has thus been illuminated by different men, proceeding along somewhat different lines, but with the same general method and to the same general end. In the light of their demonstrations, *Troilus and Cressida* reveals itself as dominated, both in the love-intrigue and in the scenes dealing with the quarrels of Greek and Trojan heroes, by earlier and contemporary narrative and dramatic conceptions, and as deeply influenced by Elizabethan social conventions and views of morality.

Application of the 'historical method' does not, however, explain completely the difficulties of this strange play. It does provide an indispensable starting-point, but it does not reveal why Shakespeare selected this unpleasant theme – for it could, as we shall see, hardly have been treated in a pleasant fashion in his day – or why, though managing it technically as comedy, he chose to offer so little relief to the intensity of the shadows. Nor does it make clear his conception of the whole. His version is like no other; what effect did he aim to produce? How did he mean his play to be understood? Like any great work of art, *Troilus and Cressida* must transcend in some degree the influences which shaped it. It is our task here, after reviewing those influences, to venture to follow, as far as we may, the course of Shakespeare's creative imagination.

I. COMPOSITION, PUBLICATION, AND STAGE PRODUCTION

Before considering the subject-matter of the play, a brief review of certain technical difficulties seems necessary: the dates of composition and production, division of authorship, revisions, a possible lost play as a source, discrepancies between the Quartos and the First Folio. While many of these questions cannot be settled, it seems advisable to determine as far as possible where the probabilities lie, as working hypotheses for subsequent discussion. This is not all tedious business; the strange way in which the Quartos were issued has the fascination of an enigma, for which I suggest a new solution, which may throw light on the history of the play. However, gentle readers who are interested chiefly in the interpretation of the text may omit this section, if they choose. It seems too important to be relegated to the honourable obscurity of notes, and its main conclusions I here state in advance.

Shakespeare probably wrote *Troilus and Cressida* in 1601 or 1602, but there are evidences of later revision. Its undramatic character and unsuitability for the public stage suggest that it was originally composed for a special audience, possibly one of the Inns of Court. It was issued in quarto in 1609 with a title-page referring to public performance by the company of which Shakespeare was a member, a reference which in a second issue in the same year was suppressed, and a foreword added commending the play to readers, and praising it as suited to the reflective, though not to the vulgar. This preface does not say, as is often stated, that the play had not been performed on the stage. The hypothesis that it was produced in 1608 or in January 1609, and proved a failure, appears to explain the puzzling variations in the Quartos. Other interpretations are, however, possible. The text of the First Folio differs in many details; its relationship to the Quarto text is not clear, but shows that the play underwent a process of revision. Scenes 4–10 of the Fifth Act are probably not by Shakespeare; they are best regarded either as relics of an old play which he was revising, or as the completion of his own work by an imitator or collaborator. There is no valid evidence, however, that these 'spurious' scenes are at variance with Shakespeare's general artistic purpose and design. The play was inserted in the Folio after the volume was made up; troubles over copyright or indecision as to its classification may provide the explanation.

We may now consider these conclusions in detail.

There is pretty general agreement that the play was first written in 1601 or 1602. The Stationers' Register, under date of 7 February 1603, contains the following: 'Master Robertes, Entred for his copie in full Court holden this day to print when he hath gotten sufficient aucthority for yt, The book of Troilus and Cressida as yt is acted by my lord Chamberlens Men.' There is no absolute proof that this was Shakespeare's play, but it seems a plausible conclusion, since the Lord Chamberlain's Men was the company of which he was a member, and since one of the Quartos mentions on the title page the acting of the 'Historie of Troylus and Cresseida' by 'the Kings Maiesties seruants at the Globe. Written by William Shakespeare'. The King's Men was of course the same company earlier known as the Lord Chamberlain's or Lord Hunsdon's Men. It seems unlikely that they would have had in their repertory two different plays on this subject. Moreover, Roberts printed in 1604 the second Quarto of *Hamlet*. He apparently never published *Troilus and Cressida*; the 'aucthority' necessary was perhaps never gained. Metrical and stylistic tests confirm a date in the opening years of the new century.

The play is not one for which success on the public stage can easily be imagined. It is fundamentally undramatic in character, as we shall see in a later analysis, and it is overweighted with reflective passages. 'Elizabethan audiences', says Wendell, 'could relish things which nowadays would put audiences to sleep. ... Even an Elizabethan audience, however, could hardly have stomached the prolonged philosophizing which fills pages of *Troilus and Cressida*.' Some of this may of course have been omitted in the acting version. Malone conjectured that the play had not been acted on the public stage, but at court, and his view has received some later approval. The subject had indeed been popular in court plays in the sixteenth century, but it does not seem likely that a piece like this could have been designed for Elizabeth and her circle. They were far from squeamish, but they would never have welcomed such impudent and intimate indecorum. As Alexander puts it, 'in *Troilus* there is much scurrility and the audience are at times addressed directly and familiarly by the most scurril character in the most scurril terms; and the play concludes with an epilogue which prevents disapproval by implying that there will be no hissing except from bawds or panders or their unfortunate customers. This was obviously not for the ears of her Majesty.'[1] Moreover, it seems unlikely that the whole acid picture of the hollowness of artificial romantic love would ever have been painted to please a court which loved to affect and practise submission to such conventions. It is far more probable that Shakespeare wrote the play for a special audience of the more sophisticated sort. 'Plays were given in private houses, as well as at court, and not only when there was a royal guest to be entertained. As the public theatres were open by daylight, the companies were easily available for private engagements after supper.'[2]

A highly reflective, philosophical, undramatic piece like this might well have been designed in the beginning for the entertainment of some noble circle of literary tastes, and later have been tried in public, despite its unfitness for the public stage, in view of Shakespeare's reputation and popularity. Even more probably, it may, as Alexander suggests, have been originally designed as part of an entertainment for one of the Inns of Court. The selection of the theme, the intellectual rather than emotional treatment, the long philosophical speeches, might be supposed to appeal to such an audience, as well as the disillusioned treatment of romantic love, the ribald jesting, the direct allusions to the sexual looseness of the time, and the familiar tone, well adapted to those who knew the shady haunts of London at first hand. There is good evidence that the revels in the Inns of Court had a reputation for indecorum. In 1594, when *The Comedy of Errors* was given at Gray's Inn, the celebrations were characterized by elaborate literary fooling, mingled with obscenity; one of the members was elected Lord of Misrule, 'Prince of Purpoole', and his domains were set down on the title-page of the printed account as the more ill-famed haunts of the city. *The Comedy of Errors* was given by

Shakespeare's own company, the Lord Chamberlain's Men, and it is worth noting that Southampton was a member of Gray's Inn. In February 1602, *Twelfth Night* was produced at the Middle Temple, as Manningham's diary informs us, and as late as 1615–1616 the All Saints' Day plays at the Inner Temple were given by the King's Men, Shakespeare's old company. In 1611 the Benchers of the Inner Temple stopped temporarily the 'lewd and lascivious plays' which had formed part of their revels.[3]

It may be, then, that we are to regard *Troilus and Cressida*, not as a story of love and war written for regular theatre-goers, and, in its disillusioned tone and extended philosophizing, failing to make a popular appeal, but rather as a special entertainment for an audience cynical about love and sceptical about the heroics of war, but nevertheless keenly interested, as even the debauchees of the Elizabethan age often were, in social and philosophical discussions, and in poetry and drama. Shakespeare was by habit clearly sensitive to the demands of his audience; is it not likely that if he had been commissioned to write for a sophisticated and intellectual gathering, he would have tried to give his hearers what he thought would please their taste?

The play was published twice in quarto in 1609. On 28 January 1609, 'A booke called the history of Troylus and Cressida' was entered on the Stationers' Register to Richard Bonion and Henry Walleys. There seems little doubt that the Quarto which we will call A, with the following title-page, was the first to be issued: 'The Historie of Troylus and Cresseida. As it was acted by the Kings Maiesties seruants at the Globe. Written by William Shake-speare.' The other Quarto, which may be called B, also dated 1609, has a title-page which reads: 'The Famous Historie of Troylus and Cresseid. Excellently expressing the beginning of their loues, with the conceited wooing of Pandarus Prince of Licia. Written by William Shake-speare.' The rest of the title-page is the same as that of Quarto A, and the text is absolutely identical. Moreover, the running title in Quarto B, 'The Historie of Troylus and Cresseida', is also the same — even to the spelling 'Cresseida' — and for these and other reasons it is clear that a change had been made in the title-page of A, the rest of B having been printed from the same set-up. But there is another highly interesting difference between the two. The second Quarto, B, has a remarkable preface, entirely lacking in A, which must be quoted in full.

A neuer writer, to an euer reader. Newes.

Eternall reader, you haue heere a new play, neuer stal'd with the Stage, neuer clapper-clawd with the palmes of the vulger, and yet passing full of the palme comicall; for it is a birth of your braine, that neuer under-tooke any thing commicall, vainely: And were but the vaine names of commedies changde for the titles of Commodities, or of Playes for Pleas; you should see all those grand censors, that now stile them such vanities, flock to them for the maine grace of their grauities: especially this authors Commedies, that are so fram'd to the life, that they serue for the most common Commentaries, of all the actions of our liues, shewing such a dexteritie, and power of witte, that the most dis-pleased with Playes, are pleasd with his Commedies. And all such dull and heauy-witted worldlings, as were neuer capable of the witte of a Commedie, comming by report of them to his representations, haue found that witte there, that they neuer found in them-selues, and haue parted better wittied then they came: feeling an edge of witte set vpon them, more then euer they dreamd they had braine to grinde it on. So much and such sauored salt of witte is in his Commedies, that they seeme (for their height of pleasure) to be borne in that sea that brought forth *Venus*. Amongst all there is none more witty then this: And had I time I would comment vpon it, though I know it needs not, (for so much as will make you thinke your testerne well bestowd) but for so much worth, as euen poore I know to be stuft in it. It deserues such a labour, as well as the best Commedy in *Terence* or *Plautus*. And beleeue this, that when hee is gone, and his Commedies out of sale, you will scramble for them, and set vp a new English Inquisition. Take this for a warning, and at the perrill of your pleasures losse, and Iudgements, refuse not, nor like this the lesse, for not being sullied, with the smoaky breath of the multitude; but thinke [thank] fortune for the scape it hath made amongst you. Since by the grand possessors wills I beleeue you should haue prayd for them rather then beene prayd. And so I leaue all such to bee prayd for (for the states of their wits healths) that will not praise it. *Vale.*

Critics have generally agreed that the writer of this jargon meant to say that the play had not been acted. Thus Tatlock speaks of 'the statement in the preface of the Quarto that the play had never been acted', and Miss Bartlett refers to 'a preface which says distinctly that it was never acted'.[4] But how is this to be reconciled with the title-page of the earlier (A) Quarto, which says that the play *had* been acted at the Globe?

The Cambridge editors suggested (1865) that the Quartos of the A type 'were first issued for the theatre, and afterwards those with the new title-page and preface for general readers. In this case the expression, "neuer stal'd with the Stage, neuer clapper-clawd with the palmes of the vulger" must refer to the first appearance of the play in type, unless we suppose that the publisher was more careful to say what would recommend his book than to state what was literally true.'[5] This is not very clear, nor very helpful. Quartos were not issued for use in the theatre, but for readers who were anxious to get a current play in print. Neilson remarks that the statement in the preface, just quoted by the Cambridge editors, 'is either a plain falsehood for advertising purposes, or is a quibble based on some alterations or omissions'.[6] Adams says, 'It may be that, since the play was by Shakespeare, they [i.e. the publishers] assumed, as was natural, that it had been acted by his company. But after publishing it they were informed that in reality *Troilus and Cressida* never had been presented on the stage; and they hurried to make capital of so remarkable a fact.'[7] Alexander holds a similar view. 'Some one must at the last minute have informed the publishers that the play they had printed had never been performed at the Globe nor indeed before any public audience: the publishers thereupon inserted the new title-page and the preface.'[8]

All these hypotheses, it will be observed, assume a misunderstanding, error, quibble, or wilful deception on the part of the publishers of the Quartos. I suggest a simpler explanation. But before we consider this the preface must be more carefully scrutinized.

Does this preface say that the play had never been acted? We must look closely at it as a whole, in order to perceive its chief aim and intent; we must give due heed to peculiarities of Elizabethan idiom; and in particular we must judge single passages in connexion with their context, and not separately by themselves. The language is certainly not lucid; this is due in part to the affected style then in vogue, and perhaps to a desire to conceal the real weakness of the plea for buying the book, while avoiding outright falsehood. The hasty reader might well be impressed by this grandiloquent puff, and not look carefully at its logic. I think the play *had* been acted, but had failed, and that the writer was trying to throw out a smoke-screen to disguise that fact. Let us now look at his arguments more carefully.

The main point of this preface is that the book ought to be bought and read, because it is full of 'wit', or intellectual quality, though it has not appealed to the rabble, and has never been cheapened by their undiscriminating applause. It is, says the writer, 'a birth of your braine, that neuer under-tooke any thing commicall, vainely'. The peculiar Elizabethan 'your' should be remembered, as in 'all your writers do consent that *ipse* is *he*'; there is no need to emend, as has been suggested. It is called a 'new' play; it had only recently been published, and other reasons for calling it new, connected with its production, will be suggested presently. Publishers then, as now, were of course anxious to assure their readers of novelties. Webster, in the 'Address to the Reader' prefixed to *The White Devil*, speaks of 'those ignorant asses who, visiting stationers' shops, their use is not to inquire for good books, but new books'. The writer of the preface says further that the play has never been 'stal'd with the Stage'. This does not necessarily mean that it has never been presented, but more probably never presented so much as to become stale. A popular piece would have been taken to the vulgar heart and applauded by the pit, but this one has never had that fortune, it has never been 'clapper-clawd with the palmes of the vulger'. Nevertheless, says the writer, it is a play full of excellent matter, like the other comedies of this cele-brated author, so that even those who like plays least value his. So buy this play – you will find one of these days when the author is dead and his comedies out of sale that people will scramble for them. This piece has escaped the curse of the applause of the groundlings, which would damn it for the intelligent, so thank fortune 'for the scape it hath made amongst you', and do not like this comedy the less for not having been so tainted, 'for not being sullied, with the smoaky breath of the multitude'.

It seems to me, then, that this preface does not necessarily convey the idea that the play had never been acted. I suggest further that the statements in the title-pages and preface may be simply explained if we assume that the piece *was* actually performed in the Globe Theatre in 1608 or January 1609, but proved a failure. On this hypothesis, everything falls into line, and it is not necessary to assume that the publishers were mistaken in their information, or were trying to deceive their readers. There is surely the best of evidence that the play was presented by Shakespeare's company on the stage; the title-page of the earlier Quarto says definitely 'acted by the Kings Maiesties seruants at the Globe'. Why should we throw this statement into the discard? What real evidence have we for so doing? Is not the assumption that Bonian and Walley (as the names are spelled on the Quarto title-pages) thought, when they issued Quarto A, that the play had been produced, but were really mistaken, extremely unlikely? Were men who were trying to make money by issuing plays so ignorant of theatrical conditions? And is it not equally unlikely that, on discovering their mistake, the publishers would have rushed out a second edition, changing the title-page and adding a preface? Was the mere fact that the play had not been produced (supposing it *was* a fact) sufficient to make this worth while? On the other hand, if the piece had been produced, and proved a stage failure, the necessity for such hasty alterations is clear. It seems most reasonable to conclude that the play had been actually staged, and that Bonian and Walley had got out the earlier Quarto for the sake of attracting readers, and put the statement that the play had been acted at the Globe as a lure on the title-page. This would have been an entirely normal and usual proceeding. What happened next? There are reasons enough for thinking that, even with the prestige of Shakespeare's name, and of the popular Globe company, the play might have failed. It was in no wise suited to gain favour with the groundlings, and upon their approval the continuance of any piece upon the public stage largely depended. If the play did fail, the publishers were in a hole. They were trying to sell a piece which had proved unsuccessful on the boards; they were commending a theatrical failure by calling attention to its stage production. So they hastily printed a new title-page, in which all reference to the performance of the play was cut out, and the innocuous sentence 'Excellently expressing the beginning of their loues, with the conceited wooing of Pandarus Prince of Licia' inserted in its place. Moreover, they added a preface, an amusing forerunner of the modern 'blurb', in which they took an entirely new tack, in order to help the sale of the book, trying to make the very failure of the play to please the crowd sell the book to readers of the better sort. In view of the unequivocal statement on the title-page of the first issue of the Quarto, and of the easy solution which the hypothesis which I have proposed offers for the apparent contradictions between that and the second issue, I believe that we are justified in assuming a strong probability that the play was again staged in 1608 or January 1609, proved a failure, and was withdrawn. The whole matter is complicated and obscure, however, and other explanations are possible. I do not wish to dogmatize.

The relation between the Quarto and Folio texts is highly obscure. The Cambridge editors maintained that 'the quarto was printed from a transcript of the author's original MS; that this MS was afterwards revised and slightly altered by the author himself; and that before the folio was printed from it, it had been tampered with by another hand'. Alexander thinks that 'the copy for the 1623 version ... consisted of a Quarto text corrected from a manuscript in the possession of Heminge and Condell', and that 'the Quarto gives a later draft of the play than that in the possession of Heminge and Condell from which it was corrected'.[9] The one point which emerges clearly is that there is ample evidence of revisions; just how and why these were made no one can tell.

More important to consider here is the strong probability that another hand than Shakespeare's is visible in the play. It has long been agreed by critics that Scenes 4–10 of Act V are 'spurious'. Both metrically and stylistically they differ from the rest of the play. Some bits in them do have a Shakespearean ring, which may be due to successful imitation of his style or to his own retouching of the work of another man. The Prologue has also been suspected; but many good critics consider it genuine, and I think with reason. Decision as to the Prologue is of minor importance; it has little bearing on the interpretation of the play. But the closing scenes are important. Tatlock, after a careful review of the whole matter, concludes that Shakespeare was probably remodelling an old play, and that he allowed the closing scenes to stand virtually as they were. The hypothesis that Shakespeare left his play unfinished, and that the spurious scenes are due to a collaborator is equally possible, as Tatlock admits,[10] and seems more in line with Shakespeare's practice in other collaborated plays. There seems no way to decide the question definitely. It is important, however, to determine whether the ending as we have it is in harmony with Shakespeare's design for the play as a whole. Both Tatlock and Rollins[11] deny that it is, and regard the ending as essentially inartistic and un-Shakespearean. I do not see adequate evidence for this conclusion, and I hope to show later that the general conception of the ending is logical and artistically defensible, even if the workmanship is inferior. It seems improbable that Shakespeare would have allowed these final scenes, no matter what their source, to run counter to the general meaning and artistic effect of a play upon which he had expended so much labour. Discussion of this point must, however, be postponed to a later stage of our analysis.

In the Folio of 1623, the play bears the title 'The Tragedie of Troylus and Cressida', and it is placed between the histories and the tragedies, immediately preceding *Coriolanus*. But it is not paged at all, excepting for the second and third pages (not counting the Prologue), which are numbered 79 and 80. The pagination of the tragedies begins properly with *Coriolanus*. The Prologue occupies a whole page, and is set in large type, in contrast to the practice elsewhere in the Folio. *Troilus and Cressida* was clearly inserted in its present place after the volume was made up. It is often said that the editors put it at the last moment between the histories and the tragedies because they were in doubt as to the propriety of classifying it as tragedy, but it is to be observed that they left 'The Tragedie of Troylus and Cressida' on the title-page, and also used it as a running title on the two numbered pages following. Some critics believe that it was originally designed for a place after *Romeo and Juliet*, but that play ends with page 79, and the paging of our piece would, according to the two numbered leaves, have to begin with page 77. The Quarto title-pages term it a history, the preface to the second Quarto a comedy. It may well have seemed to the Elizabethans as hard a play to classify as it does to us, but that scarcely explains the puzzling eleventh-hour insertion in the Folio. Perhaps difficulties with the copyright entered into the matter. Modern editors generally classify the play as a comedy.

2. PLOT AND CHARACTERIZATION

Troilus and Cressida is a difficult play to retain clearly in mind, so its
action may, in the beginning, be briefly reviewed. This action falls
naturally into two parts: the Troilus–Cressida plot, and the
Achilles–Ajax–Hector plot, which may for brevity be called respectively the love-story and the quarrels of the chieftains. The
former has usually been reckoned the more important. 'That the
love-story was Shakespeare's starting-point', says Deighton, 'is, I
suppose, generally admitted.' It is worth noting, however, that some
writers find the chief interest in the other plot. Richard Grant White
called Achilles the real hero of the play (the word 'hero' is always
ambiguous; if it means the most important male character it hardly
seems justified here), and Tatlock finds the Achilles–Ajax plot 'the
most interesting part of the play', noting that it may have been
original with Shakespeare, and that 'on its elaboration Shakespeare
spent his chief interest and did his most impressive writing'.[12] It may
well be that Shakespeare began with the Troilus–Cressida theme,
which was so popular in his own day as to command immediate
attention, and then became particularly engrossed with the other
plot. Novelists have often remarked that a character or episode un-
expectedly grips the imagination as writing proceeds, and assumes
an importance not planned for in the beginning. What is 'interesting'
in the play before us depends, of course, to a considerable extent
upon subjective impressions, varying with different individuals.
There is surely interest enough in both plots to go around. I put the
love-story second in the following analysis, since it seems to me
more vivid when viewed against the brilliant panorama of the Greek
and Trojan camps.

The siege of Troy has lasted for seven years, and both Greeks and
Trojans are tired, stale, and disillusioned. Within the walls of Troy, the
prolonged and futile waste of blood and energy over an issue relatively
so unimportant as the abduction of Helen is fully recognized. Moreover,
she is notorious in both camps as a wanton. The proposal of Nestor
that she be delivered to the Greeks and all hostilities given over is
therefore seriously considered. Hector at first favours this, and
Cassandra prophesies evil if Helen is kept. Troilus and Paris are op-
posed to ending the conflict, however, and Hector finally agrees that

while morality speaks for her return, Trojan dignity demands that she be kept.

In a council in the Greek camp, Ulysses makes the point that Troy is holding out not so much through her own strength as through the weakness of her foes; that the Greek leaders are neglecting their responsibilities, and that disobedience and lack of discipline prevail. Achilles is in love with Polyxena, the daughter of Priam, and spends his time in idleness with his favourite Patroclus. He takes no part in the fighting, and diverts himself with Patroclus by mocking the other generals. Nevertheless, he is still recognized as the greatest of the Greek warriors. Ajax, too, has grown insufferably arrogant. He is a thick-headed bruiser, who encourages his satellite, Thersites, in reviling those about him.

Hector has sent through Aeneas a challenge to the Greek camp to fight with any of their champions on the issue that 'he hath a lady, wiser, fairer, truer, than ever Greek did compass in his arms'. Although sent in general terms, this is felt to be addressed to Achilles. By the advice of Ulysses, it is settled that Ajax shall be selected, in order to humiliate Achilles. This is rendered easy by the swollen vanity of Ajax and the continued arrogance of Achilles, who refuses to enter the field again, and treats the Greek lords who come to visit him with open discourtesy. Ulysses counsels that they, in their turn, shall use him slightingly, and, in a powerful speech, reminds Achilles of the consequences of his conduct, and of his love for the Trojan princess Polyxena. Patroclus adds further reproaches: the rumour goes that Achilles stays from combat through his affection for Patroclus himself, who has 'little stomach to the war'. Achilles recognizes the waning of his reputation, but merely sends a request that Hector and the Trojan lords be invited to his tent after the combat, as he has 'a woman's longing . . . to see great Hector in his weeds of peace'.

The combat between Hector and Ajax ends indecisively; Hector refuses to fight to a finish, on the ground that Ajax has Trojan blood in his veins. He meets Achilles, and they agree to encounter each other in the future, but Achilles receives a letter from Hecuba, bringing him a token from Polyxena, and once more gives over warlike action for the claims of love.

> Fall Greeks; fail fame; honour or go or stay;
> My major vow lies here, this I'll obey.

Hector later leaves Troy again to fight the Greeks, against the protestations of Andromache, Cassandra and Priam. He spares Achilles, but

Patroclus is killed. Achilles vows vengeance; he instructs his Myrmidons to surround Hector, who is then slain in disgraceful fashion while unarmed. Achilles thereupon sends forth word that he has killed Hector.

Cressida, daughter of Calchas the Greek, has, during her enforced sojourn within the walls of Troy, ensnared the heart of Troilus, son of Priam, and, after Hector, the most brilliant of the Trojan warriors. She is a seasoned coquette, who, though taken with Troilus from the first, knows that a man is better caught if kept at a distance. Troilus is an ardent, idealistic young fellow, thoroughly under the fascination of a sensual and calculating woman. When his passion is at last gratified, by the assistance of the elderly lecher Pandarus, and Cressida has at last confessed that she cared for him from the first, Pandarus further degrades the whole affair by the coarsest of comments on their physical union.

An arrangement for the exchange of prisoners is proposed, Cressida for Antenor. Cressida at first protests that she will not return to the Greeks, but finally does so, leaving Troilus with many protestations of fidelity, and giving him a glove as a token, in return for which he gives her a sleeve. On her arrival in the Greek camp, under the escort of Diomedes, she greets the chiefs with bold coquetry, and Ulysses comments in stinging terms on her wanton character. She is soon engaged in an amorous affair with the vigorous but cynical Diomedes.

Ulysses later persuades Troilus to accompany him to the tent of Calchas, where they witness a love-scene between Cressida and Diomedes, in the course of which Cressida bestows upon him the sleeve given her by Troilus as a love-token. After the fighting is renewed, Troilus announces the death of Hector to Aeneas and the Trojans, and vows to avenge him. He has already realized the complete faithlessness of Cressida, and now repulses Pandarus:

> Hence, broker! lackey! Ignomy and shame
> Pursue thy life, and live aye with thy name!

With an obscene final speech by way of epilogue, Pandarus brings the play to an end.

Both characterization and action make a singularly disagreeable impression, which increases as the play progresses. Paris is enjoying the adulterous love of Helen, Menelaus is that shabbiest of Elizabethan butts, a cuckold, Cressida is a shameless wanton, Achilles is a slacker, forsaking his military duties for the love of a girl in the citadel of the enemy, and is accused of immoral fondness for Patroclus. Ajax is a bully and a boaster, swollen with his own conceit, Diomedes is sensual and brutal, Patroclus a weakling. But these characters, unlovely as they are, pale beside Pandarus, with his leering ribaldry, and Thersites, the foulest-spoken of all the people of Shakespeare. Yet both Pandarus and Thersites are important; each fills two functions, those of Chorus and of Clown. As though the audience might miss the sensual and calculating passion of Cressida, and be misled by the eager and youthful ardour of Troilus into setting their love upon too high a plane, Pandarus is constantly made to utter comments which no decent girl, even in Elizabethan days of unbridled speech, could hear without a protest. In comparison, the jests of Lavache in *All's Well*, to which critics have taken exception, seem like the warblings of a cherub. But Pandarus no doubt afforded the audience constant amusement. Thersites, too, is obviously the Clown in a new guise; compare, for instance, the scene in which he asserts that Agamemnon, Achilles, Patroclus and himself are fools (II.3), and Achilles challenges him, 'Derive this; come', with the badinage between Olivia and Feste in *Twelfth Night*, in which Olivia urges on the Clown, 'Make your proof', whereupon he proves logically that he is a fool (I.5). The functions of Chorus and of Clown are of course closely allied; the privileged half-wit who can utter home truths enlightens the audience while he amuses them. In the light of the comments of Thersites the Greek leaders lose all their Homeric radiance. Nestor is 'a stale old mouse-eaten dry cheese', Ulysses 'a dog-fox', Ajax a 'mongrel cur', Achilles a dog 'of as bad a kind', Diomedes 'a dissembling abominable varlet', Patroclus a 'masculine whore', and much more to the same general effect. Thersites adds the final touch of degradation to the love of Cressida and Diomedes, 'How the Devil Luxury, with his fat rump and potato-finger, tickles these two together! Fry, lechery, fry!' Of all the major characters, indeed, the only ones not bespattered with mud in one form or another are Troilus, Hector, and Aeneas. Troilus and Hector are especially brilliant, sympathetic and moving figures. They are brave and chivalrous, the chief ornaments of the Trojan camp. Hector's cruel death is deeply pathetic, but Troilus is hardly less an object for the beholder's compassion – an ardent, high-spirited boy who gives all the fervour of his idealistic young love to a false and shallow woman, and tastes the bitterest dregs in the cup of disillusion. It is noteworthy that while Pandarus gibes at the sensual element in his passion, he has no word of abuse for him, even after Troilus has uttered the most stinging of insults, and that Thersites can find nothing worse to say of Troilus than that he is a 'scurvy foolish doting young knave', 'the young Trojan ass, that loves the whore'.

The two main parts of the action may now receive more detailed attention. Since the starting point of the play appears to have been the love-story, this will be examined first.

3. THE LOVE-STORY

The most superficial reading of *Troilus and Cressida* shows that its manners are those of medieval chivalry and chivalric love, as the Elizabethans understood them. The desperate passion of Troilus, forgetting all else in the love of his lady, strikes the key-note at the opening of the play.

> Why should I war without the walls of Troy,
> That find such cruel battle here within?
> Each Troyan that is master of his heart,
> Let him to field; Troilus, alas! hath none.
>
> .   .   .   .
>
> The Greeks are strong, and skilful to their strength,
> Fierce to their skill, and to their fierceness valiant;
> But I am weaker than a woman's tear,
> Tamer than sleep, fonder than ignorance,
> Less valiant than the virgin in the night,
> And skilless as unpractis'd infancy.

The infatuation of Achilles for Polyxena, which damages his reputation as a warrior, recalls again the favourite medieval theme of the knight forgetting his duty to arms in the service of his lady. The challenge of Hector that

> He hath a lady, wiser, fairer, truer,
> Than ever Greek did compass in his arms,

a boast which he proposes to make good by combat, is wholly in the spirit of the fantastic code of chivalry. Such matters as these were thoroughly familiar to the Elizabethans from romantic narrative, the heritage of bygone days.

The observances of chivalry were not, in Shakespeare's day, merely literary survivals. The action of *Troilus and Cressida* is based mainly on literary traditions, but there was of course much of the fantastic exaggeration of medieval *fine amor* in the manners of Elizabeth and her court. Certainly in her caprices, offishness, sudden yieldings and coolings, the Virgin Queen carried on worthily the traditions of her medieval sisters. Could there be a better summary of her favourite tactics than Cressida's words?

> That she belov'd knows naught that knows not this:
> Men prize the thing ungain'd more than it is.
> That she was never yet that ever knew
> Love got so sweet as when desire did sue.
> Therefore this maxim out of love I teach:
> Achievement is command; ungain'd, beseech.
> Then though my heart's content firm love doth bear,
> Nothing of that shall from mine eyes appear.

That the exaggerated devotions and protestations of medieval lovers were repeated by Elizabeth's courtiers, even after she was old and wrinkled, is of course notorious. A favourite trick of Essex was to imitate the love-lorn medieval knight, and take to his bed, refusing all comfort, when the favour of his lady was withdrawn from him. Amusing, too, is Raleigh's attempt to drown himself, so great were 'the horrors of Tantalus' which he endured when deprived of the sunshine of the royal presence. The disease spread even beyond the limits of the court. A little London tailor, fancying himself in love with Elizabeth, 'whined himself to death' for her sake, and was doubtfully immortalized in verse by Lord Charles Cavendish. Shakespeare has his fling at these absurdities again and again; we may even see a reflection of them in *Hamlet*, when Laertes is challenged to the most extravagant of feats to show his devotion to Ophelia – to drink vinegar or eat a crocodile. As Taine puts it, 'like the tars who tattoo a heart on their arms to prove their love for the girls they left behind them, you find men who "devoured sulphur and drank urine" to win their mistress by a proof of affection.'[13] One of the adventures of Essex in Spain affords a close parallel to an episode in *Troilus and Cressida*. 'Into one of the gates of the town Essex, as a parting gesture, thrust his pike, "demanding aloud if any Spaniard mewed therein durst adventure forth in favour of his mistress to break a lance". There was no reply.'[14]

It is commonly said that the source of the love-story is Chaucer's *Troilus and Criseyde*, but this statement needs qualification. There is of course no doubt that Shakespeare made use of Chaucer's poem. As Small says, after a detailed review of the evidence: 'Shakspere's play . . . follows the order of Chaucer's story exactly, contains many passages obviously suggested by it, adopts the character of Pandarus from it without change [this must be questioned], and owes to it one aspect of the character of Troilus.'[15] Nevertheless, Shakespeare would have been familiar with the tale of Cressida if he had never read a line of Chaucer. Many contemporary references and retellings show its wide circulation. Raleigh calls it 'incomparably the most popular love-story of the earlier sixteenth century'.[16] The Cressida plot is of extreme simplicity; it can be summed up in two or three sentences. This gave a wide latitude to varying conceptions of character, and made it possible for the men of Shakespeare's day to conceive it very differently from the poets of the fourteenth century. The whole story had changed, much for the worse, and it is this new form and interpretation, strikingly reflected in sixteenth century versions and allusions, and not the delicate and sympathetic treatment of Chaucer, which appears in the work of Shakespeare. How he could have read and to some extent imitated Chaucer, and at the same time have shaped his play in accord with current traditions, can only be perceived after reviewing with care the whole development of the material. It must never be forgotten that his procedure was very different from that in *All's Well* or *Measure for Measure*, in which he was retelling a comparatively unfamiliar story, and depending almost wholly upon a single printed source.

Familiar as it is, the history of the Troilus–Cressida theme must now be briefly outlined. The tale was apparently invented, in its earliest form, by Benoit de Sainte-More, who inserted it into his great *Roman de Troie* (c. 1160). About a hundred years later, Guido delle Colonne put Benoit into Latin prose, with abridgements and alterations. Guido found many imitators, among them Lydgate, and Caxton, whose *Recuyell of the Histories of Troye* is important as a source of Shakespeare's enveloping action. The love-story was further developed by Boccaccio in his *Filostrato*. Here the episode in Benoit was made the central theme, the relations of Cressida to Troilus rather than to Diomedes emphasized, and 'Pandaro' made the go-between in the intrigue. Boccaccio's poem reflects the manners of Neapolitan society in the fourteenth century, and in particular the poet's love for Maria d'Aquino, or 'Fiammetta', the illegitimate daughter of King Robert of Jerusalem and the Two Sicilies. Medieval love-conventions control the action. Griseida is charming, voluptuous and calculating, and Pandaro a gay young courtier, cousin of the lady, who uses his good offices to secure her love for the handsome Troilo. The poem seems artificial to us today, but is a vivid and graceful picture of life in a society at once conventional and licentious.[17] Chaucer's poem was based upon Boccaccio, with some details from Benoit and Guido, but was a complete transformation, a masterpiece of sustained and subtle analysis. Troilus is not unlike the Troilo of Boccaccio, but Pandarus becomes a humorous elderly man of the world, kindly but unmoral, while Criseyde, the central figure, is so complex that critics still differ in their estimate of her character. But she is certainly treated sympathetically. The view which would make of her 'a scheming adventuress' is, as Kittredge remarks, 'so patently erroneous as to need no refutation'.[18] The poem is almost wholly devoted to the relations between Troilus and Criseyde; when Diomedes comes into the picture the poet quickly brings his work to an end. Chaucer treats Criseyde sympathetically throughout; even after she has proved faithless he does not condemn her, he only pities her weakness. He suggests the influence of Fate; the love of Troilus and Criseyde, like that of Romeo and Juliet, was star-crossed.

It is of the utmost importance to understand clearly the conventions of chivalric love which underlie Chaucer's analysis of character. These were taken over from Boccaccio, but in the fourteenth century were a commonplace alike of polite manners and of aristocratic narrative. At the court of Edward III, the practices of courtly love, best revealed in the French poetry of the twelfth and thirteenth centuries, were fast fading in a changed society and a more realistic attitude towards life. But they were still the diversion of the elegant, and a touchstone of fine manners. Their precepts were, of course, according to modern ideas, immoral. The beloved object was usually a married woman, and the granting of the last favours to the lover, after a season of devotion, was held entirely proper. Secrecy was essential, and constant discretion necessary. When once love had been granted, absolute fidelity, in the teeth of all obstacles, was obligatory. The world might be well lost for love, but it must be lost for constant, secret, and enduring love.

What is right and wrong in Chaucer's poem, then, is determined not by morality but by convention. Criseyde was not at fault in giving herself to Troilus, but she committed the supreme sin against decorum in proving faithless to him, and surrendering herself to Diomedes. There is much talk of her 'honour' in the poem, but this does not mean 'chastity'. Her 'honour' will be stained if the intrigue is discovered, but not if it is concealed. The part played by Pandarus must be clearly understood in this connexion. In theory the perfect love-affair admitted of the intervention of no procurer. Go-betweens were indeed common enough in those days, but they were usually servants, retainers, waiting-maids, and the like, persons of lower station, with whom a gentleman could not allow himself to be confused. Their services were a constant danger to the preservation of complete secrecy. As an experienced man of the world, Pandarus knows the risk in an episode of head-strong passion, which may become an open scandal. Then Criseyde's honour will indeed be stained, and he himself will suffer too. Such a disclosure would put him on the level of a common procurer or go-between acting for money, basely influencing the actions of his niece for his own gain. In a noteworthy speech in Book III he expresses his fears to Troilus (lines 239 ff.), and the latter reassures him, emphasizing the difference between 'bauderye' and 'servyse' in rescuing a friend from suffering, and, to show how far he is from holding such service 'a shame or jape', he ends by offering to gain for Pandarus the love of his sisters Cassandra or Polyxena, or of Helen. The claims of friendship, always so powerful in the Middle Ages, have a strong influence here. So in the romance of *Claris and Laris*, the knight Claris loves the married sister of his bosom friend Laris, and Laris aids him in furthering the affair. After the intrigue with Cressida has been carried to a successful climax, Pandarus has no regret for his conduct. Criseyde is no green girl; she has been a wife, she knows what she is about, and she is careful to handle the situation with the requisite amount of coyness. Nothing was in worse form than for the lady to yield too quickly; the lover's atrocious sufferings were a necessary prelude to his later bliss, and such sufferings Troilus was made to endure to the full.

The code of what was right and proper socially was, as has been noted, essentially the same for Chaucer as for Boccaccio. But their personal attitude towards this code was not the same; Boccaccio accepted it, Chaucer tested it. There is no repudiation of the system of courtly love at the end of the *Filostrato*; young people are exhorted to pray that Troilo may rest in peace, and to take care that they do not fall victims to fickle women, but rather choose ladies who are noble and constant. To Chaucer, on the other hand, the tale reveals ultimately only the hollowness of the service of Love. Troilus dies in profound disillusion; Criseyde lets passion lead her into breaking both the natural and the conventional laws of true love. What is the answer? Well, Love is not the deity for men to serve; they should put their trust in God, who will treat no man falsely.

> – sin he best to love is, and most meke,
> What nedeth feyned loves for to seke?

In short, the story is, in the hands of Chaucer, an attempt to analyse the validity of the conventions of love by minute examination of a specific instance, which leads to the decision that those conventions break down as a rule of life. The situation is much the same as if a theologian were to interpret the facts of human existence in accordance with a preconceived system, having assumed for the purposes of the experiment that the system is sound, and were to find out at the end that it breaks down in its application completely.

The most important single version of the story between Chaucer and Shakespeare was Robert Henryson's *Testament of Cresseid*, written in the late fifteenth century. It was printed in Thynne's edition of Chaucer in 1532, and was often mistaken for a work by the older master. Henryson tells us that 'to cut the winter nicht' he was reading Chaucer's poem, after which he took 'an uther quair', in which he found the fatal destiny and wretched end of Cresseid. The chances are that Henryson invented the elaboration of the story; the 'uther quair', as Skeat has noted, is probably a literary device. According to this 'book', Cresseid was deserted by Diomedes, who loved another woman.

> Than desolait sho walkit up and doun,
> And, sum men sayis, into the court commoun.

So, it is hinted, the gentle and erring lady of Chaucer has degenerated into a harlot. Henryson protests that he wishes to excuse her, and blames Fortune for her troubles. In her despair, Cresseid curses Venus and Cupid. Then in a dream she sees the gods in assembly, and Cupid demanding vengeance for her blasphemy. This is granted; Saturn strikes her with leprosy. Troilus, in the meantime, has been active in the war, and returns to the city in triumph. As he passes, he looks at the leper sitting with cup and clapper at the roadside, and seeing something in her face that reminds him of his faithless lady, throws her a purse. Cresseid makes her 'testament', and dies of a broken heart. In conclusion, the author points the moral for 'worthy wemen' – they are not to 'ming their luf with fals deceptioun'.

It is important to observe that Henryson constructed his poem on the basis of love-allegory. But the old system was breaking down, and modern ethical ideas were creeping in. The medieval notion that Cressida's fickleness is the supreme sin against love is mingled with the reprobation of the woman who gives herself to more than one man. Morality no longer countenanced even a secret intrigue like that with Troilus. Under these circumstances, the degradation of Cressida was inevitable. Gregory Smith notes that Henryson's didactic habit 'points to a declension in the spiritual force of allegory. It remains as a poetical form, but it is becoming no longer self-sustaining as a *motif* – as the mystical expression of the love-fervours of the Middle Ages.'[19] This change in the general conception of the tale was naturally hastened by its popularity. The common people, who even in the Middle Ages had had their gibes at courtly conventions, had now even less power to understand them, or desire to reverence them. They liked good stories, but they interpreted them according to their own views of life; the subtleties of courtly allegory were not for them. In the sixteenth century they summed up Cressida's character in a short and ugly word. But she fared little better at the hands of the bookish. Skelton, in his *Book of Philip Sparrow*, probably written in the opening years of the sixteenth century, is severe both upon Cressida and Pandarus.

> She was much to blame,
> Disparaged is her fame
> And blemished is her name,
> In manner half with shame.
>
> .   .   .   .   .
>
> Pandara that went betweene
> Hath won nothyng, I ween,
> But light for somer green
> Yet for a special laud
> His name is Troyllous baud,
> Of that name he is sure
> Whiles the world shal dure.

It is impossible to multiply illustrations here; one further example must suffice. Our friend George Whetstone, ever intent upon a moral lesson, took the story as the theme of his *Rocke of Regard* (1576). Cressida herself does some of the preaching,

> You ramping gyrles, which rage with wanton lust,
> Behold in me the bitter bloumes of change,

but Whetstone has young men especially in mind:

The inconstancie of Cressid is so readie in every mans mouth, as it is a needelesse labour to blase at full her abuse towards yong Troilus, her frowning on Syr Diomede, her wanton lures and love: neverthelesse, her companie scorned, of thousandes sometimes sought, her beggerie after braverie, her lothsome leprosie after lively beautie, her wretched age after wanton youth, and her perpetuall infamie after violent death, are worthy notes (for others heede) to be remembred. And for as much as Cressids heires in every corner live, yea, more cunning then Cressid her selfe in wanton exercises, toyes and inticements, to forewarne all men of suche filthes, to persuade the infected the fall from their follies, and to rayse a feare in dames untainted to offend, I have reported the subtile sleites, the leaud life, and evill fortunes of a courtisane, in Cressid[s] name. . . . [20]

This represents fairly the way in which Cressida was regarded in the Elizabethan Age. The ending which Henryson gave to the story was generally accepted; Cressida was a leprous wanton – a 'lazar kite', to use Shakespeare's own phrase. Whether Shakespeare knew Henryson's poem or not is uncertain; if he did, he may, like many of his contemporaries, have believed it a work by Chaucer.

With such a tradition as this confronting him, how could Shakespeare make the heroine of Chaucer's poem a sympathetic character for the men of his day? The story was too familiar to alter; its very popularity had stereotyped it. It is safe to say that the Elizabethans would have jeered at a pure and noble Cressida, just as the pit of an English theatre today would jeer at a self-sacrificing and high-principled Guy Fawkes. It is true that in the seventeenth century Dryden ventured the experiment of redeeming the character of Cressida in his dramatic version of the story, but conditions in Restoration days were vastly different from those at the opening years of the seventeenth century. The theatre was far less close to the people as a whole, and the tale of Troilus and Cressida had lost something of the popularity which it formerly enjoyed. Even had Shakespeare desired to do so, he could no more have whitewashed Cressida than he could have whitewashed Richard III, who was historically far from being the monster of Elizabethan tradition. He could not alter the well-known incidents of Cressida's career any more than he could have made Richard repent, and die in the odour of sanctity. How impossible it would have been for him to introduce into his work the ideals of courtly love which underlie Chaucer's poem, even if he had understood them, may be realized if we reflect that according to those ideals it would have been proper for Cassio to make advances to Desdemona, for Emilia to encourage them, and ultimately, provided strict secrecy and other rules were observed, for Desdemona to grant Cassio her love, as far as he desired. The social ethics of the Elizabethan stage were of a very different sort. Not even in his treatment of Cleopatra does Shakespeare try to justify wantonness – he strikes the key-note of the play in the opening lines, in which Philo informs us that Antony's love is dotage on a gipsy's lust, that the triple pillar of the world has become a strumpet's fool. Cleopatra's vicious instincts are unsparingly revealed, but with her extraordinary fascination

> vilest things
> Become themselves in her, that the holy priests
> Bless her when she is riggish.

This fascination, and her commanding position as a great queen, surrounded by the dazzling luxury of the Alexandrian court, and loved by the greatest soldier of the day, blind us to the coarseness of her nature and the sensuality of her intrigues. But Cleopatra was never a by-word for a loose and faithless woman, like Cressida. Sir Thomas North speaks of her 'courteous nature' and her 'noble mind and courage'. To Chaucer she was one of the saints of Cupid, the first of the procession in the *Legend of Good Women*. Chaucer intended Helen, too, for one of Cupid's saints, a female martyr to love, but Shakespeare etches her portrait in these biting words:

> For every false drop in her bawdy veins
> A Grecian's life hath sunk; for every scruple
> Of her contaminated carrion weight
> A Troyan hath been slain.

The relations of Helen and Paris in Shakespeare's play are of much significance in judging those of Troilus and Cressida. The speech of Hector, in which he defends the laws of morality, is noteworthy:

> If Helen then be wife to Sparta's king,
> As it is known she is, these moral laws
> Of nature and of nation speak aloud
> To have her back return'd. Thus to persist
> In doing wrong extenuates not wrong,
> But makes it much more heavy.

There was no place in Elizabethan ethics for adultery.

4. THE QUARRELS OF THE CHIEFTAINS

The influence of changing traditions, both popular and literary, is equally perceivable in the camp-scenes. Medieval accounts got a bad start from the debased Latin narratives known by the names of Dictys Cretensis and Dares Phrygius, and later developments of the tale suffered the same fate as other classical material: the dignity of a heroic civilization was sacrificed to the tastes of a romantic age. The great personages of Homer were remodelled according to the fashions of chivalry; they came to resemble closely the knights of the court of Arthur. Liberal provision was made for affairs of the heart; centuries before Shakespeare wrote, Achilles was made subject to the bright eyes of Polyxena, Hector had a liaison with Morgan the Fay. In a similar way, Alexander the Great was chiefly remembered in the Middle Ages as the hero of fantastic adventures in the East; he became, in Chaucer's phrase, the flower of knighthood, but devoted to wine and women as well as to war. In the Troy-story, sympathy lay with those within the walls rather than with the Greeks, since many of the western European nations loved to consider their ancestral sovereigns as related, through Aeneas, Ascanius and Brutus, to the royal blood of Troy. The Middle Ages lost all sense of the serene classic dignity of Homer, because they had lost touch with Homeric traditions. The Elizabethans were just beginning to recapture some of this, through acquaintance with the Greek text, and through translations into the vernacular.

For the work of Shakespeare, then, as for that of most men of his age, we must look mainly at medieval conceptions. Caxton's *Recuyell of the Histories of Troy* gives a good idea of these. Like the equally popular *Troy-book* of Lydgate, Caxton's work was, as we have seen, ultimately derived in the greater part from Guido delle Colonne. By the time of Shakespeare so many paraphrases and imitations of Caxton and Lydgate had arisen that, as with the love-story, it is difficult to trace source-relationships accurately. The various versions of the camp-scenes have been collected and carefully studied by Tatlock. Ovid and Vergil were frequently utilized, and the influence of Chaucer is generally apparent. Peele's *Tale of Troy*, in jigging couplets (1589), Greene's *Euphues his Censure to Philautus* (1587), in euphuistic prose, Heywood's poem, *Troia Britanica* (1609), and the stanzaic *Life and Death of Hector* (1614), attributed, probably falsely, to Heywood, illustrate the non-dramatic pieces. The last two are later than Shakespeare's play, but confirm the general tendency to tell the tale in the spirit of Elizabethan medievalism.

Much more significant is Heywood's *Iron Age*, a ten-act play of uncertain date, but probably antedating Shakespeare's work. The main source appears to be Caxton, but there are recognizable traces of other English versions of the Troy-story. Ovid and Vergil were laid under contribution, and it is worth remarking that Heywood used the Iliad, especially for the figure of Thersites, and probably the Greek text. He made small use of Chaucer and Henryson; indeed, he might have derived what he told of the love-story from current traditions. The Troilus–Cressida theme was obviously considered promising material for the stage in the sixteenth century, probably rather from its popularity than from its inherent suitability. There are records of lost court plays, and in 1599 Henslowe commissioned Dekker and Chettle to write on the subject. That astute manager twice paid them sums of money, but the fruit of their labours has not been preserved.[21] In Heywood's play the love-story is very secondary in interest and elaboration to the camp-scenes. Another point which should be remembered is that Heywood, with his ten acts, filled in a much larger canvas than Shakespeare. The earliest scenes show the abduction of Helen; the latest ones the deaths of Troilus, of Achilles, and of Ajax. Shakespeare's play, on the other hand, covers only the central part of Heywood's action. The love-story, which is of minor consequence in Heywood, is much expanded and elaborated, and the ruse of the Greek chieftains to humiliate Achilles and Ajax is added. There are, however, striking resemblances between the two pieces, especially in the disagreeable characterization of Thersites and Ajax. Apparently, Shakespeare imitated Heywood, or, more probably, both used a common source, now lost, in all likelihood an older play. The latter conjecture is supported by the borrowings from the *Iliad* in *Troilus and Cressida*, which are on the whole best explained by the assumption that Shakespeare was remodelling a piece by a man who knew Homer well. Such familiarity with the *Iliad* as is shown in *Troilus and Cressida* is to be found in none of Shakespeare's other plays, and Tatlock has shown that before 1609 Shakespeare could have used Chapman's translation only for the first seven books (though he might have consulted other versions of the *Iliad*), and that 'the play contains many Homeric particulars from outside these seven books'.[22] It is perfectly possible, of course, that Shakespeare was not revising an older play at all, but that he got his Homeric material from special reading for this particular theme, or from a hearing of the *Iron Age*, and that he found little occasion to introduce such allusions in plays dealing with other subjects. The exact relationship between Shakespeare and Heywood, and the precise sources which each used, cannot be determined with certainty.

The important point to emphasize, once more, is that in the plotting and characterization in the camp-scenes, just as in the love-story, Shakespeare was fully under the influence of medieval rather than classical conceptions of the tale of Troy. Neither the non-dramatic versions nor Heywood's play can be said to produce a 'classical' impression. Our reverence for the Homeric heroes is so great that we are inclined to exaggerate, at the present day, their nobility and bravery. A more rationalistic verdict is that of Henry Cabot Lodge, who pointed out the cowardice and meanness and self-glorification of such men as Achilles and Agamemnon. 'In a word,' says Lodge, 'the Homeric poems describe to us the doings of certain primitive tribes who were cruel and treacherous, subtle and cunning, liars and braggarts, and, withal, not over brave, although fighting was their principal business in life, and courage should have been their conspicuous and redeeming quality.'[23] This may well have been felt in the sixteenth century, especially when we consider that the current tradition arose from debased versions of the Troy-story, which deliberately belittled the Greeks, and had been shaped by a highly artificial code of manners. The degradation of Ajax and Thersites may be traced even in classical sources; it was exaggerated by the Elizabethans, who loved to gibe at the braggart and the railer. Reading of contemporary literature, then, is a wholesome and necessary corrective for attributing to Shakespeare the responsibility for the unpleasant picture of the Greek warriors, and of Cressida, who, it must be recalled, was a lady from the Greek camp. And yet, when all due allowances have been made for the influence of tradition, various problems in Shakespeare's work remain still to be explained. To these matters we must now turn our attention. What has preceded has been, indeed, a necessary clearing of the ground in order to make possible a consideration of Shakespeare's personal achievement and its significance.

5. THE ENDING OF THE PLAY

One of the strangest features of this strange play is its *dénouement*. Both of its plots terminate inconclusively. No poetic justice is meted out to Cressida, such as Henryson thought that she deserved, and such as had become, by Shakespeare's day, her traditional punishment. On the contrary, she is left, despite her faithlessness, in the full tide of her love-affair with Diomedes. In Chaucer's poem and Heywood's play, the pain and disillusion of Troilus end in death; no such solution is found in Shakespeare. As far as we can see, Troilus is left to meet, with a broken heart, the futile continuance of the great struggle into which he had thrown his best energies. Again, the elaborate plan of the Greek chiefs to shame Achilles into action misses fire completely. Achilles is indeed resentful of the slights which have been put upon him, he is indeed moved by the reproaches of Ulysses and Patroclus, but instead of sending a challenge to Hector he merely dispatches Thersites to ask Ajax to invite the Trojans to his tent after the combat. When they do meet, Hector urges him to come into the field and fight, and Achilles promises to do so, but in the next scene he tells Patroclus that he is 'thwarted quite' from his great purpose – he has received a letter from Hecuba and a token from Polyxena, his lady-love, 'taxing and gaging' him to keep an oath which he has sworn – obviously not to do battle with Hector, Polyxena's own brother. He is finally roused to action by the killing of Patroclus, and contrives the death of Hector by a base trick. But he is not punished for his arrogance or for his inaction, and he is left in triumph after having compassed the death of the most brilliant and sympathetic hero in the play. Nor does the swollen vanity of Ajax meet any rebuff. The net result of it all is, in the words of Thersites, that 'now is the cur Ajax prouder than the cur Achilles', and that all the policy of Ulysses and Nestor is 'not prov'd worth a blackberry'.

These inconclusive solutions are all the more striking when the generally skilful workmanship of the main part of the play is considered. The alternation of interest between the scenes in Troy and those in the Greek camp is deftly managed, and after the return of Cressida to the Greeks, and the visit of Hector to the Greek camp, the two plots are interwoven with much dexterity. Moreover, the play shows the hand of the practised writer in the balance between character and plot, and in the introduction of new material. The Troilus–Cressida theme is essentially undramatic. It is good stuff for a courtly romance like Boccaccio's or a psychological novel in verse like Chaucer's, but it is not well suited to the stage. Its interest lies mainly in character. In this regard it contrasts strikingly with *All's Well* and *Measure for Measure*, which are good stories, with plenty of action. Shakespeare wisely concentrated his energies, then, on the delineation of the emotions and characteristics of Cressida, Troilus, and Pandarus. Yet this left the play somewhat weak in plot-interest and suspense. Everyone knew the outlines of the love-story, and of the tale of the Trojan War. So Shakespeare (or, possibly, the author of an earlier play upon which he worked) devised the ruse of Ulysses and Nestor, which immediately arrests attention, and provokes dramatic interest. How is it all going to end? Well, it does end very strangely, to be sure. Poetic justice is in no wise satisfied; there are neither the reconciliations of comedy nor the purifying calamities of tragedy to round out the action. 'It is difficult', wrote Alden, 'to exaggerate the dramatic futility of the whole effect.'[24]

Critics have objected vigorously, from the seventeenth century on; no subtleties of modern scholarship are needed to make this point plain. Dryden's remodelling of the play is instructive. It is unblushing, like his adaptations of Shakespeare in general, but it does achieve a vivid dramatic effect which the work of the greater master lacked. The plot is greatly altered. Cressida has really been true to Troilus, but has been forced by Calchas to pretend love for Diomedes, in order that they may the more readily escape from the beleaguered city. She gives to Diomedes Troilus's ring, and Diomedes asserts that she has yielded to his love. Cressida protests her innocence, and stabs herself as a final proof. Troilus slays Diomedes, but is slain by the Greeks. The big scene in the Fifth Act, in the grand manner, is dramatically effective, but it is not a fair illustration of how Shakespeare's Fifth Act might have been written, because it wrenches the whole framework of the plot so violently askew. Dryden was very pleased with it, however; he remarks with satisfaction, 'The whole fifth act, both the plot and the writing, are my own additions.' It was fortunate for him that the tale had faded sufficiently in popular consciousness to make such radical changes acceptable.

The easy way to account for the theatrically ineffective ending of Shakespeare's play is to blame the unknown writer of the spurious closing scenes. He is a convenient scapegoat. But we have to consider with some care whether this explanation is really satisfactory. These scenes would no doubt have been better written if Shakespeare had done them, but would they have been radically different in content? We know that his habit, in retelling old tales, was to leave their plots as they were, however unplausible or ineffective these might seem, and to strive to make them reasonable and plausible by skilful characterization. This practice was of course not invariable, but his tendency was always to fit his artistic conception to the plot as he found it rather than to remake the plot to fit a preconceived effect of his own. This general point has been frequently stressed in the pages which precede. If in *Troilus and Cressida* we suppose that he was revising an old piece, the final scenes of which were allowed to stand, his retention of an apparently anticlimactic end is comprehensible, though it still remains to be explained how he planned to make these final scenes harmonize with the earlier part of the play. If, on the other hand, we assume that the whole planning of the action was due to him, we still have to inquire whether it is not entirely possible that the closing scenes are in harmony with that design, and in accord with his intentions, though actually written by another hand. It must be remembered that division of authorship does not necessarily mean looseness of construction. As Wells remarks, 'some of the most loosely constructed of Elizabethan plays, as *Old Fortunatus*, are apparently the work of one poet, while some of the best unified, as *The Maid's Tragedy*, and *Eastward Ho!*, are known to have been written by two or more poets'.[25] Why are we to conclude that the collaborator in *Troilus and Cressida* was ignorant of Shakespeare's design, or deliberately ran counter to it? Both Quarto and Folio texts agree in the final scenes, which were not reconstructed in the revisions which the play obviously suffered. Let us see, then, what is to be said for the piece as an artistic and coherent whole as it stands, and challenge Alden's statement that 'the final scenes cannot represent Shakespeare's intention'.

It will be clearest to consider the two parts of the action separately.

For the love-story, only an unhappy ending was possible. The theme was so firmly established for an Elizabethan audience by tradition, as involving the separation of the lovers, the heartbreak of the one and the bad faith of the other, that no conventional happy ending could follow. But the Shakespearean ending is not unhappy enough to suit the critics. Both Tatlock and Rollins, in their long and elaborate analyses, conclude that Cressida ought to be punished. Rollins says:

It is almost incredible that, with his knowledge of Henryson, his pre-conceived ideas of the character of Cressid and the reward of her treachery, and his respect for what the public wanted, Shakespeare should have ended his play without at least punishing Cressid. How can the present ending have pleased his audiences? Even the groundlings, however much delighted with Thersites and Pandar, surely were dis-satisfied when the play abruptly dropped the leading characters instead of carrying them on to the logical traditional *dénouement*. What American audience would care to see *Uncle Tom's Cabin* if no Little Eva appeared in the cast or if Eliza failed to cross the ice? Shakespeare, if he wrote all the play, wrenched the familiar story as violently in one direction as Dryden later did in another; neither version could have been satisfactory in 1602. . . . We could feel surer that Shakespeare was responsible for all of the play if he had punished Cressida, – if in portraying her he had shown unmistakable bitterness and hatred.[26]

Tatlock points out that in the *Iron Age*, and two other plays to which he has called attention, Cressida is punished, and in the *Iron Age* Troilus dies. 'It is hard to fancy any skilled dramatist dropping his main threads without tying them up; and harder to fancy Shakespeare writing the end of the play and bringing the Achilles-motive to nothing.'[27]

To all this there seems to me a very simple answer. Shakespeare did no violence to tradition, for the reason that he did not carry the action to its ultimate end. He chose to end it, or to let someone else end it, with the beginning of the intrigue with Diomedes, just as Chaucer did. Why was he bound to carry it on to a later time, to the beggary and the leprosy, after the break with Diomedes? Why is it wrenching the familiar story to stop short of this? When we compare Heywood's play with Shakespeare's, we can see, as has already been pointed out, that Shakespeare omits material which Heywood introduced at the beginning. Why should he not also have omitted material at the end? Moreover, he had already filled a five-Act play; I cannot see how he could have packed the desertion of Cressida by Diomedes and the smiting of Cressida with leprosy into a Fifth Act which had only just, in Scene 2, shown the love-intrigue of Cressida and Diomedes for the first time. Could things be made to move as fast as that? Heywood got it all in, after a fashion, but he had ten Acts to do it in. Even so, his treatment of Cressida's end is so sketchy that Rollins himself says that Heywood was 'sure' that his audience could finish out her story. If Heywood was sure of this, why not Shakespeare? Rollins's insistence that Cressida be punished is all the more remarkable in view of the fact that he thinks that Shakespeare dealt with her 'so mildly', and says, 'Certainly he has no apparent bitterness towards Cressida.' Other Elizabethans made her more degraded, but I do not see how anyone can be in doubt as to what Shakespeare thought of her, and meant his audiences to think, after reading the famous scene in which she kisses the Greek chieftains all round, and the scorching comments of the clear-sighted Ulysses.

> Fie, fie, upon her!
> There's language in her eye, her cheek, her lip,
> Nay, her foot speaks; her wanton spirits look out
> At every joint and motive of her body.
> O, these encounterers, so glib of tongue,
> That give accosting welcome ere it comes,
> And wide unclasp the tables of their thoughts
> To every tickling reader! set them down
> For sluttish spoils of opportunity
> And daughters of the game.

Schücking has emphasized the importance of the comments of other personages in a play for the understanding of the character of any Shakespearean figure. As for the groundlings, I agree that they might have liked to see the punishment of Cressida at the end (just as they would probably have enjoyed witnessing the torture of Iago, which Shakespeare found described in his source but did not embody in his play), but I cannot concede that the omission of her punishment is fairly paralleled by the omission of little Eva or the ice-crossing episode in *Uncle Tom's Cabin*. The appropriateness of these illustrations is, however, of no great moment. What is important to recall is that the play, taken by itself as it stands, is clearly not one which would have pleased the groundlings at all, and that there are clear indications in its stage history that it did not. The hypothesis that it was originally written for a special audience, and not for the Globe Theatre, remains highly plausible. If ever a play was caviare to the general, surely *Troilus and Cressida* was.

The ending of the camp-scenes is in full accord with the inconclusive ending of the love-story. The issue is again – failure. The Greek chieftains, with all the right on their side, with the shrewdest policy of their wisest leaders to guide them, are powerless, just like Troilus, before egotism, selfishness and lust. The cowardly bully Ajax triumphs, and Achilles, at a word from his Trojan mistress, neglects his most imperative duties as a warrior and general. Here again the cause which engages our sympathies is defeated, and Achilles, who is as little heroic as Cressida, is left, like her, in a shameful triumph. The harmony between the two actions is complete. The ending of the sub-plot, like that of the main plot, is indeed both unsympathetic and ineffective theatrically. But we cannot blame all its shortcomings upon the unknown author of the spurious scenes in Act V (4–10). The resolution of Achilles to continue his shameful inaction, for the love of Polyxena, is set forth in the opening scene of Act V, which is conceded to be Shakespeare's own work.

This fashion of ending the two actions affords a striking contrast to *All's Well* and *Measure for Measure*. In both those pieces, Shakespeare introduced a theatrically vivid climax, leading to a conventionally happy ending. Psychologically their fifth acts are weak; dramatically they are effective. This is due in part to the sources;

Shakespeare followed essentially the same lines as Boccaccio and Whetstone, though with many elaborations. The last Act of *Troilus and Cressida* affords a complete contrast; dramatically it is weak, psychologically it is strong. And here again the ending is in accord with the sources. No happy ending was possible for either part of the plot; everyone knew that the tale ended unhappily. Under these circumstances, what was Shakespeare to do? He could indeed have recast the whole play as tragedy, and deepened the poignancy of the climax. Why he decided not to do this, I shall not presume to say. But it seems clear that this was never his intention. While there is much in this play, in the relentless analysis of the darker sides of human passion, which recalls the great tragedies, there is not the intensity of emotion and violence of action which lead inevitably to a tragic climax. Try the experiment of reading the play, and imagining a fifth Act in which Troilus is killed in battle, and Cressida left in the horrors of leprosy. Would that make of it a satisfactory tragedy? I do not think so; that is not the end to crown the work as Shakespeare wrought it. Perhaps the explanation lies in this: that the whole is too detached and too observant for tragedy. Shakespeare never quite seems to let himself go, to allow the action to sweep him on to an inevitable climax. Sir Edmund Chambers observes, 'Comedy, in *Troilus and Cressida*, becomes critical.'[28] Richard Grant White called the play 'Shakespeare's only piece of introspective work'. We may question the word 'only', perhaps, but not the rest of his verdict. And Barrett Wendell remarked, 'It is a reflective, and so a bad play.' There is plenty of reflection in the great tragedies, of course, but introspection does not control the action, even in *Hamlet*.

Like Chaucer, Shakespeare seems to have been deeply interested in analysing the passion of an idealistic boy and an experienced coquette who, despite her shallowness, is touched for a moment with his own bright clear flame. But he was not free to make her in any degree sympathetic. She must be, to accord with the story as everyone in his day knew it, sensuous, calculating, temperamentally inconstant, if not worse. The purer love of Juliet is sensuous enough in some of its aspects, like normal human love generally; her speech 'Gallop apace, you fiery-footed steeds' is a marvellous expression of this, but Shakespeare could not give to the soiled and scorned figure of Cressida the idealism of a Juliet, or the magnificent royal splendour which redeems the frank sensuality of Cleopatra. No other course was open to him than to treat Cressida realistically. Romantic unreality may surround a Rosalind or a Hero or a Juliet, in spite of all the touches of reality which give them the breath of life, but it would never do for Cressida, any more than for Goneril or Regan or Lady Macbeth, or the Queen in *Hamlet*. Moreover, realistic plays were in fashion at the moment, and Shakespeare had written, or was writing, two 'unpleasant' comedies, in which, despite their romantic plots, the treatment is in a high degree realistic. With all this the artificial mythological situation invented by Henryson accords very ill – Cressida's cursing of Mars and Venus, and her punishment in being stricken with leprosy. Mythology and realism are not good yoke-fellows.

The play ends in realistic and severely logical fashion. No concession is made to theatrical effect of the obvious sort, but a very definite impression is created of the futility and misery which come of loving a worthless woman. With this the earlier part of the play is in complete harmony. The whole background of the story is armed strife over another frail lady, Helen of Troy, strife which has become futile and dreary. Hector, the greatest of the Trojan heroes, is willing to continue it, despite its lack of moral justification, through a mistaken idea that Trojan honour demands it. Achilles, the flower of the Greek chivalry, throws honour to the winds because of an infatuation for a princess in the city of his enemies. The evil influence of love without honour, then, ends in the death of Hector, in the shame and the shameful triumph of Achilles in compassing his death, and in the complete disillusionment of Troilus. 'Wars and lechery,' says the Chorus Thersites, 'nothing else holds fashion.' And, in a less quoted passage, 'What's become of the wenching rogues? I think they have swallowed one another. I would laugh at that miracle; and yet, in a sort lechery eats itself' (V.6). The shadows deepen in the closing scenes. Like many a highly emotional boy, with a strong sexual nature, Troilus suffers deeply in the very revulsion of his feeling. He is too heartsick at the faithlessness of his mistress to find harsh words for her, but he curses roundly the older man who has cynically taken advantage of his infatuation. But

Cressida, as Boas has emphasized, is to have her Nemesis, too, in the brutality of Diomedes. 'The shallow coquette pays a heavy yet just price for her selfish levity, when she exchanges a chivalrous adorer for a harsh and imperious taskmaster.'[29] Dramatic justice lies in the future, not in the cheap and illogical solution of leprosy for Cressida and sudden death for Troilus, but in the realization, for both of them, that character and conduct bring inescapable consequences in life. The ending of the tale is in accord with the facts of human experience; life often settles nothing, it leaves the innocent to suffer, and the guilty to prevail. There is nothing else in Shakespearean comedy just like the spirit of these closing scenes; and their complete analogues cannot be found even in the tragedies. Whether Shakespeare himself or another man planned them, they carry steadily to the end the relentless logic of the play, the searching analysis of a reflective criticism of life.

6. IS THE PLAY A SATIRE?

The foregoing considerations explain why *Troilus and Cressida* is so hard to classify. At the time when Shakespeare wrote it, he had forsaken the more conventional types of early comedy, but had not yet given himself over to the full current of tragedy. *All's Well* and *Measure for Measure* are in accord with its spirit, with its restless questioning of the mysteries of love and passion, despite their artificial happy endings. We may call Shakespeare's picture of the Troy-story an experiment in the middle ground between comedy and tragedy in which experience often places us; nothing is settled clearly for good or ill, we suffer from the results of our own actions and those of others, and yet can see no definite outcome, excepting in so far as we may guess at it in the future. I cannot see the justification for the view, sometimes expressed, that *Troilus and Cressida* is really to be regarded as a chronicle history. Tatlock, for example, says, 'There is absolutely no essential difference between the *Troilus* and *Henry IV*.'[30] The difference, I should think, is sufficiently striking. The Elizabethan chronicle history aims to set forth, in sequence, the chief events of a reign. Unhistorical material, comic relief, and the like, may be prominent; even, as in *Henry IV*, outweighing in interest the historical events, although the latter form the framework of the play. This gives to chronicle history an ample scope of time; *Henry IV* extends from the Battle of Holmedon in 1402 to the accession cf Henry V in 1413 – eleven years. In *Troilus and Cressida*, on the other hand, only brief contemporaneous episodes are shown. Daniel, in reckoning the time-analysis of the play, concluded that 'it is impossible to assign to it more than four days, with an interval between the first and second'.[31] Neither plot presents the extended survey of events proper to chronicle history.

Something must now be said in regard to the often-expressed conclusion that *Troilus and Cressida* was written with satirical intent. No critic has made this more plausible than Boas,[32] who perceives in it Shakespeare's manipulation of 'the materials for a merciless satire of the high-flown ideal of love, fostered by the medieval cycle of romance, whence the tale had sprung. The absolute devotion of a gallant to his mistress, which this form of literature had glorified, is transformed into the delirious passion of a youth for a mere wanton. ... The infatuation of Troilus is paralleled by that of Menelaus and Paris.... Helen and Cressida are made to figure in exactly the same light.' The keynote of the play, which brings into harmonious relation the two plots, is, according to Boas, to be found in the words of Hector, ''Tis mad idolatry to make the service greater than the god', which applies to Greeks and Trojans alike. 'In both camps sentimental gallantry is the ruling motive, with disastrous results to true national interests.'

But do not causes deeper and more universal than mere sentimental gallantry wreck the lives of these people? Was not Shakespeare rather analysing life than satirizing chivalry? The weaknesses of the system of courtly love seem, in his analysis, of secondary rather than primary importance. This is very difficult to prove, since the whole action takes place in a society ruled by chivalric conventions. But certain reservations must be made. Shakespeare could not have portrayed Greek and Roman society, in view of the form which the story had assumed in his own day, excepting as subdued to those conventions. Moreover, a very different spirit from that of Cervantes seems to have gone to the making of *Troilus and Cressida*, though from Boas's summary one might not think so. Sir Edmund

Chambers seems to have *Don Quixote* in mind when he writes of this play that 'Shakespeare goes tilting at illusions.' But surely Shakespeare's mood is very different from that of the satirist who 'smiled Spain's chivalry away'. His play is no genial exposure of absurdities, no shattering of the conventions of romance, but an earnest, concentrated, philosophical analysis of universal human passions in a corrupt society. He is not dissecting courtly etiquette, but lust, greed, selfishness, pride. Try the experiment of reading Chaucer's *Troilus* without making allowance for chivalric conventions; much of its significance is lost. But the passion of Shakespeare's Troilus, the faithlessness of Cressida, the arrogance of Achilles, the brutality of Ajax, the lust of Paris, the mistaken heroism of Hector need no such background to make them intelligible. Study of the form which medieval conventions had assumed in Shakespeare's day is essential because these conventions were inseparable from the tale as it then existed; but it does not force us to regard the whole as existing for the sake of those conventions. The experiences through which the Greeks and Trojans pass are common to every highly civilized age, no matter what its manners; they are experiences which will repeat themselves eternally, as long as the world endures. Depressing, unequal and critical as *Troilus and Cressida* is, there is in it a universality which the more perfect masterpiece *Don Quixote* lacks.

Furthermore, is it *a priori* likely, despite the assertions of Ulrici, Schlegel, Rümelin, Fleay, and Furnivall, that Shakespeare's intent was satirical at all? He had his flings at social absurdities and affectations, in dress, speech, and manners, but these are secondary; they do not determine the whole temper of any of his plays. Perhaps he comes closest to social satire in *Love's Labour's Lost* and in the portrait of Caliban in *The Tempest*. But the hits at court follies in the gay court comedy, and the remarkable anticipation of the effect of civilization upon the savage are neither of them such an attempt to 'cleanse the foul body of the infected world' as *Troilus and Cressida* must be, if its chief intent be satiric. The general question is much like that which we have already considered in discussing *All's Well* and *Measure for Measure*. We cannot prove that satire does not exist in *Troilus and Cressida*, but we must be extremely cautious about assuming that it is present, and still more that it controls the spirit of the play. The old theory that it arises from the stage quarrel between Ben Jonson and the poetasters has long since been convincingly refuted.

If any one thing is plain in *Troilus and Cressida*, however, it is that Shakespeare's attitude is singularly detached and reflective. The great speeches of the Greek chieftains in Act I, those in the Trojan council in Act II, the interview between Ulysses and Achilles in Act III, are so closely packed with thought that their dramatic value is seriously impaired. I do not agree that two styles, reflecting two different periods of composition, are observable in the play; such differences seem to me rather due to the unlikeness of the two main actions. The debates among the chieftains obviously give more opportunity for philosophizing than does the love-story, and require another sort of treatment, but it is to be observed that even the love-scenes are handled in maturer and more reflective fashion than those in earlier plays. *Troilus and Cressida* appears to have been a dramatic experiment; not a wholly successful one, to be sure, but one which must remain of great significance for the understanding of the greater creative work of this period.

FIVE

The Wager in *Cymbeline*

WITH the completion of the analysis of the three plays preceding, our main task is at an end. But certain peculiar manifestations of the technique of the problem play later on in Shakespeare's career are so important as to deserve special notice, before we gather up our results, and attempt to view them in relation to his general artistic development.

First of all we may recall the definition proposed in the opening chapter for the term 'problem play' – a piece in which 'a perplexing and distressing complication in human life is presented in a spirit of high seriousness'. When the action ends tragically, the play is better termed a tragedy; when such an ending is not present, but the temper and handling are too grave for comedy, a problem drama is likely to result. Seriousness and realistic treatment must predominate; if other elements, as for example light comedy or romance, prevail in the play as a whole, it does not fall within the scope of our definition.

It has several times been necessary to emphasize the obvious fact that *All's Well* and *Measure for Measure* are not perfect examples of this type, because serious and realistic analysis is not carried through to the very end, but yields to the romantic convention of the happy ending. This is still more true of *Cymbeline* and *The Winter's Tale* in which elements of fantasy play so large a part that no one would think of calling them problem plays. Their earlier scenes, however, deserve attention as resembling closely, in mood and technique, the three comedies which have just been studied. Then, abruptly, the picture changes, and realism and high seriousness are exchanged for romance and mirth – even for passages recalling strongly opera and masque. Intensity of feeling gives way to happy carelessness. In each play this sudden shift comes midway in the Third Act; in *Cymbeline* with the appearance of Guiderius and Arviragus at their cave, in *The Winter's Tale* with the landing of Antigonus on the coast of

Bohemia, a region which has become a byword for romantic unreality. This change is indeed so striking as to seem to demand special explanation. Thus Masefield says, 'It seems possible that *Cymbeline* was begun as a tragedy during the great mood of tragical creation, then laid aside unfinished, from some failure in the vision, or change in the creative mood, and brought to an end later in a new spirit, perhaps in another place, in the country, away from the life which makes writing alive.'[1] The earlier scenes of these two plays are generally recognized as continuing the technique of the serious comedies. Is not the presence of these scenes sufficiently explained as contributing to a deft combination of the two types of drama current in the opening decade of the century, the realistic and the romantic?

Strangely enough, Shakespeare's dramatic romances have long been conventionally regarded as contrasting sharply with the plays of the preceding 'period'. How far this is from being true of *Cymbeline* and *The Winter's Tale* has been shown by recent criticism, which is reviewed in the following chapter, in which the general course of Shakespeare's development in his later years is outlined, and the futility of 'period' divisions stressed. At the moment, we must look with especial care at the two plays just mentioned. The other dramatic romances may be dismissed with a word. There is a strong suggestion of the problem mood in the brothel scenes in *Pericles*, but these are only an episode in a long and romantic tale of adventure. So with Caliban, whose figure, while suggesting the eternal riddle of the savage and his civilized conqueror, merely affords a contrasting darker touch in a marriage masque full of the iridescent hues of fancy.

The chief 'problems' in *Cymbeline* and *The Winter's Tale* are concerned, not, as in the comedies just studied, with women, but with men. Imogen and Hermione present no difficulties; the character of each lady is a matter of common agreement among critics, and has, I think, never been attacked by moral censors. But the violent jealousy and cruel actions of Posthumus Leonatus and of Leontes have loosed the vials of wrath upon their heads – as I believe, unjustly. In particular, the case of Posthumus demands careful analysis. How shall we reconcile with his supposedly noble character the wager which he makes on Imogen's honour? Here archaic and traditional elements are of high importance for an understanding of plot and characterization. I devote particular attention to *Cymbeline*, too, because its earlier scenes seem to me more completely in the grim spirit of problem drama than the corresponding scenes in *The Winter's Tale*. The 'highly artificial society' and the 'abnormal conditions of brain and of emotion' which Boas finds characteristic of such drama are strikingly suggested in the one, but not in the other. The corrupt Britain of the venomous Queen and the lecherous Cloten, the infected atmosphere of Italy, nourishing a wily devil like Iachimo, have no parallel in the Sicily of Leontes. There the darkness lies in the soul of the tortured king, his emotions are indeed not normal, but there is nothing miasmatic about the atmosphere of his court. Moreover, in *The Winter's Tale* something of the unreality and fantasy of the later scenes invades the realistic passages earlier in the play, as in the appeal to the Delphic oracle.

I propose, then, to subject the wager-plot in *Cymbeline* to a minute analysis, in the course of which the jealousy of Leontes will be duly considered. Let us first see what the critics have said.

'Why', asked Sir Walter Raleigh, 'did [Shakespeare] create so exquisite a being as Imogen for the jealous and paltry Posthumus? He has the precedent of nature, which makes many strangely-assorted matches; and he does not greatly care what we think of Posthumus.'[2] Hartley Coleridge remarked, 'A man who could lay wagers upon his wife's virtue, and wilfully expose her to the insults of such a ribald scoundrel as Iachimo, is not only unworthy of Imogen, but richly deserving of the worst possible consequences of his folly.'[3]

'Especially repulsive to us', wrote Brander Matthews, 'is the main theme of the story, the monstrous wager which the husband makes with a casual stranger about his wife's chastity ... its abhorrent grossness is inconceivable under the circumstances in which Shakspere presents it.'[4] MacCracken finds that 'Posthumus, Imogen's husband, appears weak and impulsive, foolish in making his wife's constancy a matter for wagers, and absurdly quick to believe the worst of her.'[5] Critics who look upon Shakespeare's plays as storehouses of moral teaching are naturally severe on Posthumus; we may let R. G. Moulton speak for these. 'The wrong of Posthumus is the commonest of moral perversions, the false sense of honour that dares not refuse a challenge, whatever the moral cost implied in its acceptance. It is the perversion which is the product of social narrowness and artificiality; the duellist dreads the sentiment immediately surrounding him in the coterie that has dubbed itself "men of honour", and forgets the great world with its balanced judgements and eternal principles of right.'[6]

On the other hand, Posthumus has had his defenders. It is amusing to find that Gervinus praises him for just the quality in which Moulton finds him lacking. 'In this moral anger [during the wager-scene] Posthumus is no less the same rare being as in the rest of his conduct. His irritation on such noble grounds shows his previous calmness and discretion for the first time in its right light, and this his ever-tested moderation reminds us to consider again and again the reason which drives him exceptionally to exasperation in a transaction so indelicate.'[7] Similarly, Hudson finds in Posthumus a noble rage. 'Womanhood is to him [Posthumus] a sacred thing: the whole course of his life has been such as to inspire him with the most chivalrous delicacy towards the sex: for his mother's sake and his own, but, above all, for Imogen's, the blood stirs within him, to hear woman made the theme of profane and scurrilous talk: the stale slander of libertine tongues his noble sensitiveness instinctively resents as the worst possible affront to himself.'[8]

It would be possible to extend such illustrative quotations almost indefinitely, but the foregoing must suffice to show, in a general way, what the detractors and defenders of Posthumus think of him. I venture to think that neither party is wholly right, and that the true solution must come through methods somewhat different from theirs. The first thing which strikes one in reading comments on the play is the forgetfulness of critics that due allowance must be made for the social conventions of Shakespeare's day, and of the earlier time when the wager-story was taking shape. This is not always true, of course—for example, the statement by Brander Matthews just quoted is particularly concerned with the effect of the archaic wager-theme upon us nowadays, in contradistinction to people of earlier times. But the historical point of view is too often forgotten; Posthumus and Imogen and Iachimo are too often treated as if they were persons of the nineteenth century, and their acts interpreted like those of characters in a modern realistic novel, instead of a tale the outlines and spirit of which had been determined by centuries of literary and social tradition.

First of all, then, some of the versions of the very old and widespread story which furnished the basis of this plot must be examined, but only for the purpose of illuminating Shakespeare's work, not for the sake of collecting and classifying variants of the wager-story. The main questions which we shall have to ask are: what was the meaning of the story as Shakespeare found it? How did he alter it, and what new elements did he give to it?[9] How would the Elizabethans have understood it, as they saw it on the stage? In particular, what would they have thought of Posthumus Leonatus? Through such an analysis as this we shall, I hope, reach sound results, some of them of considerable importance. Chief of these is the substantial vindication of Posthumus, not indeed, as a man without faults, but as blameless and even praiseworthy in accepting the wager, and, in the later part of the play, one to be judged as, like Othello, 'perplex'd in the extreme' under great misfortune, and acting in accord with the ethics of his day and the conventions of romantic drama. Hardly less interesting will be the question why Posthumus has generally failed to arouse sympathy, and been regarded as weak and even vicious – the answer to which can hardly be summed up in a single phrase.

Readers who are repelled by 'sources and analogues' may omit the following section, if they choose. But some knowledge of these as a whole is desirable, if only to show how widespread and how plastic was Shakespeare's theme. A study of the wager-plot as a piece of story-telling would be full of picturesque contrasts – it has exercised its charm for centuries upon gentle and simple, the profane and the pious, upon ballad-singers, moralists, poets, dramatists, and novelists.

I. ANALOGUES OF THE WAGER-STORY

The exact source or sources used for the Imogen–Posthumus–Iachimo plot will probably never be known. This plot is of course quite independent of the pseudo-historical setting in early Britain which Shakespeare derived from Holinshed. The closest analogue – a very close one in many respects – is the ninth *novella* of the second day in Boccaccio's *Decameron*. There seems little doubt that this, or some version of it, is to be regarded as the main source. The resemblances between it and Shakespeare's own work are striking. He drew directly or indirectly upon the *Decameron* for other plays, and there is every reason to suppose that he must have been acquainted with so well-known a book.[10] On the other hand, there are great divergences. How far these are due to the dramatist himself, it is difficult to say. Boccaccio's tales had of course been retold many times in different tongues, including English, with no great fidelity to the original, and Shakespeare may have worked from one of these altered versions. Furthermore, he may have known the wager-story quite independently of Boccaccio. It had attained a wide circulation in Western Europe before Boccaccio's time, and versions quite different from his were popular in the sixteenth century. Attempts to define Shakespeare's exact dependence on his models are, then, extremely hazardous, particularly since account must be taken of versions no longer extant. But the matter need not be unduly complicated; we ought to get rid of one 'source' which encumbers introductions to *Cymbeline* – the book of tales called *Westward for Smelts*. Shakespeare's supposed indebtedness to this appears, if the expression may be pardoned, particularly fishy. After all, we ought to credit him with a certain amount of inventiveness. He did not have to get all his incidents from books.

For purposes of convenience, I shall take Boccaccio's *novella*, as the closest extant analogue, for a point of departure in analysing the main plot of *Cymbeline*. But the fortunes of the theme in other hands must first be briefly examined.

The origins of the story of the man who makes a wager on the honour of his wife or mistress lie too far in the obscurity of the past for the sharpest eye to penetrate. Versions of especial interest, showing marked analogies to *Cymbeline*, appear in Old French. In commenting on these, Gaston Paris remarked that '*un chant populaire grec conserve la forme la plus ancienne de ce thème, et indique d'où il provient*'.[11] *Li Comte de Poitiers*, a metrical romance of the thirteenth century, was probably the work of a travelling singer, who may well have drawn his material from popular sources.[12] The *Roman de la Violette*, a very charming and elaborate poem, is, on the other hand, thoroughly aristocratic, designed for a high-born audience, and full of the refinements of courtly procedure.[13] *Dou Roi Flore et de la Bielle Jehane*, a sprightly prose romance of the thirteenth century, which has been rendered into English by William Morris, shows strong ecclesiastical influence: the hero is more moved by piety than by love.[14] *Un Miracle de Nostre Dame* (late fourteenth century) is a somewhat crude popular combination of religious and secular motives, showing faint resemblances to *Cymbeline* not observable in Boccaccio. In all these versions the personages belong to the nobility, though the method of narrative often suggests a homespun audience.

Other versions reflect bourgeois society. The most noteworthy of these is that by Boccaccio, with which should be compared the probably contemporaneous tale of an unknown Italian, generally referred to as 'Anonymous'. In *Le Grand Parangon des nouvelles Nouvelles* by Nicholas de Troyes,[15] written about 1536, is a version of the theme apparently based upon Boccaccio; it would be interesting to get a French version of this date uninfluenced by the Italian. The setting among a group of merchants is represented in England by the fragment of a prose tale, *Frederick of Jennen*, in the Douce Collection in the Bodleian, which breaks off directly after the wager-scene. How it would have been continued cannot be predicted with certainty, for a group of versions with a different *dénouement* must be taken into consideration.

In these the heroine deceives the villain into believing that she has sacrificed her honour, by persuading another woman to take her place – a situation reminiscent of the central plot of *Measure for Measure* and *All's Well*. Here belong an episode in the tale of *Taliesin* in the *Mabinogion*, in its present form as late as the fifteenth century,[16] and a noteworthy German rhymed tale, of a popular character, by Ruprecht of Würzburg.[17] Both of these are obviously derived from French sources. In the German story, the bet is made with an inn-keeper, after the merchants have given unfavourable accounts of their wives. An episode in the romance of *Perceforest* shows how the lady turns the tables on her accusers; a similar episode is found in Bandello.[18]

The wager-theme was popular in Germany and Scandinavia in the sixteenth century; it was put into dramatic form by Jacob Ayrer about 1600, and it appears in Danish and Icelandic ballads.[19] The traditional versions are of great interest, comprising tales and ballads in Scottish, German, Roumanian, Venetian, Sicilian, gipsy, etc., and reflecting the theme in different ways.[20]

As already stated, it is no part of the purpose of the present discussion to attempt an analysis of the wager-story in European literature. The foregoing brief review makes it plain how complicated such an analysis would be. Different episodes are combined with one another and with extraneous material in bewildering variety, and too much has been lost to make it possible to trace a genealogy with safety. The wager-theme was constantly adapted to new settings and altered social conditions, and its motivation was correspondingly varied. As with medieval story in general, the incidents are but a framework upon which to build a structure suited to the taste of the times and the fancy of the teller. Only through a study of the circumstances and conventions which shaped it, and which influenced the author, can a given version be correctly interpreted.

2. THE WAGER IN BOCCACCIO

Our attempt to gain a better understanding of the situation in *Cymbeline* will be simplified if we first consider the wager-scene by itself, with its immediate consequences (Acts I and II), and then the later conduct of Posthumus (Acts III–V). Analysis of the wager itself must begin with a review of the closest extant analogue, which we may treat with due reservations as the source – the *novella* in the *Decameron*. The explanation of the incidents in the *novella* must, of course, be sought as much in medieval habits of thought as in Boccaccio's own convictions. Since we do not know his direct source, it is difficult to estimate the extent to which he reshaped the tale; the main outlines are in accord with tradition.

At an inn in Paris some 'very considerable Italian merchants' speak slightingly of their wives, agreeing that women amuse themselves with lovers, when left behind at home, just as men do with such girls as come their way. But one merchant, named Bernabo, maintains that he has a thoroughly virtuous and incorruptible spouse. Thereupon Ambrogiuolo of Pisa scoffs at his boast, and saying that he must 'reason with him' on thé matter, proceeds in the following vein.[21] "'Thou thyself sayst thy wife is a woman and that she is of flesh and blood, as are other women. If this be so, those same desires must be hers and the same powers that are in other women to resist these natural appetites; wherefore however honest she may be, it is possible she may do that which other women do. . . ." To which Bernabo made answer, saying, "I am a merchant, and not a philosopher, and as a merchant I will answer."' He thereupon maintains that there are 'discreet' women, and that his wife is one of them. The dispute runs on, and finally Bernabo proposes the wager. "'Since thou wilt have it that all women are so compliant and that thine address is such, I am content, so I may certify thee of my wife's honesty, to have my head cut off, as thou canst anywise avail to bring her to do thy pleasure in aught of the kind; and if thou fail thereof, I will have thee lose no otherwhat than a thousand gold florins."' Ambrogiuolo replies that he will have no advantage in shedding Bernabo's blood, if he wins the wager, but he proposes that Bernabo stake five thousand florins against this thousand, and he will undertake within three months to bring Bernabo proofs of his wife's infidelity. So the matter is arranged.

As to the social station and general type of mind represented by Bernabo there can be no doubt. He is not an aristocrat, but a merchant, and he opposes to the philosophical discussion in which he finds himself involved the simple faith of a man of the middle class, proud in the accomplishments of a wife who would make a good waiting-woman – '"moreover," said [Bernabo], "there was no sewer, or in other words, no serving-man alive who served better or more deftly at a nobleman's table than did she."' And it is noteworthy that it is he himself who proposes the wager, not the villain, as in Shakespeare's play. It is not an arrangement agreed to after provocation, but one put forward by Bernabo himself as a happy solution of the dispute. Clearly, if we are to blame Posthumus, we must bé far more severe with Bernabo.

When considered from the medieval point of view, however, the conduct of Bernabo becomes comprehensible immediately. The beginnings of the story, as we may judge from the ballads and popular tales, told of a boast as to the excellence of a wife made in much the same spirit in which a man might vaunt the superior qualities of his horse. In early days one bought wives much as one now buys animals. In a version taken down orally in Islay in 1859, which bears many marks of tradition reaching back hundreds of years, the dispute is between a young king, who has just married – and paid for – a beautiful wife, and a sea-captain. The king wishes to buy silks for her, the best in the ship.

'Indeed!' said the captain, 'thou must have an exceedingly good wife when thou must have a gown of the best silk I have on board.' 'I have that,' said the king, 'a wife many of whose equals are not to be got.' 'Wilt thou lay a wager,' said the captain, 'that with all her goodness I will not get leave to enter thy chamber?' 'I will lay a wager, anything thou desiredst [sic], that thou wilt not.' 'What wager wilt thou lay?' said the captain. 'I will put the heirship in pledge,' said the king. Said the captain, 'I will put all the silk in ship in pledge to thee that I will.' The captain came on shore and the king went on board.[22]

In Boccaccio's tale the confidence of the husband has become a virtue: Bernabo opposes his faith in his wife's constancy to sophisticated arguments about the inherent sinfulness of women. We know that he was right in his estimate of her virtue; the tale proves that. And he is willing to go to any lengths to proclaim his confidence in her; the more dangerous the test, the more perfect does this confidence appear. Nowadays we feel that to give a villain a chance to attempt to seduce one's wife, for the sake of proving to him and to others her unassailable chastity, would be the height of folly, and of cruelty to her. But the Middle Ages thought otherwise; they believed that a virtue exaggerated, as it seems to us, beyond all reason, was a virtue magnified. This explains how the wager-theme could have been so widely accepted as we have seen it to be, and how it could have been retold even by the clear-sighted Boccaccio, who perceived its essential absurdity. It is characteristic of tales exaggerating a virtue that the innocent are made to suffer, as in Boccaccio's own narratives of *Griselda* (X.10) or *The Two Friends* (X.8).[23] In the variants of the wager-story in which the heroine preserves her honour by a trick, no thought is given to the woman substituted in her place. What of *her* honour? In the version of *The Twa Knights* printed by Child the girl is the heroine's own niece – a situation repulsive in the extreme to modern feelings.

Such tales as these enable us, through their very extravagances, to understand Bernabo's act in proposing a test which seems absurd and cruel, in order to show his complete faith in his wife's chastity. He does not, indeed, stand the trial of perfect constancy to the end; he is later overwhelmed by the apparently convincing evidence of his wife's infidelity. But in the beginning he is willing to go to any lengths to show his confidence.

It may be that Boccaccio perceived the essential absurdity of the wager-story. Ostensibly he tells it to show that the deceiver is sooner or later punished for his deception. Another moral is pointed by the Sultan of Alexandria at the end of the tale, who 'praised very highly the actions, courage and virtue of Ginevra', the wife of Bernabo. But this conclusion did not appeal to the gay young Florentines of Boccaccio's party, who had small faith in women's virtue, and knew many anecdotes illustrating their frailty. So Dioneo, perhaps the most loose-tongued of them all, maintains, in telling the tale of the old husband and the young wife immediately following, 'that Bernabo in disputing with Ambrogiuolo had acted rashly and foolishly' [*cavalcasse la capra in verso il chino*]. And all the company agree laughingly 'that Dioneo spoke the truth and that Bernabo had been a great fool'. Similarly, Chaucer makes his Clerk, after telling the Virtue Story of the patient Griselda, indulge in gibes at women. The Clerk, of course, had a score to settle with the Wife of Bath. The disillusioned spirit of the fabliaux writers and of Renaissance cynics frequently made merry with the unnatural exaggerations of medieval Virtue Stories.

This does not alter the significance of the wager-story itself, even in Boccaccio. We must look at it through the eyes of those who accepted its strange morality, and told and retold it, if we are to understand its survivals in later days. So considered, it becomes plausible, however repugnant to modern feelings, and its strange popularity becomes more comprehensible. But there is much more in the situation than we can gather from Boccaccio. Shakespeare has so altered it as to make the wager seem still more reasonable, and the conduct of the husband not only excusable, but inevitable.

3. THE WAGER IN SHAKESPEARE

The chivalric discussion at the house of Philario which Shakespeare describes in *Cymbeline* is as different as possible from the contests between 'philosophy' and the pride of a bourgeois merchant in an accomplished wife in the pages of Boccaccio. It is clear at once that Shakespeare's characters are gentlemen, gathered at the residence of an Italian of wealth and social position. Their conversation is the elaborate, rather affected language of the courtier; this is particularly noticeable in the speeches of Iachimo. The social status of Posthumus is unmistakable; he is sprung from the noble stock of the Leonati and united to the daughter of a king. He is introduced to the company as an equal – as Philario puts it to his friends, 'Let him be so entertained amongst you as suits, with gentlemen of your knowing, to a stranger of his quality.' This is, to all intents and purposes, a scene from the life of Shakespeare's own time, with the social conventions of gentle-folk – just the sort of company in which a young Englishman making the grand tour at the end of the sixteenth century might have found himself. The absurdity of connecting it with early Britain hardly needs comment; as Herford puts it, 'Shakespeare clearly designed *Cymbeline* to be as much and as little a picture of Augustan Britain as *Hamlet* is a picture of eleventh century Denmark.'

Shortly after the entrance of Posthumus it is recalled that there has been a dispute, in which Posthumus maintained his lady to be 'more fair, virtuous, wise, chaste, constant, qualified, and less attemptable' than the rarest of the ladies of France. Iachimo remarks that he must not rate her above those of Italy, and Posthumus retorts that he would 'abate her nothing'. The dispute waxes, and Iachimo alleges than an 'accomplish'd courtier' could win away the lady, offering to wager thereon half of his estate against a valuable ring worn by Posthumus. Repeating his offer, he sets his own stake at ten thousand ducats. Posthumus embraces Iachimo's conditions, with the proviso that 'if she remain unseduc'd, you not making it appear otherwise, for your ill opinion and the assault you have made to her chastity you shall answer me with your sword'. Thus the wager is concluded. The scene should of course be read in full, and compared with the account of it given by the repentant Iachimo in Act V.

The important thing to note here is that Shakespeare, in making Philario and Iachimo gentlemen instead of merchants, or an inn-keeper and a merchant, has made the conduct of Posthumus far more natural. The confidence of a trusting husband, willing to go to any extreme to show his confidence in his wife's integrity, is here rein-forced by the solemn duty of a knight not to hesitate when the virtues and excellence of his lady are called in question. According to the rules of chivalry, Posthumus could have acted, as the perfect lover and gentleman, in no other way. I shall not attempt to determine how far Shakespeare, in placing the scene in an aristocratic rather than a bourgeois society, was influenced by a desire to make his story ap-pear more convincing. Thorndike has reminded us that in the dramatic romances of Beaumont and Fletcher, to which this play probably owes much, 'all the principal characters are people of the court; even those who are utterly detestable hold positions of rank'. Whether accident or design, this alteration is of the highest significance.

Various details in the conversation reveal the chivalric con-ventions which control it. Posthumus says of Imogen, 'Being so far provok'd as I was in France, I would abate her nothing, though I profess myself her adorer, not her friend', that is to say, 'If I were to be so much roused to speak my mind as I was in France, I would rate her virtue no lower than I did then, even though I were judging as one worshipping her from afar, instead of as her accepted lover.' The purity of Imogen is so compelling that even a man in the conventional chivalric attitude of loving hopelessly, as Troilus did Cressida, in the beginning, or Palamon and Arcite Emelye, would be as sure of her virtue as the man to whom she had granted her 'pity'. The reader should also observe the threat of a duel to follow, in case Iachimo cannot prove his assertions against the lady, and the words of Iachimo, referring to Posthumus at the end of the play:

> He, true knight,
> No lesser of her honour confident
> Than I did truly find her, stakes this ring.   V.5.186

The suggestion of the wager comes, it will be noted, not from the husband, as in Boccaccio's tale, but from the villain Iachimo. The 'true knight' might be loth to be drawn into a quarrel, but when the virtues of his lady were called in question, the code of chivalry gave him no choice in the matter.[24]

It is of especial interest to study the wager-scene in the *Roman de la Violette*. Of all the analogues to *Cymbeline*, this is the closest as regards its chivalric setting. Its atmosphere of courtly refinement may be gathered from the love-songs which the hero Girars sings in praise of his lady. To the proud boast of Girars in the presence of the court that he loves a lady of surpassing beauty and is loved in return, Lisiars, 'a worse man than Ganelon', retorts that he will wager his lands against those of Girars that the lady is by no means so constant, and that he will prove it within eight days. Girars, in his perfect confidence, accepts the wager immediately. The king attempts to dissuade Lisiars, telling him that he has started on a foolish venture, and that a man who attempts to shame another often finds that his efforts recoil on his own head – just the moral which Boccaccio draws from the story, in the beginning. But Girars scornfully interrupts, and tells the king to let Lisiars have his way; he himself has no fear of the outcome. So the wager is concluded.[25]

It is noteworthy that the king does not attempt to dissuade the hero from accepting the wager, since he could not in honour refuse to take it up. Instead, the king endeavours to influence the villain Lisiars not to press it. But Girars, the perfect knight and lover, cannot allow any suspicion of faithlessness to rest upon his lady, and calls for the immediate binding of the contract. So Philario, the host in *Cymbeline*, while disapproving of the wager made at his house and endeavouring to break off the discussion, never suggests that Posthumus shall reject it.

As everyone knows, *Cymbeline* was written at a time of renewed interest in romance. After an era of realistic comedy and tragedy, the English stage experienced, in the latter part of the first decade of the seventeenth century, a great revival of interest in dramatic romance. This fashion appears to have been set by Beaumont and Fletcher, and to have been imitated by Shakespeare. Many critics who have a perfect realization of this either neglect to take it into account in practice, or mistake the real nature of this romance. Arthur Symons thinks of it as a kind of children's game. 'Cymbeline is a romance, made out of Holinshed, and Boccaccio, and perhaps nursery stories, and it is that happiest kind of romance, which strays harmlessly through tragic incidents, in which only the bad people come to grief. All the time things seem to be knotting themselves up inextricably, everyone is playing at cross-purposes with everyone, as in a children's game, immensely serious to the children. ... We are following the track of a romance, and in countries where no one is sick or sorry beyond measure.'[26] Sir Arthur Quiller-Couch, reminding us to seek the truth of imagination rather than the truth of fact, refers us indiscriminately to *Blue Beard, Cinderella, Little Red Riding Hood, The Faerie Queene,* and *Pilgrim's Progress.*

It is of the highest importance to distinguish the two different kinds of 'romance' in *Cymbeline.* There is, on the one hand, a strong fairy-tale element in the play; the Guiderius–Arviragus plot has often been compared with the *Märchen* of *Little Snow-White and the Dwarfs.* But this idyllic rustic material is in sharp contrast to the main plot. There the romantic conventions are of a very definite sort, as far removed from *Blue Beard* at one end as from *Pilgrim's Progress* at the other. They are the conventions of court life, which may be studied, mingled with other material, in such plays as *Philaster,* the *Maid's Tragedy, Thierry and Theodoret,* conventions which were a survival of the Middle Ages, which had been an outgrowth and an accompaniment of the feudal system, and which were, in somewhat altered form, in the height of fashion in Shakespeare's time. They had been modified by Renaissance views of conduct, derived from Italian and classical sources, and by changes in the popular attitude towards moral questions. The Elizabethans were not ready to accept the adulterous love condoned by the twelfth and thirteenth centuries. Their treatment of the Troilus–Cressida story makes that clear. But they clung passionately to externals, and their romantic observances were full of the absurdities so characteristic of the Middle Ages.

So the wager in *Cymbeline,* in its fantastic exaggeration of confidence in Imogen's virtue, is at once thoroughly medieval and thoroughly Elizabethan. This old theme, hallowed by centuries of story-telling, happened to fit to a nicety, through its very extravagances, the spirit of sixteenth century chivalry. In the light of medieval knightly observances Posthumus Leonatus emerges fully vindicated in the making of the wager; his was the only conduct possible for the perfect knight and lover.

But what of his later actions? He receives what appears to be proof of Imogen's infidelity, it is true, but does this excuse his ready belief in her guilt – which seems to anticipate Iachimo's full revelations – his resolve to murder her, the cruelty with which he pursues his resolve, and his sudden repentance, which may seem an indication of weakness and vacillation? These questions demand separate consideration.

4. THE CHARACTER OF POSTHUMUS

After the very brilliant and carefully elaborated scenes in Acts I and II, which are beyond doubt Shakespeare's own work–the parting of Posthumus and Imogen, the making of the wager, the interview between Imogen and Iachimo, the brief but beautifully managed episode in the bed-chamber, the triumph of Iachimo over Posthumus, and the agonized soliloquy of Posthumus, in which he suspects the virtue of all women – we do not see Posthumus again until Act V. Letters from him are read, one bidding with feigned affection that Imogen meet him at Milford-Haven, and another commanding Pisanio to poison her. At the opening of Act V, it appears from his soliloquy over the bloody handkerchief that the rage of Posthumus and his desire for vengeance are quite over; he repents his command and the faithfulness of Pisanio in having, as he supposes, executed it, ending with lines of a banality that certainly make us suspect an interpolator or collaborator. The scenes on the field of battle and in the prison contain occasional evidences of his repentance, but add nothing new for his relations with Imogen, while they have often been suspected of being from another hand than Shakespeare's, especially the scene in the prison. The business in Cymbeline's tent in Act V is curiously managed: after the confession of Iachimo, Posthumus, with a fresh outbreak of repentance, strikes the disguised Imogen, who swoons, and upon reviving 'begins an unseemly squabble with Pisanio! ... Then poor old doddering Cornelius must needs be brought forward, and must tell again in prosy words what he had told us all once before, even to the very same reference to "cats and dogs"! All this while poor Posthumus has nothing to do but to shift first on one foot and then on the other.'[27]

In short, then, the development of the main plot in the last three Acts is most unsatisfactory, giving the impression of hasty and careless workmanship, as if the dramatist had lost his interest. Perhaps a collaborator was allowed too large a share here, but we must be chary of assuming that scenes were not written by Shakespeare because they seem to fall far below his usual level. There is no doubt that he did, at times, hurried and very inferior work. It seems clear, in any case, that what interested him most was the earlier part of the tale; for the punishment which Posthumus attempts to inflict upon Imogen and the final reconciliation he felt little enthusiasm.

The reason for this is not far to seek. The really picturesque and individual part of the main plot is the making of the wager and its immediate outcome; the rest is a mosaic of the commonplaces of romance. Shakespeare's creative imagination was obviously stimulated by the psychological problem involved in the wager. A devoted husband, forced by knightly conventions into a novel and dangerous situation; a scheming villain, nevertheless clear-sighted enough to admire the purity of the wife and the nobility of the husband, and a heroine of stainless virtue and surpassing charm, made to appear guilty through a cruel and unusual combination of circumstances – all this gave an opportunity for effective contrasts of character. But the ending of the story was a collocation of commonplace situations and motives, given individuality mainly by the superposition of the Guiderius–Arviragus plot. Shakespeare's poetic fancy was happily allowed full play in the lovely woodland scenes; the attention of the spectator is diverted to this attractive material, and the play is saved.

Thorndike, in a brilliant essay, has shown in detail the very close parallelism between *Cymbeline* and the romances of Beaumont and Fletcher, particularly *Philaster*, which he believes influenced it. There is no need to repeat his analysis here. Of Imogen he says, 'She is good and chaste and spirited; she resists an attempt at seduction; she wears boy's clothes; she leaves the court in search of her lover;

she remains true to him after he has deserted her, and sought to kill her; she dies and is brought back to life again; she passes through all sorts of impossible situations to final reconciliation and happiness. In all this there is little trace of an individual character; *all this can be duplicated in the stories of Bellario and Arethusa.*' Similarly, the conduct of Posthumus recalls that of Philaster; compare the jealous letter of Posthumus (III.420) with the jealousy of Philaster upbraiding Arethusa (III.2); the soliloquy of Posthumus denouncing women with that of Philaster (III.2); even the wounding of Arethusa by Philaster (IV.3) reappears in the striking of Imogen by Posthumus (V.5.228).[28] Parallels to the romantic machinery of *Cymbeline* elsewhere than in Beaumont and Fletcher have often been noted.[29] It does not appear necessary to comment upon these in detail.

Something must nevertheless be said of the sudden and terrible sexual jealousy of Posthumus, of his quick belief in the guilt of Imogen, and of his cruel order that she be put to death. What defence has he to offer?

Even if we approach these questions purely from the modern point of view, I think we can make out a pretty good case for Posthumus. Is it, after all, surprising that he believes Imogen guilty? We know that she is innocent, because we have witnessed the trick played upon her, and have perceived from all her actions and speeches that she is devoted to her absent husband. But Posthumus has not this knowledge, and the circumstantial evidence which Iachimo brings that she has sinned is very strong, quite as much so, surely, as Iago's proofs of Desdemona's guilt or Don John's of Hero's unchastity. We may indeed wish that Posthumus had recalled Imogen's ardent and loving devotion, that he had refused to credit any slander of her, and that, forced to believe against his will, he had forgiven her, instead of condemning her to death, but he is obviously not a man of the greatest strength or independence of character, and he is perplexed in the extreme by jealousy, his heart and mind poisoned by the yellow devil Iachimo. I do not think we should condemn him.

Still less would an Elizabethan have condemned him. The perfect hero was properly morbidly sensitive about the spotless purity and honour of his wife, as we have seen, and moreover he was held fully justified in putting her to death if she had proved unfaithful. It was a very old and widespread idea among the Indo-European peoples that the unchaste woman must pay for her frailty with her life, and that this is at the disposal of the husband whom she has wronged or the kinsfolk which she has disgraced; and this idea survived as a convention of the romantic drama down to the beginning of the seventeenth century, when a more humanitarian note was struck in *A Woman Killed with Kindness*. Instances of it are too common to need lengthy citation. Death, under such circumstances, was not viewed as revenge, but as just punishment, inflicted by private rather than public authority. Melantius, the brother of Evadne, the mistress of the king in *The Maid's Tragedy*, sums up the matter thus:

> EVADNE You will not murder me?
> MELANTIUS No; 'tis a justice, and a noble one,
>   To put the light out of such base offenders.   IV.I

Moreover, cruelty in inflicting the punishment, and in dealing with the guilty woman in general, was held to be only what she deserved. Our forefathers believed that to treat the sinner with consideration was to compound with sin. The erring wife or sister, like other criminals, laid herself open not only to chastisement, but to severity and insult. Othello, once convinced of the guilt of Desdemona, not only never hesitates in what he considers his duty – to kill her, but he strikes and insults her, on one occasion using such language that even the loose-tongued Emilia is revolted, and exclaims, 'a beggar in his drink could not have laid such terms upon his callat'. Parallels to the resolve of Posthumus that Imogen must die, and the means taken to put this resolve into effect, may be studied at the reader's leisure in the analogues to *Cymbeline*.[30]

In this long and crowded play, Shakespeare had of necessity to represent belief in Imogen's guilt as fastening itself rapidly on the mind of Posthumus. He did not have space to develop this at length. It was readily accepted by his audience, since in romantic drama and narrative the unjust condemnation of an innocent woman by a man not himself evil, but temporarily deceived, was so common – witness Othello, Lear, Leontes, and Claudio in *Much Ado*, to mention only Shakespearean examples. It is especially instructive to consider with some care the situation in *The Winter's Tale*.

Leontes has far less reason for his violence than Posthumus. His wife has persuaded their old and dear friend Polixenes to prolong his visit with them, which Leontes has not been able to bring about. Unfortunately she has indulged in innocent familiarities with Polixenes, such as are entirely natural in view of his intimacy with her and her husband, and of the manners of the times. The raging flames of jealousy are fed by trifles. The 'paddling palms and pinching fingers ... and making practis'd smiles' which Leontes observes with agonized dismay are done quite openly, in the presence of the king and court; we recognize immediately that only a man gone mad with jealousy would find guilt in such public and open manifestations of affection. Oddly enough, Leontes gives to Camillo a little later some further details.

> Is whispering nothing?
> Is leaning cheek to cheek? Is meeting noses?
> Kissing with inside lip? stopping the career
> Of laughter with a sigh? – a note infallible
> Of breaking honesty; – horsing foot on foot?
> Skulking in corners? wishing clocks more swift?
> Hours, minutes? noon, midnight? and all eyes
> Blind with the pin-and-web but theirs, theirs only,
> That would unseen be wicked?

These details, I think, are best explained as diseased imaginings in the mind of Leontes. They may perhaps be regarded as having some foundation in misinterpreted recollections of innocent badinage in the past. Considerable familiarity of manners was customary in Elizabethan times; kissing, for example, was a common form of social salutation. A deeper meaning may be read into the passage, however. Furness maintained that Shakespeare, having shown the jealousy of Leontes bursting forth suddenly, was then at pains to make this appear reasonable as the end of long and secretly cherished suspicions – 'after the attack of mania has once set in, I think we can detect an intention to make us lose sight of the electric flash with which it apparently began, and, apart from the memory of its utter groundlessness, which neither can, nor should, be obliterated, to make us glide insensibly into a belief that the jealousy is really the result of long observation by Leontes, who has been for many a day past watching the conduct of Hermione, and that her victory over the resolution of Polixenes to depart, was all that was needed to set the long smouldering passion in a blaze'.[31]

In attempting to decide how far Shakespeare made the jealousy of Leontes psychologically convincing, we must see what he owed to his source, the novel of Greene, and what he altered in it. In the novel, the jealousy of Pandosto is not sudden, but a gradual development. 'These and such like doubtfull thoughtes a long time smoothering in his stomacke, beganne at last to kindle in his minde a secret mistrust, which increased by suspition, grewe at last to be a flaming Iealousie, that so tormented him as he could take no rest.'[32] Moreover, Greene emphasizes the jealousy-motive in rather an extraordinary way; the opening paragraph of the novel, some fifteen lines, is devoted to this subject in general, and the gradual development of the suspicions of Pandosto is carefully indicated in the subsequent narrative. Shakespeare, then, altered his source in making the king's jealousy break forth abruptly, in the midst of gay and playful conversation, but he has left us in some indecision as to how far these suspicions had already been smouldering beneath the surface.

It is not difficult to perceive the dramatic justification of the sudden outbreak of Leontes. Shakespeare's task was, in the very beginning, to make clear to the spectator the close and intimate friendship between Leontes, Hermione, and Polixenes, which is necessary to establish the innocence of the relations between Polixenes and the queen, and to make natural and plausible their merry endearments. Had Leontes been represented as suspicious from the start, a false idea of the affection of Polixenes and Hermione might well have been created, which it would have been difficult to efface. Shakespeare first shows us the clear sky of friendship without a cloud, and then the sudden storm. The jealous fury of Leontes is dramatically most effective, breaking as it does into a charming and intimate scene between old and devoted friends. Moreover, as already suggested, the stage demands a much more rapid tempo than the novel, and the design of this particular play gives no time for the building up of the slow onset of suspicion, which is possible in a different sort of piece – *Othello*, for example. The accusation of the queen, her trial and apparent death, the order to poison Polixenes, his flight, the embassy to the oracle, with a lapse of time until its return, the vindication of the queen and the condemnation of Leontes – all this and more too must be disposed of in the space of two Acts and a half, before the scene shifts to Bohemia, and the pastoral begins.

Deighton suggested that Greene's novel, which is known to have been extremely popular, was so familiar to theatrical audiences that Shakespeare did not feel the necessity of motivating elaborately the outbreak of Leontes.[33] It seems to me more likely that Shakespeare felt such confidence rather because such sudden and unjustified suspicions were so common in popular story-telling. The direct sources of Greene's novel are not known; it is clear, however, that it is set in a framework of romantic commonplaces. Archaic details of the old and widespread Accused Queen motive were occasionally retained both by Shakespeare and by Greene. Shakespeare took no pains to persuade his hearers to accept improbabilities which they were ready to accept anyhow as the stuff of story. The sudden violence of Lear at the opening of the tragedy has often been criticized as psychologically unconvincing, but it can hardly have been so to a people familiar with the tale of a loving father violently repudiating his favourite daughter because she will not profess for him the exaggerated affection of her hypocritical sisters. Sudden and baseless rages are common in romance, and easily became a convention in romantic drama. We are not told why the Usurping Duke suddenly breaks in on Rosalind, who has been living quietly at his court, and incontinently banishes her, nor why Old Capulet treats his only child, the hopeful lady of his earth, with such violently cruel harshness, which even a crossing of his wishes does not seem to explain. We may rationalize these outbursts of passion as characteristic of self-willed old men, but they have another rationale which should not be forgotten.

Attempts have been made to show that the portrayal of the jealousy of Leontes is really psychologically accurate. Furness suggested that the sexual guilt of Leontes himself is the moving cause, that he accuses Polixenes and Hermione of a fault similar to that of which he is himself conscious.[34] Tannenbaum, who is not only a Shakespearean scholar but a professional psychiatrist, rejects this explanation, arguing that Leontes is a 'spoiled child', and that

Hermione's success in persuading Polixenes to remain, which he could not himself bring about, 'fills his heart on the instant with hatred both of his wife and his lifelong friend. Such hatred, in a person like Leontes, who must think of himself as justified in his emotions, can probably manifest itself most easily as jealousy, inasmuch as no other emotion is so little dependent upon external facts for justification.'[35] How far the details of Shakespeare's characterization agree with the results of modern study of mental disorders I shall not venture to discuss; that is a matter for experts. It seems plausible, as Tannenbaum suggests, that Shakespeare's keen observation may have anticipated modern conclusions, but there is no inconsistency in supposing that he was at the same time deeply influenced by narrative conventions. Again and again we have seen such a process at work, and there is no reason to doubt it for *Cymbeline*, *Lear*, and *The Winter's Tale*.

With these considerations in mind, let us now review the character of Posthumus as a whole. If we are to sum it up in a word, I think we must agree that he is meant to be a blameless hero. He is fully justified in the wager-business, and his subsequent procedure is entirely in accord with the ethics of romance. Moreover, Shakespeare himself tells us, in no uncertain terms, that Posthumus is a good man. In the opening scene of the play, the 'First Gentleman', that very well-informed person who tells the 'Second Gentleman' all about the situation at court, reports Posthumus as

> most prais'd, most lov'd,
> A sample to the youngest, to the more mature
> A glass that feated them, and to the graver
> A child that guided dotards; to his mistress,
> For whom he now is banish'd, – her own price
> Proclaims how she esteem'd him and his virtue;
> By her election may be truly read
> What kind of man he is.

Every audience knows that such a faithful expositor is not misleading them, but giving such information that they may understand the rest of the play intelligently. Very significant, too, is the way in which people in the play generally, even the villain Iachimo, speak well of Imogen's husband.

Yet, if all this is true, why do we feel so little sympathy with Posthumus? Why have critics almost unanimously treated him with scorn? Why does his suffering leave us cold, and his marriage with Imogen fail to suggest the mating of the eagle?

In answering these questions, several points must be kept in mind. In the first place, a hero according to a formula, whose acts are 'a mosaic of the commonplaces of romance', is not likely to be consistent or convincing. Very great brilliancy of characterization may accomplish this; a hero may be given so many little touches of individuality and naturalness that we forget the absurdity and inconsistency of his acts. It is one of the greatest of Shakespeare's marks of genius that he could do this when he liked. Old stories full of the wildest improbabilities were thus, by his magic touch, completely transformed, and made to seem psychologically sound. But at times he was too careless or too indifferent to give even very important characters this final and transforming touch. He did it for Imogen, but not for Posthumus. The noble scion of the Leonati remains a lay-figure, with all the appropriate gestures, but never instinct with the breath of life.

In the second place, modern readers and playgoers do not find the acts and expressions of Posthumus heroic. They do not share the peculiar view of chivalric obligation which sways him in the wager-scene, and they do not believe that virtue which flies in the face of common-sense remains virtue. They have learned a more humane tradition for the punishment of the woman taken in adultery. And they demand in a hero more consistency, more use of his wits, more emotional restraint. The ravings of Posthumus, his rapid fluctuations of purpose, disgust Anglo-Saxons of today, bred to repress their deepest feelings. Moreover, Posthumus has to bear all the heavier burden of reprobation because the misfortunes of Imogen are due to his conduct. Every reader of the play loves this radiant and spirited girl; what more natural than to dislike the husband who makes her suffer? 'Womanish tears' and 'wild acts' may be pardoned in Romeo, who sacrifices everything for Juliet, but not in Posthumus, who makes Imogen herself the sacrifice. It will probably make little difference to remind people that Posthumus has justification for his course of action; they will continue to think just as meanly of him. Perhaps they are right. We are all familiar with the way in which 'good' persons in real life, with virtue on their side, and a valid reason for every act, can make the innocent suffer. We wish that Posthumus had thought more of Imogen and less of social correctness. We wish, in short, that he were a man with modern notions, instead of an Elizabethan with medieval ideas still dogging him. But we must remember that the judgements which we pass on him today are probably harsher than those of the men who beheld his figure on the stage under the grey and shifting skies of London three hundred years ago.

SIX

Later Shakespearean Comedy

THE detailed analyses of plays in the foregoing chapters make certain general conclusions possible. It seems clear that the problem comedies, as we have agreed to call them, are not in their general aim radically different from the comedies of more cheerful character written, at least in the main, at an earlier time. They are romantic stories, following well-worn traditions, and arousing the interest inseparable from every tale in which human passions meet in a conflict of doubtful issue. Their meaning, in its large and simple outlines, is the same as that in the stories from which Shakespeare borrowed. There appears to be no valid reason for necessarily viewing them as satirical or ironical. There are no real ambiguities as to which characters are good and which are bad. Heroism and virtue still shine clearly forth, though sometimes in ways which appear to us strange. To this point we must hold fast, forgetting that we are of the twentieth century. We must believe that these comedies were, like Shakespeare's writing for the theatre in general, primarily designed as entertainment, in the best sense of the word, to send the spectators home, after all is over, with the feeling that they have not mis-spent their time in a world of illusion. The striking and distinctive characteristics which differentiate the problem plays from other work in comedy, and set them apart by themselves, arise from preoccupation with the darker sides of life, and a deeper and more serious probing of its mysteries, particularly those of sex. Intrigues drawn from romantic fiction are analysed with unsparing realism, even though romance may still sometimes have its way. It is the mood of the tragedies, without the ultimate tragic issue.

The questions which now confront us are those which have already been suggested. How did Shakespeare come to write such pieces? How are their peculiar characteristics to be explained, in the general development of his mind and art? And we may well again remind ourselves of the difficulty and complexity of such analysis. We are dealing with one of the most active and richly stocked minds in the history of literature, delicately responsive to external influences, not scorning to imitate and to borrow freely, and keenly sensitive to changes in public taste and literary fashion, in an age when life moved with kaleidoscopic variety and rapidity. The complex forces which governed the work of Shakespeare's maturest period cannot be set forth in a few facile phrases.

The most obvious explanation is increasing maturity. It is natural that a man, as he gets older, should feel more intensely the darker issues of life, questioning more deeply the mingled motives which control men's actions, and coming to view the world as it is rather than as a sunny optimist would have it. As G. F. Bradby puts it, in discussing the work of this period, 'hardly anybody passes from early manhood into middle age without some sense of disillusionment'.[1] In 1600, Shakespeare was thirty-six years old. Three centuries ago, men aged more quickly than they do now; there is no exaggeration in adding ten years or more, if their activities are to be interpreted in terms of modern life. One is constantly struck by the youth of Elizabethan men of action and responsibility, and by their early deaths. Shakespeare had had by 1600 at least ten crowded years of achievement, in the busy city which was the heart of England; he was to continue this for approximately ten years more, and then, his creative genius apparently burnt out, he was to live for six years more in comparative inactivity. At the opening of the new century he was approaching the very height of his powers, when he was to reveal, in the fullest degree, that marvellous and sympathetic comprehension of human life which sets his work apart from that of all his fellows. While his immediate task must have been a practical one, the filling of the theatre, he turned more and more, as an older man would, to provide entertainment which would make men think and feel more deeply, in actions transcending the interest of the ludicrous, the humorous, the romantic, and the objective presentation of the pageant of history.

All this is of course a commonplace of Shakespeare criticism. And we must also remind ourselves once more of the critical and reflective spirit appearing in his earlier work. He had given to romantic comedy a seriousness which his masters and models had never known. *Love's Labour's Lost*, one of the most artificial and 'operatic' of his plays, designedly emphasizes the dependence of the sexes upon each other, and the falseness of the celibate ideal. *The Taming of the Shrew*, for all its farcical gaiety, approaches the problem play in its discussion of the relations of husband and wife, and *The Merry Wives of Windsor*, whether or not written to gratify the queen's alleged desire to see Falstaff in love, points the conclusion that senile lechery is powerless before the wholesome hearty virtue of English country wives. The deeper, almost tragic, elements in *The Merchant of Venice* and *Twelfth Night* need no emphasis. Even the farcical main plot of *The Comedy of Errors* is tinged with seriousness. The speech of the Abbess to Adriana, 'The venom clamours of a jealous woman', deserves to be set beside Biron's words at the end of the King of Navarre's unsuccessful experiment, 'Have at you, then, affection's men at arms!', and those of Katherine the Shrew, 'Fie, fie! unknit that threatening unkind brow', at the final banquet. Lastly, in *As You Like It* a character is introduced who becomes the incarnation of the philosophic spirit in comedy, the melancholy Jaques, whose very soubriquet is a clear indication of another temperament and a soberer view of the merry world about him. As the First Lord says,

> Thus most invectively he pierceth through
> The body of the country, city, court,
> Yea, and of this our life.

The problem comedies are those in which the whole action is presented, not with Jaques as a serio-comic outsider, but in part through his very eyes.

So with the more mature of the historical plays, in which a personage interprets the action in accord with his own temper, and is at once Chorus, and a full-length study in character – Richard III, looking at life as the complete and callous cynic; the Bastard in *King John*, sturdy English man of action, revolted at the self-interest which governs the otherwise well-poised world; Richard II, interpreting his own personal tragedy in self-conscious sentimentality and theatricality; Prince Hal, coolly detached and far-sighted, manipulating destiny to his own advantage; Falstaff, trying in vain to forget the bitter realities of life and persuade himself that it is all a jest. Every Man in his Humour, and the world seen through different humours, – this is a part of the fascination of the chronicle plays on English history. The humour which prevails in Shakespeare's own heart, when the long series of plays is done, cannot with safety be deduced from the utterances of his characters, or read between the lines. There are as many ways of taking life as there are observers to see it. But no one could have created such observers who had not the philosophic spirit within himself.

Especially noteworthy in the earlier comedies is the increasing tendency to support romance by the aid of realism. The philosophical spirit has no validity in dealing with artificialities; it is impossible to criticize life and at the same time hold wholly to convention and to tradition. Romantic comedy sets forth unplausible though absorbing events in a world in which we surrender ourselves to the charm of make-believe, not examining logic or probability too closely, or distressing ourselves unduly at misadventures. Its weakness is that it does not command the sympathy which is excited by the fortunes of real people. Shakespeare, with delicate instinct, made it believable by making it real, not in such a degree as to change its essential character, but lending to it naturalness and wholesome humour and on occasion even poignancy. This is accomplished in two ways. In the first place, he introduced bodily realistic characters and scenes, of which there is no vestige in his sources – Launce and his dog, Bottom and his crew, Dogberry and the Watch, or, for high comedy, Benedick and Beatrice. In the second place, he transformed his material, giving such reality to his characters that the absurdities of their actions, forced upon him by the plots which he had borrowed, are forgotten. So Shylock and Portia and Rosalind and Viola are real, though they move in a world of make-believe. But not even Shakespeare's magic act could free them wholly from their shackles. They are still clogged by the unrealities of the world of Romance, so that a completely rationalistic explanation of their actions is impossible – one of the great stumbling-blocks of Shakespeare criticism.

The realism with which the Italian writers from whom

Shakespeare drew many of his stories had treated romance has been emphasized by Raleigh.

The Italian Novel, in its long and brilliant history from the thirteenth to the sixteenth century, foreshadowed the development and change which is seen in Shakespeare's Comedies. It began with witty and fantastic anecdote, borrowed, in large part, from the scurrilities of French minstrels. By the genius of Boccaccio it was brought into closer touch with life. He retained many of the world-old jests, gross and impossible, but he intermixed them with another type of story, wherein he moves to pity and wonder by narrating memorable histories of passion. His chief sixteenth century disciples, to both of whom Shakespeare owed much, were Bandello and Cinthio. These men carried the novel still further in the direction of realism. Bandello asserts that all his novels record events which happened in his own time; Cinthio also claims to base his stories on fact, and so handles them that they set forth difficult problems of human conduct.[2]

Here, then, in the problem *novella*, as Raleigh points out in a page of incisive criticism, is one of the sources of the peculiar character of the problem comedies, 'especially in *All's Well That Ends Well*, which is based on a story of Boccaccio, and in *Measure for Measure*, which borrows its plot from Cinthio. In these plays, as in *The Merchant of Venice*, questions of casuistry are at the root of the plot and Shakespeare uses his theme in such a way as to suggest the lessons of his own subtle and profound morality.' They recall, in their plot-machinery, the artificialities of romantic comedy – Vienna, the state governed by foolish laws, the fairy-tale caprices of the King of France, the transparent disguises of Isabella and the Duke, the absurd device of substitution in bed for setting love-complications right. But how much closer to tragedy in real life are the fundamental issues of the plots – the faithful wife spurned by an unloving husband, the too-ardent lover condemned to death, and breaking down in sheer fright before its terrors, the sister who must choose between her own dishonour and her brother's life. Such tales as these cannot be put on the stage in a vein of care-free fantasy. So with *Troilus and Cressida*, a romantic love-story not of the *novella* type, which had, through the passage of the years, gone sour, and could by no stretch of possibility be presented as sweet and romantic adventure. The very familiarity of the tale had already compelled, even before Shakespeare touched it, a clear-eyed facing of the implications of its moral issues, and the condemnation of the heroine.

It is highly instructive, also, to observe the development of realism in Shakespearean tragedy. The bounds which separate tragedy from serious comedy of the problem type are, as has already been suggested, slight. The distinction is perhaps best drawn through the situation at the end of the play; on the one hand, a continuation of the serious and realistic mood, with death as a climax, and on the other, an avoidance of this final catastrophe, sometimes indeed with a happy issue out of affliction. Perhaps the main action in tragedy, too, retains more Aristotelian pity and terror, more of a sense of impending doom than the gravest of comedy, but this point is too intangible to be helpful in a definition. In their earlier Acts, *Hamlet* and *Lear* are scarcely more harrowing than *Measure for Measure*, excepting in so far as the greater intensity of imagination and greater care in workmanship make them so. In each of those great tragedies, Shakespeare's problem was in part the same as in much romantic comedy, to give reality and validity to familiar and archaic stories, and in each of them he proceeded just as he did in comedy, by the introduction of extraneous realistic material – as for example the Grave-Diggers and the Fool – and by superb truthfulness of characterization. At the opening of the new century he busied himself with rewriting the old Kyd play on the Hamlet theme. Probably theatrical exigencies, rather than deliberate artistic choice, led him to undertake it. At about the same time Ben Jonson revised *The Spanish Tragedy*. By 1600 Kyd's work must have seemed old-fashioned and melodramatic, but its power was unquestionable. What Kyd's *Hamlet* was like may be judged well enough from the history of the story and from his technique as we see it in *The Spanish Tragedy* – an old traditional tale with romantic accretions, which had been weakened in motivation and naturalness, although theatrically strengthened by melodramatic treatment. Shakespeare made its people real, its dialogue natural, he threw over it the mantle of superb poetry, and supported it by the richest philosophy of life. He made it plausible by every art in his power, but he was hampered at every turn by the archaisms and absurdities of the action, so that its irreconcilable contradictions have been at once the joy and the torment of generations of critics.

We must now look somewhat more carefully at the general temper of literature, on the stage and off, in the years of the problem comedies.

No student of the Elizabethan drama needs to be told that it experienced, as the old century was going out and the new coming in, much the same changes as are observable in Shakespeare's own work. Comedy was extremely popular, but it became less carelessly and trustingly 'romantic'; it turned more and more to realism, often of a gross and drastic sort, to study of character, based upon observation of actual contemporary types, and to a serious, questioning, and sometimes satirical view of life. While these tendencies are not wholly absent in the decade before 1600, they are strikingly marked in the years following that date. The delightful unrealities of impossible tales, with love a pretty game, played according to artificial rules, were forsaken for the picturesque brutalities of contemporary life, with prostitutes and thieves and bawds and ruffling soldiery, and no virtue to spare in courtly circles. Vice was shown in its naked ugliness, especially the havoc made in men's lives by lust. Some manifestations of this require special notice; it must always be remembered, however, that the complexities of the many and varied pieces with which we are dealing cannot be summed up in a few generalizations. The less pleasant types of comedy are important for the general subject in hand, but the picture must not be painted too black. And the reader must again forgive emphasis on some matters which will not be new to him.

New trails for English drama were blazed by Ben Jonson's *Every Man in his Humour* (1598). Artificiality and bombast were forsaken for realism and serious study of character. Jonson's resolve, stated in the famous Prologue, to put on the stage 'deeds and language such as men do use' was carried out in many of his succeeding comedies, and imitated by Middleton, Heywood, Marston, Dekker, and others, in varying degrees and fashions. His influence did much to make comedy serious and analytical, and to turn attention to actually existing social conditions. These conditions were sometimes thinly disguised by settings in foreign lands, as in the Venice of *Volpone* or of

Blurt, Master Constable, or in the Ferrara of Middleton's *Phoenix*.
The Italian names in the earlier (quarto) edition of *Every Man in his
Humour* were, by a proper feeling for the essentially English
character of the play, later changed, and became Knowell,
Brainworm, Kitely, Mistress Bridget, and so forth. A second play
particularly deserving of careful study in connexion with Shakespeare
is Marston's *Malcontent*, published in 1604, but perhaps written as
early as 1600–1602. It was dedicated to Jonson, and shows his influence vividly. Contrariwise, the striking central figure in the play
may have given Jonson hints for Volpone, who, like the Malcontent,
is a mouthpiece for bitter revelations of the follies and weaknesses of
mankind. In Marston's play, a duke, whose place has been taken by a
usurper, returns to his court in disguise, under the name of Malevole,
and at once vents his savage humour on those about him, and exposes
the intrigues of the usurping duke, Pietro, and Pietro's lustful wife.
Middleton's *Phoenix* also employs the device of disguise. Phoenix,
prince of Ferrara, ostensibly leaves his court for travel, but remains
to study evils at home, and at the end of the piece exposes to his
father the various forms of wickedness which he has observed.
Others of Middleton's plays, *Michaelmas Term, A Trick to Catch the
Old One, A Mad World, my Masters, Your Five Gallants*, belonging
in the opening years of the seventeenth century, set the scene in
London, and present plots of realistic intrigue, with sharply drawn
studies of character.

It is extremely difficult to trace in detail 'influences' of contemporary plays upon those of Shakespeare, or the reverse, especially
since the dates of composition and production are in most cases so
uncertain. Consider, for example, the resemblances between *The
Malcontent, Measure for Measure*, and *All's Well*. The plot of the
duke in disguise, who observes and manipulates court intrigue while
he is supposed to be absent, who soliloquizes on evils of the time, who
hears courtiers abuse him as the absent duke, and who dismisses the
culprits with less than justice at the end, is common to *The
Malcontent* and *Measure for Measure*. Passarello, the bitter Fool, is
somewhat like the foul-mouthed Clown in *All's Well*. Bilioso, the
choleric soldier, has flashes which remind one of Parolles, and
Maquerelle is something like Mistress Overdone. Constant pre-

occupation with sexual matters is common to all these plays. But read Shakespeare and Marston in conjunction, and observe how unlike their work really is. Who can speak with confidence of direct influence, either way? We are repelled by the hard realism, the gibes at love and lust, the unpleasant intrigue, in the Shakespearean comedies, but they are far removed from the foulness which constantly besmirches Marston's pages. Stoll, has, with great subtlety, traced in detail some of the interinfluences in pieces written after 1600, in the main, and tried to show how Kyd affected Marston, who in his turn affected Webster and Tourneur; how Shakespeare influenced Dekker, how Fletcher and Massinger influenced Webster, and so forth. The extended and delicate analysis necessary for confirming or criticizing such conclusions can obviously not be undertaken here. What I am concerned to emphasize is the general fashion of dramatic writing from 1598 to 1608 – to set formal limits for the sake of convenience – and to urge that no dramatist writing at that time could escape being to some extent controlled by it. I make, of course, no claim to originality in emphasizing the striking changes in the drama during this period, and their effect upon Shakespeare. Thorndike has traced these tendencies more in detail than is possible here, and has more than once called attention to the gloomy comedies as 'manifestly taking suggestions from current types and fashions'.[3]

We must not make the mistake of regarding all this as a chance veering of the wind of public taste; the skies were lowering over the country as a whole. The closing years of the reign of Elizabeth were marked by a very different temper from that of the years which had preceded. The shadows darkening about the ageing queen seemed also to fall upon the spirits of her subjects. To the patriotic enthusiasm of the days of the Armada succeeded the discouragement of prolonged and only partially successful hostilities with Spain. The death of Mary Stuart had removed a national menace, but this act of shameful violence did not secure a satisfactory legitimate successor to the throne. The romantic chivalrous attachment to Gloriana at court and whole-hearted support of her leadership throughout the country was changing to toleration of a querulous old woman on account of her brilliant past. Martial enthusiasms were checked by increasing prudence and parsimony in statecraft, and by ever more cautious diplomatic jugglings. The tragic folly of the Essex conspiracy was only one of many symptoms of increasing discontent. The English had indeed won greater security at home, but they had lost the high spirit which accompanies sacrifices and adversities borne in common. The demoralization of the Stuart era began long before Elizabeth breathed her last.

The large amount of verse satire written in the very years which we are now considering reflects these conditions. This form of composition was not altogether novel, but it was new enough for Joseph Hall to assert, on the basis of his *Virgidemiarum* (1597–98) that he was the first English satirist. Certainly he was the first to see the full possibilities of adapting the methods of Juvenal to English verse. In 1598 appeared Marston's *Satyres*, in connexion with his erotic *Metamorphosis of Pygmalion's Image*, William Rankin's *Satires*, and Edward Guilpin's *Skialetheia, A Shadow of Truth in Certain Epigrams and Satires* – all coarse and vigorous pieces attacking contemporary fashions and follies. In the next year Marston published his *Scourge of Villainy*, in which the temper of the Malcontent finds expression in rough and scurrilous verse. To the influence of Juvenal in all this work must be added that of the cynical spirit of much of the Italian literature read in England, though not in the form of satire. The beginnings of character-writing, marked especially by Hall's *Characters of Vices and Virtues* (1608), and continued in the satires of John Davies of Hereford, are certainly later manifestations of the effort of realistic presentation, in formal satire and in drama, of personages and scenes drawn from English life. The influence of the pamphleteers is likewise to be reckoned with throughout this period; this had begun in good earnest with Lodge, Nash and Greene in the eighties, and found an especially prolific and able representative in Dekker, who varied his dramatic work with vivid prose descriptions of the plague in his *Wonderful Year* (1603), and of low life in country and city in the later *Bellman of London* and *Lanthorn and Candle-Light*; while his more famous *Gull's Horn-Book* (1609) provided an ironical conduct book for the young spark who would cut a dash in London by day or night. But Dekker is only one of many who would deserve mention, did space permit. We can hardly do more here than glance at the large amount of this realistic and satirical or quasi-satirical writing in prose and verse produced in the closing years of the reign of Elizabeth and the opening years of the reign of James, and note how strikingly its general tone agrees with that of many of the realistic comedies of the day.

Some caution must be exercised in the use of the terms 'satire' and 'satirical'. It is unnecessary to dwell upon the repulsive character of much of the comedy written in the first decade of the new century. Preoccupation with the darker manifestations of sexual passion brings upon the stage the denizens and frequenters of brothels, and seducers and seduced in high life, with a depiction of language and manners that leaves little to the imagination. The realistic comedies of Dekker and Chapman and Middleton, presumably written for amusement, to fill the theatres, and played in part and sometimes wholly by boys, introduce scenes and dialogue that would make a coal-heaver blush. But how far this is done with satiric intent is questionable. Not every play with bawdy scenes and loose talk, surely, is a satire, yet the term fastens itself easily on such pieces. It would appear that the method of Jonson and Marston, and to some extent that of the verse satirists, lent itself so readily to sensational dramatic effect that crass realism came to be popular for its own sake. In part there must have been a reaction against the sentimentalities and artificialities of earlier romance, and it is easy to see how this reaction might itself have brought exaggerations as great as those which had preceded. The Londoners of that day liked their spices strong, whether sweet or bitter. Occasionally the reformatory attitude characteristic of satire appears, as in the moral speeches in Middleton's *Phoenix*, or a serious effort is made to analyse the psychology of sex, as in Middleton and Dekker's *Honest Whore*, or Marston's *Dutch Courtesan*, in which we are told that 'the difference betwixt the love of a courtesan and a wife is the full scope of the play'. On the other hand, a serious attempt was occasionally made to reproduce objectively on the stage gruesome stories based upon actual events of the time. These plays are remarkable for their faithful observation of scenes and characters from English life; they fall into a very different category from attacks on contemporary manners. Some critics have discerned the hand of Shakespeare in *The Yorkshire Tragedy*. *The Miseries of Enforced Marriage* deals with the same horrid murder. *The Bristol Tragedy* and *The Chester Tragedy* are in a similar vein. In a great many pieces of this period, however, the critic must be somewhat at a loss. The presence of satiric intent is possible, but difficult to prove – or to disprove.

Some of the bitterness in comedy and tragedy is traceable to the 'melancholy' hero made popular by Kyd in the Tragedy of Blood, and again brought to prominence in the revivals of *The Spanish Tragedy* and *Hamlet*. Old Hieronymo and Hamlet apparently furnished inspiration for Marston's Malevole, a slighter study of whom appears in the Feliche of *Antonio and Mellida*. Such melancholy was recognized by the Elizabethans not only as a striking individual characteristic, but also as a disease, which led to a jaundiced view of life, disillusioned meditations, and tirades against human folly and sin. The theatrical effectiveness of the outpourings of a diseased soul is undeniable, and they appear to have had something of the fascination of stage insanity of the more violent sort. But here again there is no greater critical error than to attribute such a pessimistic view of life to the dramatist himself. The popularity of the melancholy type throws a strong light on the creations of Shakespeare, but it should not lead to the conclusion that Shakespeare became a melancholy hero himself. The type affected his work in some degree as early as *As You Like It*, but Jaques is, as we have seen, a very different sort of person. There was much in the 'melancholy' mood which was in harmony with the increasing seriousness of an older man, but the chief reasons for Shakespeare's 'gloom', we must believe, were external influences. Contemporary dramatic fashion decreed that life should be seen without rose-coloured spectacles, and Shakespeare proceeded, as was his habit, to suit the public taste. His whole attitude, so far as we can judge it from his earlier work, was singularly objective; the mirror is held up to nature, but the wicked are not scourged or lectured. Critics who discern in the problem comedies a personal ironic, or satiric, or despondent, mood must reckon with the fact that the leading dramatists of the day were all exhibiting similar moods. Shakespeare's 'bitterness' was certainly not deep enough to last until the end of *Measure for Measure* or *All's Well*, which he ended in the conventional way – everybody happy, and the villainy all but completely forgiven. *Troilus and Cressida* was first written, in all probability, for a sophisticated audience fond of coarse pictures of contemporary sexual laxity. It sets forth the disillusionment of idealistic youth by wanton beauty. But even here there was not enough *saeva indignatio* to carry Shakespeare through to a conclusion which modern critics demand as logical, the punishment of Cressida. If the Countess in *All's Well*, who is universally considered a fine and high-bred lady, sympathetically portrayed, lets the Clown jest coarsely in her presence, does that mean that Shakespeare's view of womanhood has changed? Rather, I think, that the tone of jesting popular on the stage had changed, and that Shakespeare was willing to turn from the merry quips of Feste or Touchstone to unsavoury jokes like those of his brother dramatists.

So with the selection of the themes of the problem comedies, it may well be that these themes were not congenial to Shakespeare, but that he adopted them and did his best with them because there was a demand for that sort of thing. Perhaps their very uncongeniality is the cause of the hardness and mechanical quality occasionally observable in the completed plays. We may not like to think of the godlike Shakespeare as bowing to whims or fashions which did not please him, but the conclusion is inescapable. In the *Merry Wives* he clearly produced inferior work on account of external pressure. Dennis, in 1702, stated that the play was written in fourteen days at the queen's command, and Rowe and Gildon add that she wanted to see Falstaff in love. 'So plausible is the tradition', remarks F.P. Emery, 'that it is now accepted by most critics.'[4] Certainly it affords a reasonable explanation for the degradation of Falstaff and the feebler treatment of other old favourites, as well as for the often noted impression of haste, in spite of technical competency, which the whole play gives. In general, I do not think that sufficient allowance is made for the influence of external circumstances and for accident and chance in the selection of the subjects of the various plays. John Jay Chapman, in a highly suggestive little book, notes that Shakespeare 'to the end of his life was always at the mercy of his theme', and, pointing out that the great tragedies were written through the same years as *Troilus and Cressida*, *Measure for Measure*, *Timon of Athens* and *Pericles*, continues: 'Is there another example of a very great artist who did his best and his worst work during the same decade? I do not know how to explain the matter, except by imagining that Shakespeare's instinct in the choice of tragic themes was unreliable ... it seems to have been an accident with him whether he hit upon a theme that was suitable to his genius or not. If he happened to choose a bad theme, it ruined his play.'[5]

It has been usual to assume that Shakespeare selected his subjects to fit his artistic moods, but the chances are rather that he had to fit his moods to his subjects. Consider *Timon of Athens*, which Wright calls 'one of the bitterest of tragedies'.[6] This is true, but the play is bitter because the subject makes it so. Shakespeare had to do his best to portray pessimism, and not being himself a pessimist, succeeded indifferently. It looks as if Timon might have been chosen in part because he was the Malcontent sort of figure popular at the time, and also partly because he moved through the pages of Plutarch, a source which Shakespeare had already brilliantly utilized for *Julius Caesar* and *Antony and Cleopatra*, and less happily for *Coriolanus*. So with Holinshed, from whom was drawn, after *Lear* and *Macbeth*, the feeble background of scenes of Roman Britain in *Cymbeline*. After these mines had been worked awhile, they did not yield the same pure ore as in the beginning.

How little the change in mood in Shakespeare's middle comedies was due to personal feeling is further illustrated by his treatment of the Dramatic Romances.

The tendencies which we have just been examining brought, in their turn, their own reaction. Men tire, after a time, of a gloomy, realistic, satirical attitude towards life, especially in the theatre, where, after all, they go to be entertained. And so one of the first signs of a change appeared on the stage. With the *Philaster* of Beaumont and Fletcher (1608?), Romance spread its golden banners to the winds once more. Again the hearts of men turned gladly to idyllic scenes in far-off lands, to happy issues out of affliction, to graceful and poetic verse. The success of *Philaster* led to the production of other plays of similar character. A convincing demonstration of the probable effect of this on Shakespeare's latest plays has been given by Thorndike. The impossibility of dating *Philaster* exactly makes absolute proof impossible, but it is clear that nothing else so well explains Shakespeare's scenes of happy abandonment to unreality, in the characteristic manner of the younger dramatists.[7]

Earlier criticism stressed a different explanation, which still finds wide acceptance. It held that the shift of mood in the Dramatic Romances, like that earlier in the tragedies and the darker comedies, was due mainly to alterations in Shakespeare's temper and view of life, resulting from personal experiences. This point of view is extremely familiar; it has been set before generations of students, from Dowden's *Shakspere Primer* down, and it has enjoyed great vogue. Energetic attacks have been made upon it, but it still continues to find favour in high places, and to colour much current Shakespearean criticism. Some consideration of it appears imperative here. We cannot, I think, escape the conclusion that it has been greatly exaggerated, but we cannot deny it all validity. 'Personal experiences' is rather a vague terms; critics have viewed the events which they believed to have affected Shakespeare's life after 1600 in a variety of ways, attaching greater importance now to one circumstance or train of circumstances, and now to another. We do not know where the truth lies, but no one, surely, would be so rash as to deny to external events all effect on his creative powers. The question is mainly one of emphasis, and this, I think, has been wrongly placed.

It does not seem necessary to weary the reader with a long series of citations to show the general acceptance of this theory, or to illustrate its variations in detail. I will therefore confine myself to two quotations, one from the eminent scholar who gave it widest currency, and the other from one of the foremost authorities at the present day, showing particularly the bearing of this view upon the Dramatic Romances, which are at present under consideration.

Dowden's method of distinguishing his four 'periods' may be recalled from the following passage:

During this [second] period Shakspere's work grows strong and robust. It was the time when he was making rapid advance in worldly prosperity, and accumulating the fortune on which he meant to retire as a country gentleman. I name the second period therefore *In the world*. THIRD

PERIOD. – Before it closed Shakspere had known sorrow: his son was dead; his father died probably soon after Shakspere had written his *Twelfth Night*; his friend of the Sonnets had done him wrong. Whatever the cause may have been, the fact seems certain that the poet now ceased to care for tales of mirth and love, for the stir and movement of history, for the pomp of war; he needed to sound, with his imagination, the depths of the human heart; to inquire into the darkest and saddest parts of human life; to study the great mystery of evil. . . . The tragic gloom and suffering were not, however, to last forever. The dark cloud lightens and rolls away, and the sky appears purer and tenderer than ever. The impression left upon the reader by Shakspere's last plays is that, whatever his trials and sorrows and errors may have been, he had come forth from them wise, large-hearted, calm-souled. . . . And it will be felt that the name which I have given to this last period – Shakspere having ascended out of the turmoil and trouble of action, out of the darkness and tragic mystery, the places haunted by terror and crime, and by love contending with these, to a pure and serene elevation – it will be felt that the name, *On the heights*, is neither inappropriate nor fanciful.[8]

This was written some fifty years ago; Sir Edmund Chambers may speak for the present day.

The evidence of [Shakespeare's] profound disillusion and discouragement of spirit is plain enough; and for some years the tide of his pessimistic thought advances, swelling through the pathetic tragedy of *Othello* to the cosmic tragedies of *Macbeth* and *King Lear*, with their Titan-like indictments not of man alone, but of the heavens by whom man was made. . . . The period closes with *Antony and Cleopatra* and *Coriolanus*, in which the ideals of the love of woman and the honour of man are once more stripped bare to display the skeletons of lust and egoism, and in the latter of which signs of exhaustion are already perceptible; and with *Timon of Athens*, in which the dramatist whips himself to an almost incoherent expression of a general loathing and detestation of humanity. Then the stretched cord suddenly snaps. *Timon* is apparently unfinished, and the next play, *Pericles*, is in an entirely different vein, and is apparently finished but not begun. At this point only in the whole course of Shakespeare's development is a complete breach of continuity. One can only conjecture the occurrence of some spiritual crisis, an illness perhaps, or some process akin to what in the language of religion is called conversion, which left him a new man, with the fever of pessimism behind him, and at peace once more with Heaven and the world. The final group of plays, the Shakesperian part of *Pericles, Cymbeline, The Winter's Tale, The Tempest,* all belong to the class of what may be called idyllic romances. They are happy dreams, in which all troubles and sorrows are ultimately resolved into fortunate endings, and which stand therefore as so many symbols of an optimistic faith in the beneficent dispositions of an ordering Providence.[9]

It is extraordinary how little the fallacies of this view of the Dramatic Romances have been observed. The detailed analysis in the preceding chapters has shown that *The Winter's Tale* and *Cymbeline* are composites of sunny romance and of the gloomiest realism. They end in the vein of fantasy, but they begin, and are long maintained, in the vein of *All's Well* or *Measure for Measure.* Try the experiment of reading the first two Acts of either play, and see how easily it might have been continued as a problem comedy. Consider the brutalities of these 'happy dreams' – the cruelty of Posthumus Leonatus and the sufferings of Imogen, the raging jealousy of Leontes and the atrocious treatment of Hermione, scarce risen from childbed. Read the dreadful speech in which Leontes speaks to Mamillius of his mother's supposed dishonour, or the foul imagery of Posthumus, as he imagines the details of his wife's lasciviousness. Have these scenes any darker parallels in the period preceding? It seems clear that Shakespeare was not undergoing a marvellous change from pessimism to serenity, but that he was combining two forms of dramatic entertainment which had proved popular, the realistic and the romantic. *Cymbeline,* as we have seen, is a particularly striking instance of utilization of all kinds of dramatic tricks and situations. No one can lay much stress on *Pericles,* a collaborated play of inferior quality, as showing whether Shakespeare's spirit was serene or not, but so far as the evidence goes, it is in line with the argument which I am here advancing. The Hogarthian brothel scenes are certainly not sunny, and I agree with Alphonso Smith and others that Shakespeare's participation in them must certainly be admitted.[10] *The Tempest,* by its very nature, stands out of the reckoning. A marriage masque cannot admit the problem mood, or unpleasantly realistic scenes. Caliban, surely, was designed to provide the contrast of the rough 'anti-masque', rather than to turn the minds of wedding-guests to social problems.

Lytton Strachey has protested, in an incisive and too little known essay, against what he calls the universal opinion, fortified by Dowden, ten Brink, Gollancz, Furnivall, Brandes, and Sidney Lee, that 'after a happy youth and a gloomy middle age Shakespeare reached at last a state of quiet serenity in which he died'.

It may, indeed, be admitted at once that 'Prince Florizel and Perdita' are charming creatures, that Prospero is 'grave', and that Hermione is more or less 'serene'; but why is it that, in our consideration of the later plays, the whole of our attention must always be fixed upon these particular characters? Modern critics, in their eagerness to appraise everything that is beautiful and good at its proper value, seem to have entirely forgotten that there is another side to the medal; and they have omitted to point out that these plays contain a series of portraits of peculiar infamy, whose wickedness finds expression in language of extraordinary force. Coming fresh from their pages to the pages of *Cymbeline*, *The Winter's Tale*, and *The Tempest*, one is astonished and perplexed. How is it possible to fit into their scheme of roses and maidens that 'Italian fiend' the 'yellow Iachimo', or Cloten, that 'thing too bad for bad report', or the 'crafty devil', his mother, or Leontes, or Caliban, or Trinculo? To omit these figures of discord and evil from our consideration, while Autolycus and Miranda dance before the footlights, is surely a fallacy in proportion; for the presentment of the one group of persons is every whit as distinct and vigorous as that of the other. Nowhere, indeed, is Shakespeare's violence of expression more constantly displayed than in the 'gentle utterances' of his last period. . . . Nowhere are the poet's metaphors more nakedly material; nowhere does he verge more often upon a sort of brutality of phrase, a cruel coarseness.[11]

There is another and better reason for doubting that personal emotions and experiences were the controlling reason for changes in the tone of Shakespeare's work: the fundamental assumption underlying this view appears to be false. What we know of actual imaginative composition does not justify us in concluding that cheerful writing necessarily accompanies or follows cheerful experiences, or gloomy writing gloomy experiences. Consider how little the tragic sorrows in the life of Charles Lamb appear in his essays, or the family troubles of Mark Twain, which his friends knew caused him the deepest dejection, in his tales. That gay and sparkling comedy, *The Beaux' Stratagem*, was written on Farquhar's deathbed. The same holds in music: some of Beethoven's sunniest pages were written in deafness and loneliness; Mozart composed the enchanting *Magic Flute* in illness and poverty, with the shadow of death upon him. Or turn the pages of Shelley's *Cenci*, surely one of the grimmest tragedies in any language, and then read his own words, 'In writing *The Cenci* my object was to see how I could succeed in describing passions I have never felt, and to tell the most dreadful story in pure and refined language.... *The Cenci* is a work of art; it is not coloured by my feelings.'[12]

This whole question is somewhat related to the vexed problem of how far the Sonnets are autobiographical, and how far artificial performances in a fashionable literary form. Probably the wisest position to take is that the Sonnets are a combination of artistry and subjectivity; it is certainly true that a conventional type does not exclude personal experience and emotion, as Dante and Boccaccio may teach us. But Elizabethan sonnets must be judged in a very different way from Elizabethan plays. By its very nature, as a lyric, the sonnet reflects personal feeling; the drama, as an essentially objective type, excludes it. The Sonnets of Shakespeare are highly personal in expression; his plays never so. Because the Sonnets show disillusion through the faithlessness of a friend and the inconstancy of a mistress, which may conceivably reflect intimacy with Southampton and love of a Dark Lady, it cannot be concluded that the studies of sensual young men or the portraits of heroines in the problem comedies are bitter reactions of a wounded heart. Still less plausible is the theory that the plays contain subtle references to political events; that *Julius Caesar*, for example, is in any way connected with the Essex conspiracy. Shakespeare was wise enough to see the dangers in any such procedure. There is not a single clear reference in his plays, from beginning to end, which could have given offence to the Crown at the time when it was written; indeed, he goes rather far in flattering the susceptibilities of Elizabeth, and, in passages less clearly to be interpreted, of James I.

I claim, of course, no originality in the general point of view here presented. But, in the widespread prevalence of contrary opinions, it seems important to restate it, and to show how the evidence of the problem comedies supports it. The whole matter was vigorously summed up by the late Raymond Alden.

If our survey of Shakespeare's life, as given us through external sources, exhibited any biographic reasons why he should have written chiefly comedy in one period, and chiefly tragedy in another, it would no doubt be significant to find that he actually did so; but in the absence of such evidence, the passage from the types of his work to the facts of his personal life is one only for acrobats of the imagination. . . . The point to remember is that there is no obvious and determinable relationship between objective and subjective conditions. We have no reason to suppose that Shakespeare found the writing of tragedy easiest when he was at odds with the world. He is quite as likely to have passed upstairs from a merry bout of words with Mistress Mountjoy, his landlady's daughter, to work out the agonies of Othello's temptation, as to the writing of a pastoral or a clownish scene.[13]

This leads to a final caution in regard to the dangers of dividing Shakespeare's dramatic achievement into 'periods'. Such an arrangement serves to some extent a useful purpose, particularly for the critic or teacher, whose concern is to clarify and to simplify. It gives an air of system and finality. But it leads easily to the false assumption that Shakespeare's creative activity followed a succession of well-marked stages, each different from the preceding, and each containing within it plays set apart by distinctive characteristics. It neglects the obvious possibility that a literary artist, and still more a busy dramatist, may turn quickly from one style of writing to another, and back again, that relaxation from the strain of tragedy may be found in light comedy, and that external conditions such as literary fashion and theatrical supply and demand may be more potent than personal interests and artistic preoccupations. It has led students of Shakespeare to feel that all the cheerful comedies must belong in the period of cheer, all the gloomy ones in the period of gloom, and that nothing but serenity characterizes the plays written in the period of serenity. Thus in a well-known manual appears the remark, 'All the plays of this [final] period end happily and are wholly free from the bitterness of the Third Period comedy.'[14] Dating of doubtful plays has, indeed, been much affected by period divisions; critics have run cheerfully around in a vicious circle.

The evidence for dating the plays of Shakespeare which apparently lie immediately after the turn of the century is not sufficient to enable us to separate one period from another, unless we admit that the boundary lines are extremely hazy. The gloomy comedies may all have been written after the cheerful ones, but we do not know that this is so. *Troilus and Cressida* apparently belongs in 1601 or 1602, but we do not know that it was composed after *Twelfth Night*. It may have preceded that joyous comedy. The usual dates for *All's Well* and *Measure for Measure* are 1602 and 1603 respectively, but neither is certain. Many critics have held that *All's Well* was first written in the early nineties, and later revised. If we put it with Lowes before 1598, it is hard to see how it could, even in its earlier state, have been full of sunny cheer, while the later limit of its revision, 1608, groups it with *Pericles*. So with the 'Fourth Period', there is no controlling reason for putting *Coriolanus* before *Cymbeline*; the evidence for dating either play is exceptionally scanty. The assignment of *Coriolanus* to 1609 and of *Cymbeline* to 1610 has undoubtedly been influenced by the neatness with which each play will fit into the period in which it is satisfactory to have it.

If, then, the old division into periods must be kept, it should be thought of as indicative merely of general tendencies, vague in its boundaries, and admitting, under the different rubrics, plays which do not fit the categories in which they are placed.

A final word may be added, by way of summary, after the long investigation which has preceded.

The place of the problem comedies in Shakespeare's dramatic development will now, perhaps, appear in a clearer light. Their characteristic features – preoccupation with the darker sides of life, serious and searching analysis of character and conduct, and drastic realism – which are found also in the great tragedies and in the Roman plays, are naturally due in part to the larger vision and broader philosophic insight, perhaps also to the loss of youthful illusions, which come to most men with advancing years. But they are also due, far more than is usually supposed, to the influence of prevailing literary and dramatic fashions. At just the time when the problem comedies were written, realistic plays of sexual intrigue were occupying the stage, and satirical verse was engaging the attention of poets. The temper of the English people was very different from what it had been at the time when Shakespeare began to write. Something was wrong with the world; the effort of the day was to strip away glittering illusions and expose the ugliness of vice. To healthy honest frankness of speech succeeded brutal coarseness of language, and to robust joy in active life and to delight in the world of illusion, a passion to reveal, often for melodramatic effect, the baser forms of sin, and a feverish desire to expose the hidden mysteries of sex.

Shakespeare's mind, we must believe, was singularly healthy. His writing up to the turn of the century has a sanity, a cheerfulness, a broad tolerance which need no emphasis here. When we find the same changes in his later work as in that of contemporary dramatists, changes which are too far-reaching, too much in accord with the general spirit of the times to be due to his own influence, we must conclude that he was deeply affected by what was going on about him. Still more inescapable is this conviction when we observe how, with the revival of romance under Beaumont and Fletcher, he altered his work once more, while not giving over the gloomy and realistic scenes which had found, and were to some extent still finding, popular favour. His greatest plays in the darker vein are those in which his broad tolerance still shines out; his weakest are those in which he affects an attitude foreign to his true nature.

Problem comedy is a kind of bastard brother of tragedy. In Shakespeare's hands it never wins undisputed sway over any play from start to finish, but combines, now well and now ill, with the unrealities of romantic story. In tragedy the complications of the action can be pushed to their logical conclusion; in comedy the effort to achieve a happy ending wrenches matters askew, or leaves difficulties unsolved. Problem comedy was never really congenial to Shakespeare's genius; it never called forth his highest faculties, or produced a single masterpiece to be ranked with his greatest work. It has never won the love and admiration, either on the stage or on the printed page, which even his minor achievements in other types of drama command. But it is none the less worthy of the most careful attention and study. The plainest of Shakespeare's vestures has an interest which transcends for us the most gorgeous robes of his fellow workers in Elizabethan drama.

NOTES

W. W. Lawrence's original Notes have been retained except where they refer to matters no longer of current interest or where, on factual matters, they might give a misleading indication of the state of present scholarship.

I. INTRODUCTION

Pages 19 to 42

1. F. S. Boas, *Shakspere and his Predecessors*, London, 1896, p. 345.
2. *Plays Pleasant and Unpleasant*, revised ed., London, 1931, vol. I, p. xix.
3. F. H. Ristine, *English Tragicomedy*, New York, 1910, p. xiv.
4. *The Cambridge Shakespeare*, Boston and New York, 1906, p. xviii.
5. *Op. cit.*, p. 446.
6. Ashley H. Thorndike, *English Comedy*, New York, 1929, p. 128.
7. *The Limits of Verbal Criticism of Works of Art*, New York, 1928, pp. 28–9.
8. From a private letter to the author dated 4 January 1921.
9. See Joseph Jacobs, *Barlaam and Josaphat*, London, 1896, pp. lxiv ff. for a full discussion of early analogues to the Caskets story. The passage just quoted will be found on pp. cvii ff.
10. E. E. Stoll, *Shakespeare Studies*, New York, 1927, pp. 255 ff.
11. *Gesta Romanorum*, ed. Hermann Oesterley, Berlin, 1872; Tale 195, cf. p. 603.
12. *Dolopathos*, ed. Hermann Oesterley, Strassburg und London, 1873, pp. 57 ff. The date of the collection (late twelfth century) is discussed in the Introduction, p. ii.
13. *The Renaissance*, London, 1873, pp. 8 ff.
14. The proper explanation seems first to have been suggested by Sampson, in his edition of the play for the *Tudor Shakespeare*, Introduction, p. xv (1912).
15. Karl Young, 'Samuel Johnson on Shakespeare: one Aspect', in *University of Wisconsin Studies in Language and Literature*, No. 18.
16. Levin L. Schücking, *Character Problems in Shakespeare's Plays*, London, 1922.

17. *Shakspere, a Critical Study of his Mind and Art*, London, 1875, pp. 2, 7.

18. A. C. Bradley, *Shakespearean Tragedy*, London, 1904, p. 2.

19. Émile Legouis, 'La Réaction contre la critique romantique de Shakespeare,' *Essays and Studies by Members of the English Association*, vol. XIII, pp. 74–87 (1928). The passage quoted is on page 87.

20. Feuillerat, *Litteris*, vol. III, pp. 16 ff., 1926. See also the discussion of *Measure for Measure* below.

2. ALL'S WELL THAT ENDS WELL

Pages 43 to 79

1. *History of Prose Fiction*, London, 1888, vol. II, p. 86.

2. *Harper's Magazine*, 1892, vol. LXXXV, p. 213.

3. *Shakespeare as Dramatist and Moralist*, New York, 1901, p. 390.

4. *William Shakespeare*, London, 1911, p. 147.

5. For the quotation from Lowes, see Introduction to *All's Well* in the *Tudor Shakespeare*, p. xiii; for that from Neilson, Neilson and Thorndike, *Facts about Shakespeare*, New York, 1913, p. 83; for that from Elton, *A Book of Homage to Shakespeare*, London, 1916, p. 161.

6. George Philip Krapp, in *Shakespearian Studies by Members of the Department of English and Comparative Literature in Columbia University*, New York, 1916, p. 291.

7. Barrett Wendell, *William Shakspere*, New York, 1901; W. Osborn Brigstocke, Introduction to *All's Well* (old *Arden* edition) p. xv.

8. Gervinus, *Shakespeare Commentaries*, translated by F. E. Bunnètt, London, 1903, p. 182; Walter Raleigh, *Shakespeare*, London, 1908, p. 185, Levin L. Schücking, *Character Problems in Shakespeare's Plays*, London, 1922, pp. 195–6; Seccombe and Allen, *Age of Shakespeare*, London, 1903, vol. II, p. 81 f.

9. For the reader's convenience, I quote the following from Lowes's edition of the play: 'The Countess, Parolles, the Clown and Lafeu are all added; Giletta of the story is rich, has refused many suitors, and has kinsfolk of her own; on her arrival in Paris, her first step is to see Beltramo; the King and not Giletta suggests as her reward the bestowal upon her of a husband, whom Giletta merely requests, thereupon, that she may choose; the choice of Beltramo is not made in his presence, but he is called in later to hear of it; after Beltramo's desertion (which is not motivated beforehand, as in the play), Giletta

returns to Rossiglione, and devotes herself to the care and improvement of Beltramo's estate, rendering herself greatly beloved by his
subjects; as Beltramo does not return, Giletta sends him word that
she is willing to leave Rossiglione, should that insure his return, and
it is in reply to this message of Giletta that Beltramo writes his
letter; when Giletta leaves, she does so publicly, telling her subjects
that she has determined to spend the rest of her days in pilgrimages
and devotion; the widow at whose house she stays in Florence is not
Diana's mother, but a neighbour of her mother, who is also a widow
and a gentlewoman; Giletta remains in Florence, after Beltramo has
returned home, until the birth of twin sons; in the dénouement
neither Diana nor the King is present, but Giletta simply appears, in
poor apparel, with her two sons in her arms, at a feast which
Beltramo is giving, and, weeping, claims her rights; there is no
mention whatever of a second ring.' Professor Lowes is in error in
saying that Beltramo's desertion is not motivated beforehand; it is
clearly due to Giletta's lower birth, which was not 'convenable to his
nobilitie'.

The most thorough study of the process of revision has been made
by Professor Lowes, to whom I am indebted for friendly counsel.
Through his kindness I have been privileged to examine the unpublished MS. of this study, and to utilize some of its results here. It
is noteworthy, in connexion with the point made above, that according to Professor Lowes, Bertram, the most unpleasant character in
the main plot, was not retouched. The chief alterations made Helena
more womanly and less girlish. Some of the conclusions of Professor
Lowes are summarized in his edition of the play for the *Tudor
Shakespeare* (pp. vii ff.). He believes that the play was first written
'from 1598 to 1600 or 1601', and worked over 'at a date very near
that of the latest tragedies, and not long (if at all) before the
Romances, say 1606–1608'. I do not feel fully convinced of this, but
it would obviously be unfair to discuss unpublished work.

10. Maive Stokes, *Indian Fairy Tales*, London, 1880, 'The Clever
Wife', Tale XXVIII, p. 216.

11. W. Radloff, *Proben der Volkslitteratur der nördlichen türkischen
Stämme*, vol. VI, Dialect der Tarantschi, St Petersburg, 1886, 'Die
Kluge Wesirs-Tochter', pp. 191–8.

12. Cf. the *Mágussaga*, below. Anger at the division of the cock, which
is imposed upon Hlothver by his bride Ermenga, leads to his setting
her the tasks which form the main theme of the episode.

13. M. B. Landstad, *Norske Folkeviser*, Christiania, 1853, 'Kong Kristian og hans dronning,' No. LXXIII, pp. 585 ff.

14. Gaston Paris, *Romania*, 1887, vol. XVI, p. 98. It should be observed, however, that the intimacy of the Count and Countess extends over a considerable time in the romance, not a single night.

15. F. J. Wolf, *Über eine Sammlung spanischer Romanzen in fliegenden Blättern auf der Universitäts-Bibliothek zu Prag*, Wien, 1850, p. 42.

16. Antin-Pacha, *Contes populaires de la Vallée du Nil*, Paris, 1895, 'La Fille du Menusier', tale XX, p. 239.

17. *English and Scottish Popular Ballads*, vol. I, p. 8. The whole of this introduction to the ballad of the Elfin Knight may be read with profit.

18. Cf. Bolte and Polívka's analysis of Grimm's tale 'Die kluge Bauerntochter, *Anmerkungen zu den Kinder- und Hausmärchen der Brüder Grimm*, Leipzig, 1915, vol. II, pp. 349 ff., which tells of the girl's cleverness both before and after marrying the king. A very large number of variants are registered. The whole discussion of this story by Bolte and Polívka serves to show how complicated a study of the sources of Boccaccio's *novella* might be made, and how impossible any such exhaustive study would be here.

19. J. Barrois, ed. Paris, 1837, pp. 188 ff.

20. *Percy Folio Manuscript*, ed. Hales and Furnivall, vol. III, p. 422.

21. Creizenach, *Geschichte des neueren Dramas*, Halle, 1909, vol. IV, pp. 306 ff. Italics are mine. I am indebted to Schücking for this reference.

22. For analogues illustrating this, see Bolte and Polívka, *op. cit.*

23. *Berichte über die Verhandlungen der kgl. sächs. Gesellschaft der Wissenschaften zu Leipzig*, Phil.-hist. Klasse, vol. XII (1860), pp. 125–8. A parallel folk-tale recovered from the Roumanian gypsies is summarized by F. Miklosich in *Über die Mundarten und die Wanderungen der Zigeuner Europas*, Part IV, *Denkschriften der Kais. Akademie der Wissenschaften zu Wien*, Phil.-hist. Klasse, Band XXIII.

The tale, 'The Jealous Man', is on pp. 321–4. It begins with the *Cymbeline* wager-theme, with recognition by a mark beneath the heroine's left breast. The husband, on discovering the supposed infidelity of his wife, sets her adrift on a boat on the Danube, and himself takes service with the Jews as a water-carrier. Upon coming to land, the wife disguises herself as a man. She tarries in a city where the Emperor is blind. It is revealed to her in a dream, as she sleeps beneath a tree, that he may be healed, and how this may be done. She performs this service, the Emperor gives her his entire kingdom, she finds her husband, and makes him emperor, while she reigns as his consort. This little tale is instructive in showing how easily such a theme as the one under discussion may be combined with another episode, here the *Cymbeline* motive.

24. Paisley and London, 1890, vol. II, pp. 327 ff.

25. *Variorum Shakespeare*, Philadelphia, 1888, p. 316.

26. D. S. Fansler, *Filipino Popular Tales*, Lancaster and New York for the American Folk-lore Society, 1921, p. 55.

27. L. Gautier, *La Chevalerie*, Paris, 1884, chapter IX. For Helissent, see p. 343.

28. Except perhaps in his telling the king that he is going to return to his own country, and then riding off to Italy, and in his reply to the messengers later sent from his wife: '*Alli quali esso durissimo disse: "Di questo faccia ella il piacer suo, io per me vi tornerò allora ad esser con lei, che ella questo anello avrà in dito, et in braccio figliolo di me acquistato."*' Paynter renders '*durissimo*' as '*chorlishlie*', which gives a somewhat different meaning.

29. See Note 9, above.

30. Krapp, *loc. cit.* (see Note 6, above), p. 299. This study is important in offering reasoned excuses for Parolles, and its contentions cannot be neglected. But there is more to be said of the significance of Parolles for the character of Bertram, and for the play as a whole.

31. *Shakspere, a Critical Study of his Mind and Art*, London, 1875, p. 76.

32. 'Honesty' may mean either upright conduct, honourableness, decency, or chastity (Schmidt). Since the word is here used of woman, the meaning 'chastity' seems most probable. 'Puritan' has of course an unfavourable connotation in Shakespeare. 'A big heart' signifies pride. 'The puritans abominated the surplice as a rag of iniquity, and were great sticklers for the black gown, which was to them the symbol of Calvinism. Some of them, however, yielded so far as to wear the surplice over the gown, because their consciences would not suffer them to officiate without the latter, nor the law of the church without the former.' (Herford, quoted by Brigstocke, in *Arden* ed., p. 31). I do not think the alternative explanation, making 'honesty' refer to the Clown, is admissible: an honest man like myself, though he be no sanctimonious fellow, will do no hurt when woman's commands are laid upon them; he will cloak his pride under humility. The possibility of 'doing hurt' in the opening sentence is clearly that woman might do it to man, not man to woman; the whole

tenor of the Clown's preceding meditations shows that plainly enough.

33. No. 1030, 31 October 1921, p. 650.

34. Boas has well emphasized the medieval conception of 'service' in *All's Well.* '[Helena] feels throughout that as a dependent of the great house she stands in a feudal relation to Bertram, and that in return for the protection extended to her, she owes him, in the technical sense, "service".' The reader may follow the development of this argument at his leisure; he will note how completely it disposes of the conclusions of Gervinus. Due allowance has to be made for changes in the Elizabethan attitude towards chivalry; *Troilus and Cressida* marks a distinct shift in the point of view. But this does not mean that Shakespeare had reached anything like our modern convictions about social ethics. He was on the whole far nearer to the days of Chaucer than to those of Tennyson.

35. *Shakespearean Tragedy*, p. 252.

36. New York and London, 1903, p. 5.

37. Cf. Note 8, above, Raleigh, pp. 195, 197.

38. Cf. Schücking, Note 8, above.

39. *Elizabeth and Essex, a Tragic History*, London, 1928, pp. 8 ff.

40. Professor Thaler (*Shakespeare's Silences*, p. 70) thinks that this suggestion of mine is plausible 'on the face of it', but questions if it goes to the root of the problem. He reminds me of the jig following a serious play, a custom of which I was not unmindful when I wrote this passage. It seems to me that an audience who were looking forward to a fresh diversion like a jig to follow would be likely to be more restless rather than less so, while listening to dramatic material which no longer occupied their entire interest.

41. Introduction to *Waverley*, Boston, 1892, p. lxxxiv.

3. MEASURE FOR MEASURE
Pages 80 to 114

1. For the quotation from Saintsbury, see *A Short History of English Literature*, New York and London, 1898, p. 323; for that from Raleigh, see his *Shakespeare* (English Men of Letters), London, 1909, pp. 219–20.

2. *Measure for Measure*, Cambridge (England), 1922, p. xiii.

3. Edgar C. Morris, ed. *Measure for Measure* (*Tudor Shakespeare*), New York, 1912, p. xiv.

NOTES

4. This is challenged by Hart, old *Arden* edition, Introduction, p. xxvi. (Cf. Note 9, below.) Hazlitt remarks that 'there is in general a want of passion' in the play, a view still harder to accept.

5. *Loc. cit.*, pp. xxviii ff. Other disparaging remarks about Isabella by Charlotte Lennox and Sir George Greenwood are there quoted.

6. A. C. Bradley, *Shakespearean Tragedy*, p. 78; J. S. P. Tatlock, *Sewanee Review*, April 1916, p. 14.

7. *Character Problems in Shakespeare's Plays*, Gloucester, Mass., 1959, p. 197 f.

8. *Shakespeare as a Playwright*, New York, 1913, p. 227.

9. See Hart's edition of the play for the *Arden Shakespeare*, London n. d., p. xxii. L. Albrecht, *Neue Untersuchungen zu Shakespeares Mass für Mass*, Berlin, 1914, p. 82. For a review of criticisms of the play, cf. W. H. Durham, 'Measure for Measure a Measure for Critics,' in *Essays in Criticism by Members of the Department of English, University of California*, Berkeley, 1929.

10. For a convenient reprint of the original text, see Hazlitt, *Shakespeare's Library*, London, 1875, vol. III, pp. 169 ff.

11. Sidney Lee, article 'George Whetstone', *Dictionary of National Biography*.

12. Albrecht, pp. 112 ff.

13. Series VIII, vol. IV, 29 July 1893, pp. 83–4.

14. Translated in Hazlitt, *loc. cit.*, vol. III, pp. 167–8.

15. Albrecht, p. 298.

16. See F. Douce, *Illustrations of Shakespeare*, London, 1807, vol. I, pp. 152–60; vol. II, p. 274; and Albrecht, pp. 295–8, who gives further references.

17. Hazlitt, vol. VI, p. 204.

18. At a first reading, the secondary material appears so different from that in *Measure for Measure* that Shakespeare's dependence upon it seems questionable. But I think that Albrecht is right (pp. 34 ff.) in insisting that there are suggestions of Mistress Overdone in Lamia, of Pompey in Rosko, of Elbow in Gresco, and possibly some other correspondences. Much of the subsidiary material, in Whetstone, as in Shakespeare, serves to suggest sexual corruption among the lower classes.

19. Albrecht, pp. 81–94; 294. I do not agree with Albrecht that the Duke's disguise as a monk was derived from this source; a point which is discussed above, p. 92.

20. '*la legge di quella Città, che uolea, che tali fossero condannati alla pena della testa, se bene anco si disponessero a pigliarla per Moglie.*'

21. Sidney Lee, article cited from the *Dictionary of National Biography.*
22. Albrecht, p. 126; Creizenach, *The English Drama in the Age of Shakespeare*, London, 1916, pp. 221 ff. Creizenach cites Middleton's *Phoenix* and Day's *Law Tricks*, but these are probably later than *Measure for Measure* and influenced by it. In Chapman's *Blind Beggar of Alexandria* a banished Duke remains among his people disguised as a beggar; cf. also *The Blind Beggar of Bednal Green*, and Marston's *Malcontent.*
23. The exhibition of the head, as was pointed out years ago by Simrock (*Quellen des Shakespeare*, vol. I, p. 154), is an old folk-tale theme; a servant is employed to do a murder, and deceives his master by producing false proofs. See also Albrecht, p. 127.
24. The ballads afford illustrations. In *Gil Brenton* (Child, vol. I, No. 5, pp. 62 ff.) a lady who has been dishonoured through no fault of her own by a seducer in the greenwood is to be married to Gil Brenton. Sweet Willy, 'a widow's son', who runs at her stirrup-foot, advises her, if she is no maid, to hire some woman to take her place. So she says to her bower-woman,

> Five hundred pounds, maid, I'll gi to thee
> An sleep this night wi the king for me.

The blankets and the pillows betray to Gil Brenton the presence of the substitute; the heroine tells of her seduction, and shows tokens from the unknown lover in the greenwood, who proves to have been no other than Gil Brenton himself, and all ends well. In the ballad of *The Twa Knights* (Child, vol. v, No. 268, pp. 21 ff.), a lady who gets into the power of a seducer, through her husband's wager on her honour (see below, in the discussion of *Cymbeline*), hires her niece Lady Maisry to take her place. The niece later on has the choice of killing the seducer or of wedding him, and chooses the latter alternative.

> And a' the ladies who heard o it
> Said she was a wise woman.

The implication in the ballad clearly is that both the wife and Lady Maisry acted as heroines should. The most famous example of the substitution of one woman for the preservation of the honour of another is of course the Brangaene episode in the Tristram story. The motivation and treatment of this differ in the various versions.
25. C. L. Powell, *English Domestic Relations, 1487–1653*, New York, 1917, p. 4.

26. Joseph Quincy Adams, *A Life of Shakespeare*, Boston and New York, 1923, pp. 69 ff. For the situation in *Cymbeline*, see chapter v.
27. Quoted from the English translation, p. 198.
28. In *The Shakespeare Library*, New York, 1907, cf. pp. v and vii.
29. Cf. E. K. Chambers, *The Elizabethan Stage*, London, 1923, vol. II, p. 211; vol. IV, pp. 119, 171, and S. A. Tannenbaum, *Shakespeare Forgeries*, New York, 1928, pp. 1, 21, 46.
30. *Shakespeare* (English Men of Letters), p. 219–20.
31. *Lectures and Notes of Shakespeare and other English Poets*, London, 1890, p. 299.
32. Introduction to the play in the *Leopold Shakspere*, London, 1877.
33. J. Huizinga, *The Waning of the Middle Ages*, London, 1927, p. 16.

4. TROILUS AND CRESSIDA

Pages 115 to 155

1. Peter Alexander, *Library*, vol. IX, December 1928, pp. 267–86; see especially p. 278.
2. E. K. Chambers, *Elizabethan Stage*, London, 1923, vol. I, pp. 219–20.
3. See Alexander and Chambers, *loc. cit.*, and J. Q. Adams, *Life of Shakespeare*, Boston and New York, 1923, pp. 209 ff.
4. Tatlock, preface to edition of play for the *Tudor Shakespeare*, p. ix; Henrietta C. Bartlett, *Mr William Shakespeare*, New Haven, 1922, p. 40.
5. Reprinted in *The Cambridge Shakespeare*, ed. W. Aldis Wright (1895), vol. VI, p. viii.
6. *Shakespeare, Complete Works*, Boston and New York, 1916, p. 260.
7. *Loc. cit.*, p. 348.
8. *Loc. cit.*, p. 268.
9. Cf. Notes 1 and 5 to this chapter.
10. Tatlock, 'The siege of Troy in Elizabethan literature, especially in Shakespeare and Heywood', *P.M.L.A.*, vol. XXX.
11. Rollins, 'The Troilus-Cressida story from Chaucer to Shakespeare', *P.M.L.A.*, vol. XXXII.
12. Tatlock, *P.M.L.A.*, vol. XXX, p. 756.
13. *History of English Literature*, New York, 1871, vol. I, 227. I cannot verify the reference to Middleton with which this is supported.
14. Lytton Strachey, *Elizabeth and Essex*, London, 1928, p. 35.

15. R. A. Small, *The Stage-Quarrel between Ben Jonson and the So-Called Poetasters*, Breslau, 1899, p. 155.

16. *Loc. cit.*, p. 115.

17. See the translation with parallel text by Griffin and Myrick, Philadelphia, 1929.

18. *Chaucer and His Poetry*, Cambridge, 1915, p. 133.

19. G. Gregory Smith, *The Transition Period*, New York, 1900, p. 45.

20. Quoted by Rollins, *loc. cit.*, p. 408. See his discussion for further details.

21. Rollins, *loc. cit.*, pp. 389, 417.

22. Tatlock, *loc. cit.*, p. 739.

23. *Certain Accepted Heroes and Other Essays*, New York, 1897, p. 21.

24. R. M. Alden, *Shakespeare*, New York, 1922, p. 295.

25. *Publications of the Modern Language Association*, vol. XLIV, March 1929, p. 123.

26. P. 428.

27. P. 756.

28. *Shakespeare, A Survey*, New York, 1925, p. 191.

29. *Shakspere and his Predecessors*, p. 376.

30. P. 769, note.

31. Quoted in Rolfe's edition of the play, New York, 1882, p. 217.

32. See Boas, pp. 373 ff.

5. THE WAGER IN 'CYMBELINE'

Pages 156 to 180

1. *William Shakespeare*, London, 1911, p. 223.

2. *Shakespeare*, London, 1909, p. 185.

3. Quoted by Furness, *Variorum* edition of *Cymbeline* (1913), p. 498.

4. *Shakspere as a Playwright*, New York, 1913, p. 335.

5. *Introduction to Shakespeare*, New York, 1910, p. 200.

6. *The Moral System of Shakespeare*, New York, 1903, p. 79.

7. *Shakespeare Commentaries*, translated by F. E. Bunnètt, London, 1903, p. 667. According to the view of Gervinus, *Cymbeline* 'treats uniformly throughout two opposite ideas or moral qualities, namely truth in word and deed (fidelity), and untruth and faithlessness, falseness in deed or perfidy, falseness in word or slander' (p. 671). The story of Little Red Riding Hood treats uniformly throughout two opposing ideas or moral qualities also, trusting innocence and

scheming villainy, but nobody has ever supposed that a desire to contrast these moral concepts as such had anything to do with the evolution of the story.

8. H. N. Hudson, *Shakespeare, his life, art, and characters*, Boston, 1882, vol. II, p. 443.

9. There are strong indications that Shakespeare's chief interest was centred on the Posthumus–Imogen plot. Many of the inconsequences of the sub-plots seem due to another hand. Dr Furness stated his convictions: 'Regarded broadly, I believe that the Imogen love story and all that immediately touched it interested Shakespeare deeply: the Cymbeline portion was turned over to an assistant, who at times grew vainglorious and inserted here and there, even on the ground sacred to Imogen, lines and sentiments that shine by their dullness.' Such conclusions are, of course, insusceptible of proof. But we may feel confident that the earlier scenes of the main plot interested Shakespeare deeply. Upon them he lavished some of the most brilliant writing in the play.

10. It is worth noting, however, that the *Decameron* made its way in English and French somewhat more slowly than is usually supposed. It was translated into French in 1414; into English in an incomplete version in 1566, in a complete version in 1620. See the interesting article by Willard Farnham, 'England's Discovery of the *Decameron*', *Publications of the Modern Language Association*, vol. XXXIX, pp. 123–39.

11. *Littérature française au moyen âge*, Paris, 1905, p. 89.

12. Ed. F. Michel, Paris, 1831.

13. Ed. F. Michel, Paris, 1834.

14. Moland et d'Héricault: *Nouvelles françaises en prose du xiiime siècle*, Bibl. Elzev., 1856, pp. 83 ff.

15. Ed. E. Mabille, Paris, 1869.

16. See the edition by Nutt, 1902, pp. 301 ff.

17. F. H. von der Hagen, *Gesammtabenteuer: Hundert altdeutsche Erzählungen*, Bd. III, No. LXVIII, pp. 356 ff., Stuttgart and Tübingen, 1850.

18. R. Köhler, *Jahrbuch für Romanische und Englische Litteratur*, 1867, vol. VIII, pp. 51 ff.

19. Gollancz, *Temple Shakespeare*, Introduction, p. x, note.

20. See especially the Introduction to the ballad of *The Twa Knights*, Child, *English and Scottish Ballads*, vol. V, pp. 21 ff. (No. 268).

21. I use the translation in the Furness *Variorum*.

22. J. F. Campbell, *Popular Tales of the West Highlands*, Edinburgh, 1860, vol. II, No. 18, pp. 1 ff.

23. See above, chapter I, p. 36.

24. Cf. the *Morte d'Arthur*, Bk. IX, chapter XIV.

25. Michel, p. 18.

26. *Works of Shakespeare*, ed. by Sir Sidney Lee, New York and Boston, 1911, Introduction to *Cymbeline*, p. xi.

27. Furness, *Variorum Cymbeline*, Introduction, pp. xiv f.

28. Ashley H. Thorndike, *The Influence of Beaumont and Fletcher on Shakspere*, Worcester, Mass., 1901; see pp. 139, 153.

29. See the old *Arden* edition of *Cymbeline* (Dowden), pp. xxxiv ff. The play *The Rare Triumphs of Love and Fortune* deserves, according to Dowden, special attention.

30. Boccaccio arranges the matter thus: '... on the ensuing day Ambrogiuolo was paid in full, and Bernabo, departing Paris, betook himself to Genoa with fell intent against the lady. When he drew near the city, he would not enter therein, but lighted down a good score of miles away at a country house of his and dispatched one of his servants, in whom he much trusted, to Genoa with two horses and letters under his hand, advising his wife that he had returned and bidding her come to him; and he privily charged the man, when as he should be with the lady in such place as he should seem best to him, to put her to death without pity and return to him.' In the *Roman de la Violette*, the hero tries to kill the heroine in a wood, but is prevented by the appearance of an enormous serpent; the warning cry of his wife saves his life, and he cannot bring himself to kill her. In the *Comte de Poitiers*, the serpent is replaced by a lion. In *Florus and Jehane*, with its religious colouring and rather namby-pamby hero, the killing is omitted. In the *Miracle*, the hero says he would put the heroine to a shameful death if he could,

> '*et certes, se la puis tenir*
> *a honte la feray mourir.*'

(Monmerqué et Michel, p. 460.)

In the work of the so-called 'Anonymous' Italian *novella* writer, the husband sends his wife to a country estate, and charges a servant to drown her. (Ohle, p. 35.)

31. Furness, *Variorum*, p. 384.

32. *ibid.*, p. 326.

33. *ibid.*, p. 384.

34. *ibid.*, p. 43.

35. *Philological Quarterly*, October 1928, vol. IV, p. 359 f.

6. LATER SHAKESPEAREAN COMEDY
Pages 181 to 203

1. *About Shakespeare and his Plays*, London, 1926, p. 57.
2. Raleigh, *Shakespeare*, pp. 214 ff.
3. Especially in his *English Comedy*, New York, 1929, chapters VII and VIII.
4. Introduction to edition of the play in the *Tudor Shakespeare*, p. xi.
5. *A Glance towards Shakespeare*, Boston, Atlantic Monthly Press, pp. 87, 88.
6. E. H. Wright, *The Authorship of Timon of Athens*, New York, 1910, p. 15.
7. Ashley H. Thorndike, *The Influence of Beaumont and Fletcher on Shakspere*, Worcester, Mass., 1901. For the dating of the play, see p. 65.
8. *Shakspere Primer*, chapter v.
9. *Encyclopaedia Britannica*, 14th edition, 1929, article 'Shakespeare', vol. XXIV, p. 447.
10. Introduction to the play in the *Tudor Shakespeare*, p. xi.
11. *Books and Characters*, London, 1922, pp. 57 ff.
12. Trelawney, *Records*, I, 117, quoted by G. E. Woodberry, ed. *The Cenci*, Boston, 1909, p. xii.
13. R. M. Alden, *Shakespeare*, New York, 1922, p. 103.
14. MacCracken, Pierce and Durham, *Introduction to Shakespeare*, New York, 1910, p. 103.

INDEX

This index covers proper names in the main text. A few of these, of minor significance, have been omitted, and the Notes, with a few exceptions, have not been included. The principal characters in the problem comedies are indexed as in the appropriate chapters; references of special importance within those chapters, and occurrences elsewhere, are listed separately. Quotations and analyses have not been indexed.

Abbess (in *The Comedy of Errors*), 183

Achilles, 127, 129ff., 144, 149, 151

Adams, Joseph Quincy, 96, 122

Aeneas, 130

Agamemnon, 130

Ajax, 127, 130, 144, 149

Albrecht, Louis, 84, 87, 92, 104, 210–11

Alchemist, The, 73

Alden, R. M., 147, 200

Alexander, Peter, 119, 122, 125

All's Well That Ends Well, 20, 21, 22, 24, 25, 26, 32, 41, 43–79, 80, 93, 100, 130, 149, 156, 162, 185, 188, 193, 197, 201

Amis and Amile, 35

Angelo, 24, 80–114, esp. 107ff.

Antonio and Mellida, 192

Antony and Cleopatra, 20, 24, 115, 194

As You Like It, 20, 100, 105, 183, 192

Aurelia (Whetstone), 85

Ayrer, Jakob, 163

Bandello, Matteo, 32, 162, 185

Barlaam and Josaphat, 33

Barnardine, 110

Barrie, J. M., 60

Bartholomew Fair, 73

Bartlett, Henrietta C., 121

Basilikon Doron, 104, 114

Beatrice, 26, 184

Beaumont, Francis, and Fletcher, John, 168, 169, 172, 194, 202

Beaux' Stratagem, The, 199

Beethoven, Ludwig van, 199

Bellman of London, The, 190

Benedick, 184

Benfey, Theodor, 64

Benoit de Sainte-More, 133

Bertram, 24, 43–79, esp. 69, 78

Bilioso, 188, 206

Biron, 183

Blackstone, Sir William, 108

Blurt, Master Constable, 188

Boas, F. S., 21, 116, 152, 153, 158, 209

Boccaccio, Giovanni, 32, 35, 48ff., 57, 62, 65ff., 133–4, 136, 161–2, 185, 199

Bonion (Bonian), Richard, and Walleys (Walley), Henry, 120, 124

Bottom, 184

Bradby, G. F., 182

Bradley, A. C., 40, 83

Bragtha-Mágus saga, 53

Brandes, Georg, 198

Brink, B. ten, 198

Bristol Tragedy, The, 191

Brooke, Arthur, 74

Caliban, 157, 198

Cambridge editors, 122, 125

Campbell, J. F. (*Popular Tales of the West Highlands*), 63

Capulet, 177

Caxton, William, 134, 141
Cenci, The, 199
Chalmers, George, 104
Chambers, Sir Edmund K., 26, 150, 153, 196
Chapman, George, 191
Chapman, John Jay, 193
Characters of Vices and Virtues, 190
Chaucer, Geoffrey, 25, 133ff., 167
Chester Tragedy, The, 192
Child Waters, 58
Cinderella, 60
Cinthio, Giraldi, 85ff., 89–90, 185
Claris and Laris, 135
Claudio, 80–114
Clerk's Tale, The, 167
Clown (in *All's Well That Ends Well*), 46, 50, 68–71, 78–9, 193
Coleridge, Hartley, 158
Coleridge, Samuel Taylor, 25, 38, 41, 44, 111–12, 115
Comedy of Errors, The, 19, 100, 119, 183
Comte d'Artois, Le, 54ff., 57, 60
Comte de Poitiers, Li, 161, 215
Coriolanus, 20, 126, 194, 201
Countess (in *All's Well That Ends Well*), 50, 67, 70, 78, 193
Cox, Captain, 98
Creizenach, Wilhelm Michael Anton, 61, 74, 92
Cressida, 26, 115–55
Cymbeline, 22, 24, 26, 32, 42, 58, 96, 156–80, 194, 197, 201, 207, 213, 214

Daniel, P. A., 153
Dante Alighieri, 199
Dares Phrygius, 141
Darling of the Gods, The, 81
Davies of Hereford, John, 190
Decameron, 35, 48, 60, 65ff., 161ff., 214, 215
Deighton, Kenneth, 116, 127, 177
Dekker, Thomas, 187, 189, 190–91

Dennis, John, 193
Desdemona, 139
Diana, 44, 77, 101
Diarmaid and Graidhne, 56
Dictys Cretensis, 141
Dimock, Sir Edward, 35
Diomedes, 130, 148
Dogberry, 184
Doll's House, A, 22
Dolopathos, 34
Don Quixote, 154
Dou Roi Flore et de la Bielle Jehane, 162, 215
Douce, Francis, 87
Dowden, Edward, 40, 70, 195, 198
Dryden, John, 139, 145
Duke (in *As You Like It*), 177
Duke (in *Measure for Measure*), 25, 84, 91, 99ff.
Dunlop, John Colin, 44
Dutch Courtesan, The, 191

Edward III, 34
Elbow, 105, 113, 210
Elizabeth, Queen, 35, 190, 199
Elton, Oliver, 46
Emery F. P., 193
Encyclopaedia Britannica, 26
Enemy of the People, An, 22
Epitia, 85
Essex, Earl of, 35, 132, 133
Euripides, 29
Every Man in his Humour, 187

Fair Annie, 58
Falstaff, 68–9, 71, 193
Farquhar, George, 199
Feliche, 192
Feste, 193
Feuillerat, Albert, 41
Filocolo, 60
Filostrato, 134
Fleay, F. G., 154
Fletcher, John, 189. *See also* Beaumont, Francis, and Fletcher, John

Florus and Jehane: see Dou Roi Flore et de la Bielle Jehane
France, Anatole, 73
Franklin's Tale, The, 60
Frederick of Jennen, 162
Furness, H. H., 177, 214
Furnivall, F. J., 108, 154, 198

Gautier, L., 65
Gervinus, G. G., 38, 74, 159, 209, 213
Gesta Romanorum, 34, 64
Gil Brenton, 211
Giovanni, Ser, 33
Goethe, Johann Wolfgang von, 41, 115
Gollancz, Sir Israel, 198
Grand Parangon, Le, 162
Greene, Robert, 141, 176–7, 190
Gresco, 105, 210
Griselda, 58–9, 165
Guido delle Colonne, 133
Guilpin, Edward, 190
Gull's Horn-Book, The, 190

Hales, J. W., 58
Hall, Joseph, 190
Halliwell Phillipps, James Orchard, 96
Hamlet, 20–21, 24, 39, 118, 132, 168,
Hart, H. C., 84, 101
Hathaway, Anne, 96
Hazlitt, William, 25, 38, 44, 82, 96, 101
Hecatommithi, 85, 87
Hector, 127, 130, 131, 151
Hedda Gabler, 22
Helen, 115, 129, 140
Helena, 24, 25, 43–79, 97, 99, 113
Helissent, 65
Henry IV, 69, 152
Henry V, 19
Henryson, Robert, 136–7
Heptameron of Civill Discourses, An, 85, 89

Herford, C. H., 87, 168
Hermione, 175ff., 197
Heywood, Thomas, 141ff., 148, 187
Hieronymo, 192
Holinshed, Raphael, 161, 194
Homer, 141ff.
Honest Whore, The, 191
Hudson, H. N., 26, 159
Huizinga, Johan, 111

Iachimo, 115–55
Ibsen, Henrik, 22, 25, 75
Imogen, 96, 158–80, 197, 214
Inns of Court, 119
Iron Age, 142ff., 147
Irving, Henry, 23
Isabella, 24, 25, 72, 80–114
Isham, Samuel, 31

James I, 25, 35, 84, 103–4, 114, 199
James IV, 85
Jameson, Mrs Anna Brownell, 82
Jaques, 183, 192
Johannes de Alta Silva, 34
Johnson, Samuel, 25, 38, 45, 47
Jonson, Ben, 69, 155, 187–8, 191
Juliet, 150
Julius Caesar, 20, 194, 199
Jungfrau von Orleans, Die, 73

Katherine, 183
Kemble, John Philip, 47
Kilhwch and Olwen, 63
King John, 96
King Lear, 24, 76, 115, 186, 194
Kiss for Cinderella, A, 60
Kittredge, G. L., 134
Krapp, George Philip, 47, 69
Kyd, Thomas, 39, 186, 189, 192

Lafeu, 50, 205
Lamb, Charles, 38, 199
Lamia, 105, 210

Landau, M., 62
Lang, Andrew, 25, 45, 69, 79
Lanthorn and Candle-Light, 190
Launce, 184
Lavache: *see* Clown
Lee, Sir Sidney, 116, 198
Legouis, Émile, 40
Lennox, Mrs Charlotte, 38
Leontes, 157, 175ff., 197
Lodge, H. C., 143
Lodge, Thomas, 190
Lounsbury, Thomas Raynesford, 45
Love's Labour's Lost, 19, 73, 154, 183
Love's Labour's Won, 19
Lowes, J. L., 46, 201, 205
Lucio, 71, 89, 92, 105, 11 2–13
Lydgate, John, 134, 141

Mabinogion, 63, 162
Macbeth, 115, 194
MacCracken, H. N., 158
Mad World, my Masters, A, 188
Magic Flute, The, 199
Mágussaga, 53
Maid's Tragedy, The, 174
Malcontent, The, 188, 194
Malevole, 188, 192
Malone, Edmund, 103, 118
Malvolio, 23
Mamillius, 197
Maquerelle, 188
Mariana, 83, 93ff., 108ff.
Marston, John, 187ff., 191
Masefield, John, 25, 45, 157
Massinger, Philip, 189
Matthews, Brander, 69, 83, 158, 159
Measure for Measure, 20–21, 22, 24, 26, 32, 42, 59, 71–2, 75, 80–114, 149, 156, 162, 185, 188, 192–3, 197, 201
Menelaus, 129
Merchant of Venice, The, 19, 23, 33, 64, 100, 183, 185
Meres, Francis, 19

Merry Wives of Windsor, The, 19, 183, 193
Metamorphosis of Pygmalion's Image, The, 190
Michaelmas Term, 188
Middleton, Thomas, 187, 191
Midsummer Night's Dream, A, 19, 100
Miracle de Nostre Dame, Un, 162, 215
Mirour for Magestrates of Cyties, A, 90, 210
Miseries of Enforced Marriage, The, 191
Mistress Overdone, 105–6, 113, 188, 210
Morris, E. C., 82, 88
Moulton, R. G., 26, 75, 158
Mozart, Wolfgang Amadeus, 199
Much Ado About Nothing, 19, 92, 96, 174
Müller, Max, 50

Nash, Thomas, 190
Neilson, W. A., 24, 46, 116, 122
Nestor, 130, 145
Nicholas de Troyes, 162
Notes and Queries, 86, 90
Nut-Brown Maid, The, 58

Oliver, 111
Olivia, 34
Orsino, 34
Othello, 85

Paid in Full 81,
Painter, William: *see* Paynter, William
Palace of Pleasure, The, 48
Pandarus, 115–55, esp. 130–31
Paris (in *Troilus and Cressida*), 129, 140
Paris, Gaston, 161
Parolles, 46, 50, 68–71, 72, 78–9, 99, 188, 205

Parzival, 25
Passarello, 188
Pater, Walter, 35
Patroclus, 130
Paynter, William, 48
Pecorone, Il, 33
Peele, George, 141
Perceforest, 162
Pericles, 63, 157, 193, 197, 201
Philaster, 172–3, 194
Phoenix, 188, 191
Pinero, Arthur Wing, 25
Pistol, 71
Plutarch, 194
Polixenes, 175, 176ff.
Pompey, 71, 105–6, 113, 210
Portia, 26, 34
Posthumus Leonatus, 26, 96, 111, 156–80, esp. 169ff., 173ff., 178ff., 197
Prince Hal, 69, 184
Promos and Cassandra, 85, 88, 89
Proteus, 35, 111
Puccini, Giacomo, 81

Quiller-Couch, Sir Arthur, 25, 81ff., 96, 102, 170

Ragozine, 93
Raleigh, Sir Walter (died 1618), 35, 132
Raleigh, Sir Walter (died 1922), 31, 47, 75, 80, 158, 185
Rankin, William, 190
Richard II, 183
Richard III, 183
Ristine, F. H., 23
Robert Laneham's Letter, 98
Robinson, Richard, 34
Rollins, H. E., 126, 147–8
Roman de la Violette, 162, 169, 215
Romeo, 34
Romeo and Juliet, 19, 74, 92, 100, 126
Rosalind, 24, 26
Rosaline, 34

Rosko, 105, 210
Rosmersholm, 22
Rümelin, Gustav von, 39, 154
Rymenhild, 65

Sardou, Victorien, 81
Schiller, Friedrich von, 73
Schlegel, August Wilhelm von, 38, 154
Schücking, Levin L., 39, 40, 47, 76, 78, 83, 96, 98, 148, 204
Scott, Sir Walter, 79
Scourge of Villainy, The, 190
Seccombe, Thomas, and Allen, John, 48
Ser Giovanni, 33
Shakespear Illustrated, 38
Shakspere Primer (Dowden), 195
Shelley, Percy Bysshe, 199
Shylock, 23, 34
Sidney, Sir Philip, 35
Skelton, John, 138
Skialetheia, 190
Smeaton, Oliphant, 87
Smith, Alphonso, 197
Smith, G. Gregory, 137
Somadeva, 62
Sonnets (Shakespeare), 199
Sophocles, 29
Southampton, Earl of, 199
Spanish Tragedy, The, 186, 192
Strachey, Lytton, 77, 198
Strindberg, August, 75
Sudermann, Hermann, 25
Symons, Arthur, 170

Taine, Hippolyte, 132
Taliesin, 162
Taming of the Shrew, The, 19, 96, 183
Tannenbaum, S. A., 103, 177
Tate, Nahum, 75
Tatlock, J. S. P., 25, 83, 116, 121, 125–6, 141–2, 147, 152
Tempest, The, 20, 154, 197

Tennyson, Alfred, Lord, 74
Testament of Cresseid, The, 136–7
Thaler, Alwin, 209
Thersites, 115–55; esp. 130–31
Thorndike, A. H., 26, 169, 172, 189, 194
Timon of Athens, 20, 194
Titus Andronicus, 19
Tosca, La, 81
Touchstone, 193
Tourneur, Cyril, 189
Trick to Catch the Old One, A, 188
Tristan und Isolde, 25
Troilus, 115–55
Troilus and Cressida (Shakespeare), 20–21, 22, 24, 25, 32, 41, 43–79, ·185, 192, 201, 209
Troilus and Criseyde (Chaucer), 25, 134ff.
Twa Knights, The, 167, 211
Twain, Mark, 199
Twelfth Night, 20, 23, 73, 96, 100, 120, 130, 183, 201
Two Gentlemen of Verona, The, 19, 35, 100

Ulrici, Hermann, 38, 154

Ulysses, 130, 145, 148

Valentine, 35
Viola, 24, 26
Virgidemiarum, 190
Volpone, 187
Voltaire, 37

Wagner, Richard, 25
Webster, John, 123, 189
Wells, H. W., 146
Wendell, Barrett, 47, 115, 118, 150
Westward for Smelts, 161
Whetstone, George, 83ff., 88ff., 92, 93, 105, 111, 138
White, R. G., 127, 150
Winter's Tale, The, 32, 96, 156ff., 174ff., 197
Wolfram von Eschenbach, 25
Woman Killed with Kindness, A, 174
Wonderful Year, The, 190
Wright, E. H., 194
Wynkyn de Worde, 34

Yorkshire Tragedy, The, 191
Young, Karl, 38, 204
Your Five Gallants, 188

MORE ABOUT PENGUINS, PELICANS
AND PUFFINS

For further information about books available from Penguins please write to Dept EP, Penguin Books Ltd, Harmondsworth, Middlesex UB7 0DA.

In the U.S.A.: For a complete list of books available from Penguins in the United States write to Dept DG, Penguin Books, 299 Murray Hill Parkway, East Rutherford, New Jersey 07073.

In Canada: For a complete list of books available from Penguins in Canada write to Penguin Books Canada Ltd, 2801 John Street, Markham, Ontario L3R 1B4.

In Australia: For a complete list of books available from Penguins in Australia write to the Marketing Department, Penguin Books Australia Ltd, P.O. Box 257, Ringwood, Victoria 3134.

In New Zealand: For a complete list of books available from Penguins in New Zealand write to the Marketing Department, Penguin Books (N.Z.) Ltd, Private Bag, Takapuna, Auckland 9.

In India: For a complete list of books available from Penguins in India write to Penguin Overseas Ltd, 706 Eros Apartments, 56 Nehru Place, New Delhi 110019.

NEW PENGUIN SHAKESPEARE

General Editor: T. J. B. Spencer

All's Well That Ends Well   Barbara Everett
Antony and Cleopatra   Emrys Jones
As You Like It   H. J. Oliver
The Comedy of Errors   Stanley Wells
Coriolanus   G. R. Hibbard
Hamlet   T. J. B. Spencer
Henry IV, Part 1   P. H. Davison
Henry IV, Part 2   P. H. Davison
Henry V,   A. R. Humphreys
Henry VI, Part 1   Norman Sanders
Henry VI, Part 2   Norman Sanders
Henry VI, Part 3   Norman Sanders
Henry VIII   A. R. Humphreys
King John   R. L. Smallwood
King Lear   G. K. Hunter
Macbeth   G. K. Hunter
Measure for Measure   J. M. Nosworthy
The Merchant of Venice   W. Moelwyn Merchant
The Merry Wives of Windsor   G. R. Hibbard
A Midsummer Night's Dream   Stanley Wells
Much Ado About Nothing   R. A. Foakes
Othello   Kenneth Muir
Pericles   Philip Edwards
The Rape of Lucrece   J. W. Lever
Richard II   Stanley Wells
Richard III   E. A. J. Honigmann
Romeo and Juliet   T. J. B. Spencer
The Taming of the Shrew   G. R. Hibbard
The Tempest   Anne Righter (Anne Barton)
Timon of Athens   G. R. Hibbard
Twelfth Night   M. M. Mahood
The Two Gentlemen of Verona   Norman Sanders
The Two Noble Kinsmen   N. W. Bawcutt
The Winter's Tale   Ernest Schanzer